The Life Transforming Power of
# NLP

Your True Power Lies within Your Mind
Nothing Is Impossible

## Manoj Keshav

INDIA • SINGAPORE • MALAYSIA

**Notion Press**

Old No. 38, New No. 6
McNichols Road, Chetpet
Chennai - 600 031

First Published by Notion Press 2018
Copyright © Manoj Keshav 2018
All Rights Reserved.

ISBN 978-1-64429-064-4

This book has been published with all efforts taken to make the material error-free after the consent of the author. However, the author and the publisher do not assume and hereby disclaim any liability to any party for any loss, damage, or disruption caused by errors or omissions, whether such errors or omissions result from negligence, accident, or any other cause.

No part of this book may be used, reproduced in any manner whatsoever without written permission from the author, except in the case of brief quotations embodied in critical articles and reviews.

I dedicate this book to:

1. Aporesh Acharya—founder, McGrath Institute of Leadership Training (MILT)—who brought me out of my shell and helped me gain self-confidence.

2. Dr. Rajan Muthukrishnan—founder, Indian Academy of Training and Development (IATD)—who encouraged me to become a Trainer and whose advice led me to places I never thought I would go.

3. Richard McHugh—an amazing gem of a person, my NLP guru and my inspiration—who made me fall in love with NLP and helped me transform the deepest core of my being.

# Contents

| | | |
|---|---|---|
| **Chapter 1:** | What is NLP (Neuro-Linguistic Programming)? | 1 |
| **Chapter 2:** | The NLP Beliefs of Excellence | 19 |
| **Chapter 3:** | New Level of Awareness Through Sensory Acuity | 38 |
| **Chapter 4:** | Anchoring | 69 |
| **Chapter 5:** | Circle of Excellence | 101 |
| **Chapter 6:** | Swish: Reprogramming Habits | 108 |
| **Chapter 7:** | Clearing Confusion With Visual Squash | 123 |
| **Chapter 8:** | Outcome Frames | 129 |
| **Chapter 9:** | Advance Listening Skills with Metamodel | 147 |
| **Chapter 10:** | The Predicates: Brain's Building Blocks | 198 |
| **Chapter 11:** | Submodalities: Key to Transformation | 213 |
| **Chapter 12:** | NLP: Belief Change Exercise | 230 |

*About the Author*   *281*

# Chapter 1

# What is NLP (Neuro-Linguistic Programming)?

## Are we Free Beings or are we Preprogrammed?

**NLP: Neuro**

### What Does Neuro Mean?

Neuro refers to nerves or the nervous system. The nervous system includes both the central nervous system and peripheral nervous system. The central nervous system is made up of the brain and spinal cord, and the peripheral nervous system is mainly made up of nerves that connect the central nervous system to every other part of the body.

Earlier, science suggested that the brain cannot change. Scientists believed that if a part of the brain was damaged due to an injury or if a person was born with a mental condition, nothing could be done. According to earlier theories, the brain is like a machine. Just as a machine has a fixed structure and cannot change itself, the brain cannot do so either. The cellular structure remains fixed and therefore cannot change or modify itself.

### Can the Brain Change Itself?

Today, scientific research points to the fact that the brain changes its very structure based on the way an individual lives his or her life. The brain constantly adapts itself to the person's daily activities and lifestyle. Because of neuroplasticity, the brain's ability to continually adapt, anything is possible. If a person chooses to do something different in life, the brain adapts itself to help that person cope with the new internal and external environment.

The fact that the brain can reorganize itself is one of the most significant discoveries of the 20th century.

*"The idea that the brain can change its own structure and function through 'thought' and 'activity' is, I believe, the most important alteration in our view of the brain since we first sketched out its basic anatomy and the working of its basic component, the neuron."*

**– Dr. Norman Doidge, author**—*The Brain That Changes Itself*

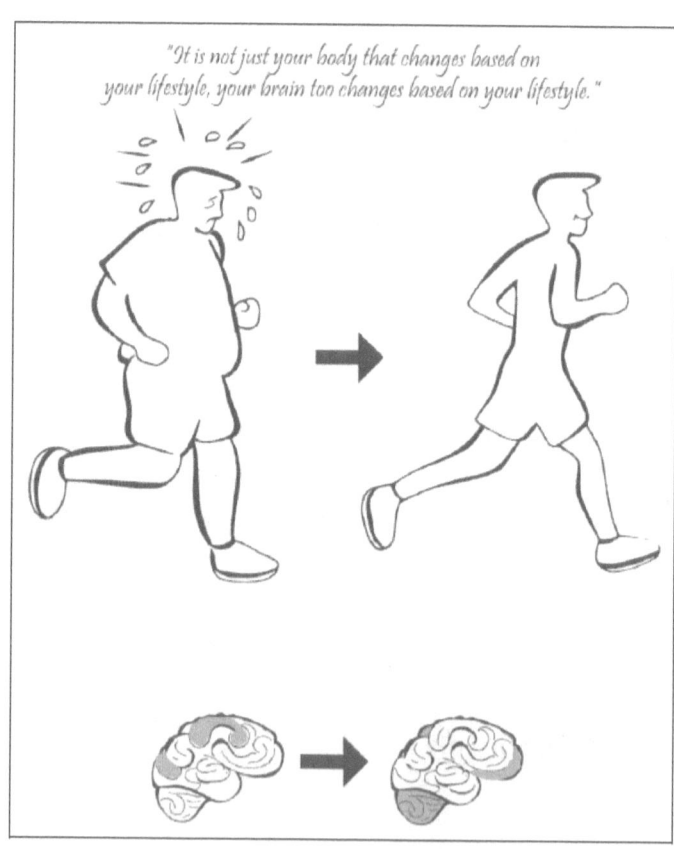
"It is not just your body that changes based on your lifestyle, your brain too changes based on your lifestyle."

The human brain has the amazing ability to reorganize itself by forming new connections between brain neuron cells. When we specialize in a set of particular skills, the part of the brain that deals with this ability grows, literally.

## Any Example to Showcase the Fact That Brain Can Grow Literally?

Neuroscientist Eleanor Maguire of the University of London was fascinated to know that a part of the brain called hippocampus (which is crucial for long-term memory and spatial navigation) is larger in animals (e.g., squirrels) and birds that store food in secret places to be dug up later. These animals need to remember the locations of all their hiding spots. This interesting fact led Maguire to wonder whether the hippocampus would grow in those organisms that had to memorize lots of visual locations. This led him to study a group of London cab drivers who end up memorizing roughly 25,000 city streets, a number much larger than that of bus drivers.

The result of the study (Maguire, Woollett & Spiers, 2006) is stunning. London taxi drivers had a larger hippocampus than London bus drivers. The reason being that taxi drivers must navigate through various routes around the city whereas bus drivers had to follow a limited, predetermined set of routes.

When a lazy person takes to athletics and stays with it for years, her/his strength, ability to accelerate and balance improve. Such folks also enhance their cardiovascular endurance, mental toughness and self-discipline, which in turn brings about a change at the cellular level in the body and neural level in the brain. As Michael Merzenich explains in his book, *The Brain That Changes Itself*, practicing a new habit under the right conditions can change hundreds of millions of connections (neural pathways) in the brain.

The same would be the case of a married couple who has been having severe conflicts for years together. As the conflict and the resulting anger, bitterness and stress stay unresolved for years, it brings about a change at the neural level of the individuals. Both body and mind would undergo definite changes at the cellular and neural level. The destruction that is happening deep within the psyche would show up as loss of enthusiasm toward life, lack of productivity at work and/or as psychosomatic illness. Our thoughts, beliefs and our lifestyle are literally (physically) changing and shaping our brain continuously.

### The King and the War Within

*Although the people of the kingdom of Malesh slept, and there was total silence in the kingdom, the king himself was awake. Not only was he awake, but he also heard a noise. The noise was not coming from outside but from within his head. No enemy has ever been able to defeat him. The fortress around the kingdom was impenetrable, but the king felt something has taken over him. Yes, it was anxiety; wave after wave of dread took over him. He had not slept for the last two days, and he knew that he would not be able to sleep tonight.*

*When the sunrays lit up his palatial bedroom, he instantly made a decision: I must consult my spiritual guru. He had not consulted him for over a decade now. The king thought of the last conversation he had had with him and how it had not gone well. The king had offered his spiritual guru a place in the palace for him to stay, but his guru declined the offer and chose to continue to stay in his small hut. The king left in anger after having failed to convince the guru to shift to the palace and never went back after that day. But now, as the sun rays filled the room, he knew he needed to see his guru.*

*By noon, the king's chariot reached his guru's hut. The king asked his soldiers not to follow him. He entered the hut only to find few young disciples performing prayers. The king looked at one of the disciples and asked, "Where is the guru? Go fetch him and tell him the king has come." All the disciples stood up and looked at the king with astonishment. He felt perplexed. He couldn't make sense of the silence in the room. So, he asked again, "Where is the guru?"*

*One of the disciples took a step forward and bowed. "Long live the king," he muttered in a weak voice. The king started getting impatient and paced the room. The disciples were still standing in the same place. The king stopped pacing and gave a stern look at the disciple who had taken a step forward. The disciple looked at the floor and said in a sad voice, "With due respect, the guru passed away a year ago. He died in his sleep. He had even said, ahead of time, that his time to renounce his body had come and that he would leave soon."*

*The king felt a deep sense of sadness and disappointment. "The guruji was probably 108 years old," thought the king. Maybe his time had indeed come. He felt weak in his knees and reached out to a bamboo pillar near him to find support. Regaining balance, he asked in a stern voice, "Why was I not informed?" The disciple responded, "Before he passed away, Guruji said you will visit this hut when the time is right." Feeling an unexplainable sorrow, the king turned to leave when another disciple came forward with a wooden scroll in his hand and explained, "Guruji had asked us to give this to you and said that you would need it." The words in the scroll read: "The more you do it, the more you want to do it; the less you do it, the less you want to do it."*

*That night, the king wanted to sleep desperately. He closed his eyes and lay still in bed, but he couldn't sleep. Waves of anxiety took over him. Although there was no threat to his kingdom, the king sensed a fear that he might lose everything—his kingdom, family and people. The king told himself a thousand times that there is nothing that suggests he is going to lose everything, but the feelings were there. The fear was just there. "Oh! God! How to let go of this fear? How to let go of these anxiety waves?" thought the king. "And the whole thing doesn't make sense. There are no enemies who have surrounded the kingdom. There are no enemies within the kingdom who are likely to challenge me. My army, my people and above all, my family are absolutely loyal to me," pondered the king. But the fear that he will lose everything was real and robust and was growing day by day.*

*Worry and fear had taken the place of sleep. One thing the king clearly understood was that the problem was not out there; the problem was inside his head.*

*The king's eye fell on the scroll. "The more you do it, the more you want to do it; the less you do it, the less you want to do it." "Hmmm. What does that mean? The more I worry about losing everything, the more I want to do it? Is that so? Why do I want to do something that is unpleasant? Fear is not pleasant. Not being able to sleep is not pleasant. The knots of worry and tension in my stomach are not pleasant. Then why would I want to do it? The more you do it, the more you want to do it? Is there something within me that wants me to worry? And the more I worry, the more it wants me to worry?"*

*"Oh god! If only the guru were with me. He could have guided me through these dark times. Is it true? The more we do something, the more we want to do it? Hmmm… Maybe in this inscription, I might find my solution."*

*The king tried to sleep, but waves of anxiety swept through him. "Oh! The more I feel these anxiety waves, the more I want it. Well, that's what the inscription says. Well, how do I not want it?" He turned in the bed, deep in thought, "What do I really want?" Slowly, the foggy pictures in his head cleared and a realization dawned on him that he genuinely wanted to fine-tune his sword fighting skills. He had craved that for years and somehow could not find the time to do it. "Let me do what I genuinely want to do, and the more I do, the more I would want to do it." The king called out for a soldier nearby and ordered him to make arrangements so that he could practice sword fighting immediately.*

*The king got ready in a few minutes and walked into an open space which was reserved for martial arts practice. He was happy to see his trusted general waiting to welcome him at this time of the night. The king practiced with his sword for the next six hours. He didn't realize the sun had appeared in the sky and had painted the sky orange.*

*The king felt alive and joyous. He was sweating and physically tired, but he felt good. "After so many nights, this was the first night I felt good. Hmm... So, the secret is to do something different when an anxiety attack happens," thought the king. The king ordered his men to keep the martial arts practice lawn ready for him all the time.*

*Any time the king felt a little worry or anxiety, he would go to the martial arts practice lawn and practice sword fighting with his soldiers for hours until he felt great and physically exhausted. Week after week, he kept up his sword practice. Whether it was daytime or night-time, the moment he felt anxious, he would take his sword and practice for hours till he was physically exhausted.*

*After months of practice, he lost the habit of worrying. He couldn't figure out precisely when, but the worrying had gone. He could slip into a deep sleep just like that. Although there was no worry to prompt him into a sword fight practice, he still decided to keep up his training because that was something he really wanted to do. The king had understood what the scroll meant. "The more you do it, the more you want it. And this time, I am doing just the right thing, and if I want it more, it is just fine," thought the king and slipped into deep, peaceful sleep.*

– Manoj Keshav

## The Continuously Changing Brain

By practicing new ways of thinking, we can reshape our brain and change the way our brain works. At this point, it's important to note that irrespective of intentions, the brain works in patterns. A person who continually thinks out of the box because his or her job demands it will become better at it over a period of time. Her or his ability to come up with creative ideas will become easier and more effortless. The brain will literally change to suit this way of life, and she/he would transition from an average linear thinking person to a highly creative person.

Similarly, a 'worrier' would get better and better at worrying and would find it easier and quicker to get into a state of depression. The more you do it, the more you want to do it. And the more you do it, the better you are in your ability to do the same. Somebody who picks up conflicts with others on a regular basis will become better at picking up disputes with others. Somebody who gets frustrated over little things would get better at it over a period of time, and he or she would find it easier to get frustrated.

## NLP: A Tool to Bring Change at the Neural Level

There may be unhealthy patterns and habits that have established themselves very deeply in a person's psyche, but no matter how deep a pattern or habit might be, the brain can reorganize itself. NLP is all about bringing about a change at the neural level so that you can be the person you want to be. You have this incredible power to change any thought or behavioral pattern, and NLP shows you how.

# NLP: Linguistics

*"The gift of speech and a well-ordered language are characteristic of every known group of human beings. No tribe has ever been found which is without language."*

**– Edward Sapir (Anthropologist-linguist)**

The iconic bitten-fruit has now become a universal symbol that we instantly recognize as the brand Apple Inc. The Red Cross symbol, Shell's red-and-yellow emblem and the Nike swoosh are other examples of symbols that are instantly recognized around the globe.

Just the way a logo or symbol represents an organization, words represent a thing or a concept.

We can use language to represent something to ourselves or to others. When we use language to express to ourselves, we call it reasoning, thinking, fantasying, rehearsing, etc. When we use language to describe our experiences or thoughts to others, we call it talking, discussing, writing, lecturing, singing, etc.

## Do Plants and Animals Communicate with Each Other?

Bees dance to other bees in order to communicate their current location and in which direction they are heading. Birds and monkeys employ a sophisticated system of sounds to alert each other of intruders. The loudness and the frequency are proportional to the distance and probably to the size of the intruder. Language is actually quite widespread in nature. All animals communicate; even plants have some rudimentary form of interaction with each other by releasing odorous chemicals called volatile organic compounds (VOC), secreting soluble chemicals, etc.

The key insight, though, is that language is not only used to express thoughts but also to shape thoughts. The goal of language is to transmit a neural pattern from one brain to another. It is a pattern that already exists in the mind of the speaker, and he or she wants to recreate it in the brain of the listener.

## Are Languages More Alike or Different from Each Other?

Language is common to all humans; we seem to be hard-wired for it. Animals don't have spoken languages like us humans. Many social scientists say it's the ability to use language symbolically that makes us 'human.' Though it may be a universal human attribute, language is hardly simple.

What traits do all human languages have in common? We represent our experiences to ourselves and others through language. The most authoritative source on the world's languages is *Ethnologue* (published by SIL International), whose detailed classified list as of 2009 included

6,909 distinct languages. Linguists have discovered that all these languages are more alike than different from each other.

Although there are differences among all languages, there are characteristics and properties that are common in all languages. These shared properties are contained in the universal grammar, which gives a common structure to all human languages. Regardless of the language we speak, the way we form words and sentences has a universal structure.

## Does Quality of Life Depend on the Choices of Words That We Use Every Day?

*"You cannot revolutionize your mind and your thoughts until you revolutionize the language that you use."*

— **Noam Chomsky**

The quality of our relationship with ourselves and the world around us depends a lot on our choice of words and the way we use language. NLP guides us in understanding the structure of language and the role it plays in transforming our lives.

## Words Can Change Your Life

Susan got on the bus. She was slightly anxious. It takes the bus about 40 minutes to reach her workplace. She looked at her watch. If there wasn't heavy traffic, she could still make it on time. Luckily, there was less traffic, and she reached just in time. Right as she was about to enter the campus, she realized she had stepped on dog poop. The smell was dreadful. "Oh, shit! My day is spoiled. It is a bad day. A terrible day," thought Susan with complete disgust and anger. By the time she cleaned herself and got rid of the odor, she was 30 minutes late.

"It's a terrible day. It's a terrible day," muttered Susan to herself as she walked to her seat. Indeed, it turned out to be a terrible day for her. She got fired from her job that very day.

The moment Susan reached her apartment, she cried out loud. This is not the first time she was fired from a job. She could never hold a job for more than six months. "Oh! It is a terrible day. Life is terrible!" she kept muttering this sentence till she dozed off. Her cheeks remained wet with tears until the breeze coming from the window erased it all.

The next day, she woke up at noon and felt thirsty and hungry. She opened her apartment door to pick up the milk packet that gets delivered every day at her doorstep. To her surprise, the milk packet was not there. "Oh, shit! How come they didn't deliver the milk packet? Oh! God! What a terrible day. My life is so terrible." She went back to her bed, got consumed by self-pity and began chanting 'What a terrible day' till she slept off again.

In the evening, she dragged herself out of bed. She decided to go to the market nearby to buy a milk packet and some groceries. As she got off the lift, a little boy gave her a broad toothless smile and greeted her, "Hello, What-a-terrible-day aunty!" He then waved and ran off to the playground. She stood there speechless. She was so struck by his greeting that she took a minute to recover and find her voice again. She then walked to the playground and went up to the boy who greeted her and asked him, "Why did you call me What-a-terrible-day aunty?" The boy again gave her a broad smile and said, "Well, you always murmur that when you walk by. Looks like you are chanting some mantra. My grandfather always chants the name of God."

"Oh, shit! What a terrible day!" she muttered in irritation. The boy gleamed. "Oh! There you go again with 'what a terrible day.' What does 'terrible' mean, aunty? Is it the name of a god? Does it have some magical power?" The boy innocently asked. Susan just stood there with lips tightly closed, but in her head, she was indeed chanting 'What a terrible day.' Just that this time, she was aware of it. With no response coming from Susan, the little boy joined his friends to continue playing.

She sat on the park bench and contemplated her life. The boy was right. Whenever anything goes wrong, even if it is a tiny issue, she gets into chanting 'What a terrible day.' And somehow, her day ends in a terrible way. And recently, every day has been ending in a terrible way. "Does a simple statement—what a terrible day—have such power that it can indeed turn a normal day into terrible day and that too every time? Does language have that much power?" She sat there confused, bewildered and shocked. "One statement—what a terrible day—turns my life upside down. Everything has gone wrong for me for god knows how long. I am single and now without a job. Oh god! What a terrible d—" She stopped herself, "Oh! Come on, Susan. Stop saying that."

Then an idea hit her like lightning. "What if I start saying the opposite of 'What a terrible day'? How about 'Wow! What a great day!' Will that change my life?" Every time something goes wrong, she decided to say 'Wow! What a great day!' She felt energized and felt positive about transforming her life back in order. She would get up in the morning and say 'Wow! What a great day!' and then think of a couple of reasons why the day is indeed a great day. Every time something went wrong, she would say 'Wow! What a great day!' and then look for some reasons as to why it was a great day.

> *A few weeks later, she walked into a large corporation for a job interview. She really wanted to work for this great company. She kept murmuring 'Wow! What a great day.' Finally, her turn came, and she was called inside the conference room for an interview. The interview lasted for more than an hour. Finally, the main interviewer looked straight into her eyes and said, "I need to be very straightforward with you. You don't qualify for the position that is vacant. Hence, you are not selected." Susan's face lit up naturally. With a sparkle in her eyes, she said, "Wow! What a great day!" The interviewers were puzzled. One of them asked, "Why is it a great day? Are you saying this sarcastically?" Her eyes continued to radiate. "Wow! What a great day! I am saying this because I really wanted this job, and I couldn't qualify. Me not qualifying is a great opportunity to lift myself to higher standards. Isn't that something great to look forward to? That's why it is an excellent day. You will see a better and wiser Susan soon. Thanks for letting me know that I need to work on myself. Wow! It is a great day. Thank you, gentlemen." She got up to leave. The main interviewer requested her to sit once again. The interviewers interviewed her for another 20 minutes, and by the end of it, they reversed their decision and confirmed to her that she got the job.*
>
> *She walked out of the interview room and straight away headed to the bathroom. Tears rolled down her cheeks. She didn't want anyone to see her crying. Of course, they were tears of joy. "Wow! What a great day," she muttered to herself.*
>
> – Manoj Keshav

## NLP: Programming

Technologists, scientists and software programmers are creating technological breakthroughs almost every day. Siemens recently unveiled a driverless forklift truck that uses lasers to find its way around in factories. In the UK, the police use a system called Automatic Number-Plate Recognition technology. How does it work? When a vehicle passes an

ANPR camera, its registration number is read and instantly checked against database records of stolen cars or vehicles known to be used by criminals. The system does this recognition of registration numbers and checking it out with the database in a matter of few seconds. Police officers then can intercept and stop a vehicle, check it for evidence and make arrests when it's necessary.

The Lely group of the Netherlands has invented a machine that milks cows without human intervention. Cows learn to saddle up to this robot milking device on their own when their udders feel full, letting themselves in and out of a particular stall to do so. For the first time since humankind has domesticated animals, farmers don't have to rise before dawn to milk the herd.

Self-driving cars, robots and drones may give the impression that machines are self-aware and intelligent, but they just do what programmers want them to do. When a machine executes a man-made program, the machine gives the impression that it is a thinking machine, but they are nothing but pieces of metals and plastics put together along with instructions on what they need to do. Of course, in the years to come, machines are likely to become self-aware, but today their behavior reflects the instructions and programs that are fed to them.

It's true, technology has made our lives better, but technology did not self-evolve. It is just doing what it is programmed to do. It is the humans that created technology who deserve our appreciation.

**Humans and Machines: Do They Both End up Doing What They Are Programmed To Do?**

The critical difference between machines and humans is that machines are not self-aware and they only do what they are programmed to do. What about humans? Is there a difference? Are we like machines? Do we just execute programs that are installed in us by our parents, society, culture, traditions and life experiences? Are we self-aware or do we do what others or circumstances have programmed us to do just like robots?

## Behave Like a Girl

*Revathi was a naughty 6-year-old girl born in a wealthy family. She loved to run, dance and chatter nonstop for hours. She hardly saw her dad; he was often away on business tours. But today, she was happy that her dad was coming back home. She climbed on the sofa and jumped down screaming, "Dad is coming home! Hurraaay!" She ran from one room to another, screaming with joy, "Daaaad! Daaaad!" It was only in the evening that Dad came home. Later that evening, just as her dad entered, she ran to him with a big smile on her face and called out loudly, "Daaad!" Her father sat on the sofa and told his wife that he was tired and could do with a drink.*

*Revathi climbed on to her dad's lap and pulled his big mustache. As she did that, his face appeared to change to that of a funny monkey, and she laughed out loud. At once, her dad put her down with a stern voice saying, "Behave yourself. Girls don't laugh loudly in our culture." Little Revathi got scared to see her dad's angry eyes. She recoiled with fear. Nevertheless, she wanted to climb back on her dad's lap. But as she tried to climb back, her dad pushed her away. He said, "I don't want to see you laughing loudly ever again. Is that understood? Behave like a girl. Is that clear?" Revathi nodded with tears in her eyes. She never laughed wholeheartedly ever again.*

*Time went by. Revathi grew up, went to college and then got herself a job in a reputed firm. Despite her excellent performance, a feedback that she often got in her workplace was that she had a serious demeanor and that she never laughed, socialized or joked around with her colleagues. Revathi did try to let go and laugh just because it was in her feedback form. But something pulled her back.*

*She got married, had kids and got old. One night, in her sleep, she passed away. Her grandkids found one of her diaries under her pillow. She had scribbled down her thoughts, and as they read the journal, one theme came back again and again. That theme was: 'Although for onlookers I was an educated woman from a well to do family, I went through life as if I am a dead piece of wood. Wish I was more joyful, a little naughty and laughed my heart out.'*

**– Manoj Keshav**

Let me take the audacity to say that Revathi, although human in body, was just a machine executing her programmer's code. To onlookers, she might have appeared as an educated and intelligent lady, but she was not self-aware. She was not even aware that her natural ability to laugh had been suppressed by an externally installed program that came in the form of her dad's stern reprimand.

Let's look at another story:

## You Can Never Sing

*A little boy was asked to sing in the music class in school. The moment the music teacher looked at this boy with her stern eyes, the little boy experienced a wave of fear going through his body. His lips went dry, his*

> *throat constricted and he felt knots tighten in his stomach. "Come on, Ravi, sing now," the music teacher said impatiently. The boy wanted to sing, but his mouth wouldn't open out of fear. He saw the teacher's facial muscles tightening, and with a lot of effort, the little boy managed to open his mouth and sing the first line of the song. The whole class laughed. His voice sounded croaked and funny even to him. The teacher asked him to sit in a corner and told him to bring comic books next time he came to music class. She told him that he could never sing. And this little boy grew up to be a man, and the one thing he was very sure about himself was that he could never sing.*
>
> *If you ask him to pay attention to the voice in his head that tells him that he cannot sing and ask him whose voice he hears in his head when he believes he can't sing, he would be surprised to discover that it is his music teacher's. Is he self-aware?*
>
> *– Manoj Keshav*

Machines run preprogrammed programs. What about human beings? Do we execute a set of programs like machines?

What is programming in terms of human behavior? What is programming regarding thought patterns? What is programming regarding who I am as a person?

## Who Writes the Human Behavioral, Thought and Emotional Programs?

A computer program is written by humans. Who writes human behavioral, thought and emotional programs? Life does. Experience does. Consciously or unconsciously, we create our own programs. Machines cannot re-write their programs, but human beings can.

Most people are not aware of the programs within them that run their lives. They don't realize that they have the power to re-write the program if they are unhappy with their own behavior or life situation. You might say,

*"I do try and change my programs, but they relapse to the old patterns."* Well, you need to re-write your program at the 'neuro-linguistic' level and not merely change at the surface, New Year's resolution level. Welcome to the amazing world of NLP.

# Chapter 2
# The NLP Beliefs of Excellence

## Do Beliefs Manifest Into Reality?

The NLP beliefs of excellence are also called presuppositions. The word 'presuppose' means 'to suppose beforehand.' In the context of NLP, presuppositions are rules or principles or beliefs that facilitate change and self-empowerment. For example, when an athlete presupposes or believes that she is not going to win, she won't do her very best and hence is likely to lose the race. On the contrary, if an athlete presupposes or believes she is going to win, she is likely to feel more energy and give her best, which enhances the possibility of her winning.

There are beliefs or presuppositions that we have in our head that empower us, and there are also presuppositions that can disempower us. For example, if a person believes that someone doesn't like him, his defensive manner can make it a reality.

**Here is a list of key beliefs of excellence or presuppositions in NLP that facilitate change and self-empowerment:**

### 1. The Map is Not the Territory

The phrase was coined by Alfred Korzybski, an engineer, mathematician and a great thinker. A map can never be precisely accurate; otherwise, it's size would be the same as the ground it covers. The map of London is not London. Although a map can never be precisely accurate and can never capture all the information of the territory it represents, it is still very useful. A map is also contextual. A railway map may show all the key railway stations and routes but not every single stop on the way, and it is likely to exclude other milestones like bus stops. Yet, a railway map has its utility.

Similarly, for the city we reside in, we have a map of that city in our head. We may not have captured every street, every building and all the details of the city in our head, but the map that we have of the city is enough to get us through the day.

## All That We Believe In – Are They True?

It is not just a city map that we carry in our head but a life map. Everything we experience in our life, we add to this mental map and keep updating it based on our experiences. However, we might draw a few lines too soon. For example, a person travels to Hong Kong and gets tricked by a local. Based on this episode, he concludes that all the people of the country are cheats and Hong Kong is not a safe place to travel. Another person who goes to Hong Kong finds the locals very helpful and trustworthy. He concludes that all of the country's people are wonderful and Hong Kong is a great place to travel. Both of these individuals have created a different map or 'representation' of the same territory.

A little boy fails an exam and gets reprimanded by his teachers and parents. His friends laugh at him and crack jokes about him. The little boy concludes that he is not capable and that his intelligence is lower than that of others. This conclusion becomes a part of his self-map that he carries in his head. He lives his entire life as a mediocre person because he believes that he is not a capable person and his intelligence cannot compete with others. To him, it is the absolute truth (mental map) although the facts (reality) might be different.

'The map is not the territory' is a life-transforming belief of excellence. The stuff that we carry in our head—thoughts, beliefs, opinions and views—may not be accurate. Yet, we respond to this flawed map that we carry in our head, not the actual territory (reality). Understanding that the map is not the territory helps us question our thoughts. It encourages us to take our thoughts with a pinch of salt. It gives us a chance to update our maps on a regular basis, which includes letting go of outdated thoughts and beliefs and creating a new set of thoughts and beliefs that are more in tune with the current reality.

## 2. People Work Perfectly

Think about a car engine that has a part which is out of place or flawed due to wear and tear. Because of this, the engine makes much noise when the car is being driven. One way to look at it is that the engine is not working perfectly; it needs to be repaired. Another way to look at it is that the engine works perfectly fine, given its situation—one of its parts is out of place or flawed. It continues to run in the best way possible, given the current restriction.

When a person begins to limp after an injury, one view is that he is not walking properly. Another view is that he is walking perfectly, given his current conditions. He wouldn't have walked any differently in this situation at this point in time if his circumstances were the same as before.

Every being is a product of his or her experiences, circumstances, education, cultural and societal influences, etc. When a person takes a decision or action, he or she is doing the best, given his or her background, understanding and resources at that point in time. They couldn't have done anything differently.

> ### Weighs Like a Piece of Paper
>
> *Sathish always felt his life was messed up because he quit college before getting his degree. He did odd jobs throughout his life, and now at the age of 55, all he could think of was his unfinished degree. "How stupid of me to have walked away from such a good college," thought Sathish. This unfinished degree was eating him from inside. "Had I been an engineer, I would have been in a very good position and in an excellent company," thought Sathish.*
>
> *As he became older and older, he became more and more bitter about life. All he could think of was his unfinished degree and the deep remorse he felt about it. One night, as Sathish was sleeping, the God of Death visited him because his time had come. The God of Death lifted him from the bed and found Sathish too light. "How come this person weighs like a piece of paper?" thought the God of Death. The God of Death then poked his finger through Sathish's skin and found nothing inside. His innards had been eaten away by remorse.*
>
> — **Manoj Keshav**

When we look at a laptop we used 15 years ago, we can now say that it was too slow and cumbersome. Yes, today's laptops are faster, sleeker and more efficient. But the laptop that we used 15 years ago worked perfectly at that point in time, given the software and hardware that it came with.

Similarly, when we look back at life, we are filled with regrets, guilt and shame. But we couldn't have done anything differently at that point in time, given the experience, maturity and understanding of life we had at that point in time.

Every human being is doing their best at any given point in time, given the software (mind) and hardware (body) that one possesses. This doesn't mean that we don't have any flaws; not that we cannot improve ourselves. But we don't have to feel guilty or regret the decisions we made in the past because we did our best, given the circumstances, knowledge, skills and awareness we had.

This belief of excellence can completely change our perception of ourselves and others. It can help us accept people the way they are and at the same time help us identify the root causes of our apparent flaws in order to re-design our lives.

## 3. Every Behavior Has a Positive Intention

Positive intention is the conscious or unconscious benefit we derive from a behavior. We all have reasons for what we do. Sometimes, we are aware of the reasons at the conscious level. Sometimes, we may not be conscious of it. Everything we do, we do for some benefit for ourselves. Without a purpose, reason or self-interest, there is no motivation to act or behave in a certain way.

**Few examples:**

| S.no. | Behavior | Positive Intention |
|---|---|---|
| 1: Person 'A' | Drinking Alcohol | For A, the primary intention is to beat stress and feel a sense of mental relaxation, which happens to be through alcohol. |

Reducing stress and restoring mental well-being is a human need. It's natural for someone under too much stress to do something that helps restore a sense of comfort and wellness. Although the intention here is positive, the means (drinking alcohol) to achieve this objective can lead to addiction and health problems.

Going for a walk, listening to music, talking about your stress to a friend or therapist, meditation, etc., are healthier ways to beat stress without adverse side effects. This also reveals that although we don't agree with how a person behaves, which we might find annoying or even unhealthy, we can connect with and appreciate the positive intention behind the behavior.

| S. no. | Behavior | Positive Intention |
|---|---|---|
| 1: Person 'B' | Asthma attack: Psychosomatic disease. For B, her mind creates the health issue. | For B, the positive intention is meeting her need for belongingness and love with her family. |

As a child (Person B), whenever she was sick and had an asthma attack, her family showered her with love and affection. As an adult, whenever she felt a deep need for love, which she was not receiving from her husband, and felt unappreciated by her kids, her mind unconsciously triggered an attack. True to her belief, her family then gave her time and care. Whenever she was healthy and fine, they tended to ignore her amidst their busy lives. Her subconscious mind has learned to trigger an attack in order for her to meet her need for belongingness and love.

Although we may not approve of how her mind copes with the lack of love by causing a physical issue, we can be compassionate and agree that her need for love and connection is real, and the intention to meet those needs is positive.

All our actions and behaviors have some purpose that we value. By identifying the intention, establishing a rapport with it and exploring healthier alternatives to satisfy our positive intention, we have better chances of working on our unwanted behavior and changing it.

## 4. People Make the Best Choice They Can at the Time

A woman resolves to diet and eats healthy food to reduce weight. She manages to diet right through the day. She has a party to attend in the evening, so she decides to not eat cake or any sweets; she is going to eat right. At the party, her friend brings her a large slice of red velvet cake. This woman looks at the cake, which looked delicious. She couldn't resist taking a bite. "Just one bite," she tells herself. But it was so yummy that she couldn't help but take another bite and another until she finished the entire slice.

To an outsider, it might look like she made a wrong decision. She didn't know how to make the best choice at that point in time. But the truth of the matter is that we all make the best decision at any given time. Taking into account her subconscious mind's deep craving for red velvet cake, her weak willpower, which is in beginning stage when it comes to food, lack of strategies on how to avoid unhealthy food and go for healthier options when in a group, considering her past experiences with saying NO to others and her deep-seated habits encoded in her brain, she couldn't have taken any other decision.

A person takes a decision to buy shares from a particular company. The market collapses, and he regrets his decision. But the fact is that while buying the shares with all the information that was available at that point in time, with all his previous experiences and considering his mental and emotional maturity at that point in time, he couldn't have taken any other decision.

Every decision that we have taken and every choice we have exercised in the past, we couldn't have done in any other way. Yes, we can improve our decision-making skills by working on our attitude, but it's important to remember that 'people make the best choice they can at the time.'

This NLP belief of excellence helps us to accept our past and work on our mental software to improve decision-making skills rather than just regret certain decisions.

5. **There is No Failure, Only Feedback – All Results and Behaviors are Achievements, Whether They are Desired Outcome for a Given Task/Context or Not**

The Wright brothers wouldn't have known any success if it wasn't for their repeated failures. Even though they were close to powered flight, unforeseen setbacks brought them to the brink of yet another defeat.

The Wright brothers never let a crash set them back. Instead, they took what they learned to make their prototype more effective. The Wright brothers' success laid the foundation of the ever-growing multi-billion-dollar aviation industry.

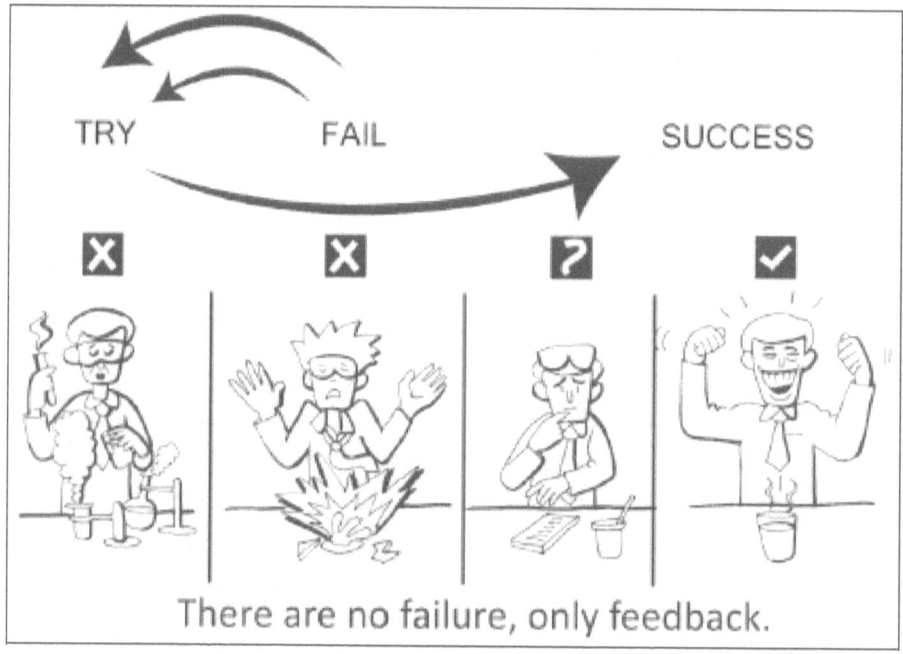

Every prototype that the Wright brothers built is an achievement; every failure is an achievement. All these achievements led to the final outcome—a successful powered flight. Hence, all results and behaviors need to be considered as achievements.

Sigmund Freud was booed from the podium when he first presented his ideas to the scientific community of Europe. He returned to his office and kept on writing.

As an inventor, Edison made 1000 unsuccessful attempts at inventing the light bulb. When a reporter asked, "How did it feel to fail 1000 times?" He replied, "The light bulb was an invention with 1000 steps."

Henry Ford failed and went broke five times before he succeeded. Failure contains within itself invaluable lessons. Learning these lessons are essential to success. Hence, it would be appropriate to say that success lies concealed within failure. In other words, we open the treasure box of success with a key that we found while looking out for lessons learned from failures.

## 6. The Meaning of Communication is the Response You Get

How do we know if a salesman is good or not? By looking at the results. If he is able to sell, he is a good salesman, and if he is not able to sell, he is not. A salesman can never blame the customer for his failure. How do we know if a person is an excellent communicator or not? By looking at the response she or he receives. If the communication is misunderstood and does not produce results, then the communication is not effective. A communicator can never blame the receiver or the audience for failure in communication just like a salesman cannot hold a prospective customer responsible for failing to sell.

For example, a father communicates with his son in order to motivate him to study, but the end result is that the son feels demotivated and irritated by the father's words. In this case, the meaning of the father's communication is in the response he received. In other words, what the father conveyed through his communication is, "Hey, son! I want you to get demotivated and irritated." How can we be sure that's what the father communicated? Because that's the response he got. **The meaning of communication is the response you get.**

If the father understands this belief of excellence, he will then change his choice of words and style of communication until he gets the desired result that he wants, and his son will feel motivated to do well in school. Otherwise, he will go on communicating in the same old way, and the son will continue to feel demotivated and irritated.

Master communicators are not born but made. The best way to improve your communication skills is to know when we fail at communication and take responsibility for it. We can gauge this by the response we get. By learning from failures and being flexible in how we choose to communicate, we can become master communicators and produce excellent results.

## 7. The Resources an Individual Needs to Effect a Change are Already Within Him/Her

The cells of your body start from just a single cell. The first replication gives two cells. The second replication gives four and so on. By the 50$^{th}$ replication, you have 100, 000 billion cells in your body, and that's where the replication stops. Scientists are still puzzled by how that single cell ends up dividing into so many different kinds of cells, which then are able to organize themselves into a stomach, a brain, skin, teeth and all other highly specialized parts of the body.

Our muscles are made of muscle cells, our liver of liver cells and there are even very specialized types of cells that make the enamel of our teeth or the clear lenses in our eyes. Each cell does a few million things per second just to keep functioning, like breaking glucose down for energy to building cell walls, constructing new enzymes and allowing the cell to reproduce. Every single cell is supremely intelligent. All these trillions of cells coming together and working together is nothing short of a miracle. It's a definitely a sign of the super intelligence that is present in every cell of your body.

The human brain has extraordinary abilities. The human brain is a self-learning system which adapts continuously to continually changing environmental conditions and situations. Most people feel awed by the value of a precious diamond or a Rolex watch but don't appreciate one of the greatest gifts that we are born with: the amazing human brain. Most people underuse it, misuse it, underestimate its power and take its abilities for granted.

You do not have to measure the distance between you and another person when you shake hands with them. You do not have to measure the distance between you and the television set to adjust your vision. You do not have to measure the distance between your car and the other car and its speed while overtaking it. You do all these without even thinking about it because of your brain's incredible capacity to crunch numbers at unimaginable speeds. Your brain performs trillions of computations in the blink of an eye. Every human being is endowed with super brains. We are all super intelligent. Some of us may not use our intelligence entirely, but just being humans, we are super intelligent. We have to learn to trust our incredible potential and intelligence to solve problems, change our self and enjoy a fuller life.

The resources an individual needs to change are already within them. Accepting this belief of excellence will kill the blame game. We blame our apparent lack of intelligence or lack of charisma for our failures. We tell ourselves, "I am not that talented," or "I am not lovable," or "I am not creative." We carry low self-esteem and berate ourselves for not being smart enough. But the truth of the matter is that each human being has incredible potential and talent. We have all the resources to change and be what we want to be. We have all the resources already within us to go after our goals and dreams. The only question is, "Are we willing to recognize the immense power that we have and are we willing to tap into the abundant reservoir of intelligence and talent within?"

## 8. Most Distinctions Human Beings are Able to Make Concerning Our Environment and Our Behavior Can Be Usefully Represented Through the Visual, Auditory, Kinesthetic, Olfactory and Gustatory Senses

The five senses are the five main tools that humans use to perceive the world. These senses are sight (Visual), hearing (Auditory), smell (Gustatory), touch (Kinesthetic) and taste (Gustatory).

Today, science has listed much more than five senses—anywhere from 9–21. These include things like perception of heat, pressure, pain and balance among others. But the five primary senses are the most fundamental tools that we use to make sense of our surrounding. Although our five senses seem to operate independently as five distinct modes of perceiving the world, in reality, they collaborate closely with each other to enable the mind to better understand our surroundings.

A brain in a jar has never experienced anything. There is no experience where there is no consciousness. Life is experienced through the five senses—the sight of beautiful flowers during springtime, the taste of biting into a piece of fresh ripened mango, standing in the beach and listening to the sound of the waves or the soothing touch of someone you love.

We take these five senses for granted, but they are incredible. Our eye alone consists of more than two million working parts. A person with normal vision can recognize candlelight from up to 14 miles away. Although our sense of smell is inferior to the sense of smell possessed by animals, we can still smell about 10,000 odors. When you ride a bike on a busy street, your sense of hearing helps you to see approaching vehicles from behind even before you actually see them. Life is not possible without the five senses.

When we are thinking, dreaming, remembering and memorizing, we are using these senses internally. Just for a moment, pay attention to what's going on in your mind. You might come across an image which might be as vivid and colorful as an image in real life. Or you might recall an image from the past, which is gray and unclear, not how the image was in real life back then. The quality of the visual images that come and go, which are part of your thinking, plays a crucial role in how you perceive life within your head.

Sometimes when we think of a past experience, we recreate all the visuals, sounds and odors that came with it. In memories, you see, you touch, you smell, you hear, you taste—none of it is real; they are just memories. Take away the five senses of those memories, and there is nothing much left.

Whether our attention is on the external world around us or our internal world, the five senses are the medium through which we experience life. Understanding the way we use our five senses is crucial to understanding our personality and our behavior.

## 9. The Person With the Most Flexibility in Thinking and Behavior Has the Greatest Influence

There are people who are very rigid about their approach to doing things, communicating, solving problems, etc. Imagine a salesperson who makes the exact same presentation to every prospective client he meets. And he is rigid about it. Even if a potential client is in a hurry, he sticks to his style of presentation and cannot make a short sales pitch.

Now consider, in contrast, a salesperson who customizes his presentation to the needs of the client. He speaks more about technology when a client is more interested in it, he focuses on durability when a client is more concerned about that, and he talks about value for money when a client's priority is the price. If a client wants a lot of information, he makes a detailed presentation. If a client wants a concise presentation, he makes a presentation with only the key points.

The second salesperson will be more influential compared to the salesperson with the rigid approach. To be able to modify our approach to match changing circumstances and expectations is the key to success and influence. Flexibility in thinking and behavior also helps a person to deal with unexpected events in an ever-changing environment. Changing strategies to match the reality of the situation, unlearning and letting go of approaches that are no more useful, embracing change, being open to new ideas and developing the ability to work with a broad spectrum of people are the keys to power and impact.

Holding on to the notion of 'That's how I always do…and will do it' indicates a preference to live in the past and pining for the good old days. Continuing to keep doing the same thing when it isn't working is a sure path to getting stuck in life. The road to success is never straight; it is full of twists and turns, unexpected roadblocks and potholes. Learning from mistakes, improvising your approach and trying again, building resilience and willingness to shift views and seeing problems with a new perspective are the keys to success.

## 10. What We Recognize in Others is True About Ourselves

"My wife does not appreciate me. She is so critical. She always finds fault in me," said a man to his colleague. "Isn't that what you are doing right now? Being critical of your wife," asked the friend. The man was taken aback. "What do you mean? Are you saying that I am the one who does not appreciate her? Am I the one who is constantly critical?"

"If you feel the need to find faults in her, isn't it likely that she too will find faults in you? What about when you speak to yourself? Do you criticize yourself? Do you find faults and look for things that you didn't do right instead of all things you did well? How many times have you appreciated yourself in the last week?" asked the colleague. "If you haven't appreciated yourself even once in the last week, how can you expect your partner or somebody else to find something to appreciate in you?"

Everyone you meet is a mirror. We can only see things in others that we see within ourselves. To say 'somebody is very judgmental' is to recognize being judgmental ourselves. What you say about others says a lot about you. Your perceptions of others reveal much about your own personality. What we hate in others is what we hate in ourselves. The traits that we tend to dislike in others are usually the traits we do not like about ourselves. **"What we recognize in others is true about ourselves."** This NLP belief of excellence helps us truly understand ourselves and brings far-reaching changes within.

## 11. The Way to Understand is to Do

Children are so good at learning. A child can learn a language much faster than an adult. A child can adapt to a new city or culture very fast. He/she can learn the cultural nuances of the new city faster than an adult. One reason why children learn things fast is that they don't wait for total understanding. They just jump right into action. For example, a child learns a little bit about a new language and starts speaking without any hesitation or worry about grammar or mistakes. The more the child speaks the new language, the more the child learns it.

An adult wants to understand everything about the language before speaking (doing) the language. In the process, they never get to learn the new language. To resist putting into action something 'new' till we fully understand it sounds quite logical, but in the learning arena, it just comes in the way of learning.

Do first, understand later; that's the secret to learning. Whether it is public speaking, mathematics, meditation, learning to sing or learning to dance, we learn by doing, making mistakes, doing it again, correcting mistakes and finally understanding and doing it correctly. If you want to understand meditation fully before doing it, it is never going to happen. Do first and understand later.

Even to master NLP, trial and error is the only way to do it. Even though you don't understand it fully in the beginning, if you keep going, the understanding deepens. Making mistakes, learning from failures, trying it again and correcting the mistakes and doing it again are all part of the process. There are no failures, only feedback. That's how you master any skill. ***The way to understand is to do.*** This NLP belief of excellence is the secret to success.

## 12. The Ability to Change the Process By Which We Experience Reality is More Often Valuable Than Changing The Content of Our Experience of Reality

Take the case of a woman for whom every positive experience in her memory is fuzzy and gray. She cannot recall the details. It could be an experience back in school or an experience from last week. Recalling a happy experience takes time, and when she does recall it, the picture is unclear, hazy and gray. On the other hand, every unpleasant experience is vivid, bright and rich in detail. She can quickly recall a bad experience whether it happened years ago or in the recent days. It's easier for her to speak about her bad experiences because she has vivid memories of the same.

There is a structure to the way she is unconsciously storing her experiences in her head. All pleasant memories are hazy, gray and unclear, while all unpleasant memories are in color, vivid and easy to recall.

Suppose we change the way she stores her experiences; suppose we train her mind to consciously store all the pleasant memories in color and the unpleasant memories in gray, what would happen? There will be a huge shift in her personality and behavior. A woman who doesn't smile, doesn't look happy most of the time and has difficulty feeling joyful will undergo a huge change when how she processes reality changes. This is life transforming because the change is at the process level, not just at the content level of experiences.

*Hence, the ability to change the process by which we experience reality is often more valuable than changing the content of our experience of reality.*

## 13. Every Behavior is Appropriate in Some Context

If a behavior does not work, it is useful to re-contextualize it than to fight against it. The more you resist a behavior, the more it persists. The more you use that behavior in an appropriate context, the more that behavior becomes useful.

For example, let's take procrastination. A student might want to do his school assignments, but he procrastinates. He wants to get up in the morning and jog, but he delays. He wants to stop eating junk and begin eating healthy food, but he procrastinates again. And over a period, procrastination becomes a strong habit, which he tries hard to get rid of but cannot.

Let's take another example. A hardworking individual wants to find himself wanting to make an impulse purchase of a fancy car on credit, but he procrastinates. He feels like going to the casino and gambling away the extra bonus he received at work, but he procrastinates. When he gets angry, he wants to curse and scream at a colleague, but he delays again. While working late on a project, he wants to sleep, but procrastinates sleep and completes the project.

Procrastination can be wise and healthy or self-destructive based on the context. The hardworking individual does not give in to unnecessary impulses, does not overspend and diligently does his work, all because of procrastination. A few very successful stock-market traders' secret success formula: procrastinate the impulse to sell when you see the market going crazy and everybody is selling in a panic. Stay for the long term, and you will make big money in the market.

Every action can be considered useful or unhealthy based on the context. In rare cases, even injuring someone turned out to be the action which saved one's own life or saved others from danger. Instead of trying to get rid of a behavior, it would be more appropriate to use a particular behavior in the right context. Even a wonderful thing like a smile is not appropriate in every circumstance. For example, smiling during a funeral may not bring out the right reaction even if it was well-intended.

Whenever there is an inner dialog that goes, "I want to get rid of this behavior of mine," change that inner dialog to, "When will this behavior be valuable?" and "When is this behavior inappropriate?"

***Every behavior is useful in some context.*** This NLP belief of excellence helps us to take note of the circumstances and context while taking decisions rather than follow blind rules or a predetermined code of conduct all the time, in every context, without conscious thinking.

Flexibility and adaptability help us survive, rigidity keeps us stuck. To be flexible, we need to consider the appropriateness of our behavior based on the context.

## 14. You Cannot Not Communicate

Some people say nothing to remain safe. But not saying anything is also communication. Whether we like it or not, we are always communicating, either verbally or non-verbally, even when we do not intend to. Even by remaining silent, a message is conveyed. Our physical posture, the tone of voice, facial expressions, breathing, hand gestures, muscles tension, moving a step forward or backward, the way we dress, stand, walk—everything is communicating something about us to the world around us.

If you have ever been on the receiving end of a fellow driver's angry fist, a colleague's contemptuous smile, a friend's scowl or a child's sad face, you know how much can be conveyed without uttering a word.

In therapy, what a client conveys non-verbally is far more important than what he or she reveals verbally. Becoming aware of non-verbal communication is essential to understand the real message. For example, when a client speaks about his mother and suddenly his breathing changes, his muscles tighten and his voice becomes slightly strained, it is imperative that the therapist picks up the non-verbal cues because verbally he might be saying wonderful things about his mom, but his non-verbal communication paints a different picture.

It is also important to know that we are communicating all the time whether we are actively speaking and participating or not. It would be appropriate to ask, "What message am I sending non-verbally right now? Is it appropriate? Can I work on my non-verbal and verbal communication?"

If there is a misunderstanding, if the result of your communication is something you are not happy with, then it is time to become aware of your non-verbal communication, which includes your facial expressions, tone of voice, posture, how fast or how slow you are speaking and most importantly, what your body language conveys when you are not verbally speaking.

Bringing awareness to what you convey when you are not saying anything and how your non-verbal language compliments or restricts your verbal communication is the key to improving your interaction with others.

# Chapter 3

# New Level of Awareness Through Sensory Acuity

*"There is ecstasy in paying attention."*

**– Anne Lamott**

The term 'acuity' refers to the physical ability of the sensory organs to receive input. The physical ability of the sensory organs is different for different species. What a dog can smell, humans cannot. A honeybee can see ultraviolet light, humans cannot. Humans can see the colors of the rainbow, cats cannot. Cats can hear ultrasonic frequencies, humans cannot.

A person's visual acuity refers to the person's ability to see; we characterize one's visual acuity as 20/20 vision and use numerical digits to denote the accuracy of the eyes' ability to see both close and distant objects. Auditory acuity is the person's ability to hear and indicates one's hearing ability with numbers that denote the decibels one can hear accurately.

## What Is the Difference Between Sensory Acuity and Perception?

It is important to understand the distinction between 'acuity' and 'perception.'

**Sensory Acuity** is the process of receiving sensory input accurately. For example, eyes receive visual information, ears receive auditory information, etc. Acuity is restricted to receiving the physical information and not the interpretation of the received data.

**Perception** refers to the person's ability to understand or make meaning out of the sensory input received through the sensory organs such as the eyes and ears. The perceptual process occurs through mechanisms in the brain that link the current sensory information with similar memories of past experiences and knowledge.

### My Guru – Hero or Villain?

*Ria and Renu worked for AirTight Security Services. They were in the organization's mini-auditorium. Both of them were software engineers and had about three years of service in the company. Also, they were now close friends and were seated next to each other. There were about 150 staff members of AirTight Security Services in the auditorium waiting for the program to start. They all knew that it would be a 2-hour motivational seminar, but nobody knew who the speaker was.*

Suddenly, there was some activity on the stage. Both Ria and Leela looked at the stage, and both knew the speaker of the evening would appear on the stage any minute. Then they saw the speaker walking toward the center of the stage. He was an old man clad in a saffron dress from head to toe, looking like a Hindu spiritual guru. The whole auditorium stood up in reverence to the holy guru except Leela. Ria, who noticed that Leela was still sitting, leaned toward her and asked," What happened, Leela? Are you ok?" Leela couldn't say anything. By then the spiritual guru had asked the crowd to be seated, hence everybody sat down. Ria again looked at Leela, she was breathing hard and there were beads of sweat on her forehead. Leela looked at Ria and said, "I am perfectly fine. You focus on what the guruji is saying." "Ok Leela, I got sacred. Thought you are not feeling well. Ok, let's listen to the Guruji."

Ria was looking at the guruji with respect and admiration. She was listening to his every word with total attention. On the other hand, Leela was looking down with clenched fists, feeling angry, scared and disgusted with the guruji although she was seeing that old man in the saffron dress for the first time.

The reason Leela was in this state was because, as a 14-year-old girl, her parents brought an old man clad in a saffron dress home to conduct a prayer to ward off evil spirits. They told her that this old man was a spiritual master and that she should touch his feet and seek his blessing. This spiritual master, after performing the prayer, asked for a large sum of money as the evil spirit was stronger and said that he needed to stay in the house for two weeks and do prayers regularly to ward off the evil spirit. Those two weeks were hell for Leela.

Every night, the old man in the saffron dress would come into her room and molest her. He told her that if she told anybody about it, the evil spirit would take her away to a dark forest far away, and she will never be able to

> *return to her parents. Although she didn't believe in evil spirits, the mean and dangerous look in his eyes froze her in fear, and she never told anybody about the horrific suffering she had gone through those two weeks. After that terrible experience, she could not trust another spiritual or religious guru. The man speaking on stage is not the same man who had molested her, but Leela hated all men of religion. For her, they were all evil spirits who had come from the dark forest.*
>
> *On the other hand, unlike Leela, Ria had fallen very sick as a teenager. One night, the situation deteriorated very severely, and she started shivering. She was taken to a hospital, but her condition worsened further. Ria reached a state when she felt she might die. Thinking of death made her cringe with fear. Tears started rolling down her cheeks. She didn't want to die. It was then that she saw her mother bringing a spiritual guru clad in a saffron dress. This guruji applied sandal paste on her head and started chanting mantras. She couldn't remember all the religious rituals he performed, but she remembers his eyes. The eyes had a divine spark, kindness and purity. She woke up the next day feeling better, and in a few days, she was fully alright. Ever since, every time she saw a spiritual or a religious person, she bowed with gratitude for one of them had saved her life.*
>
> *– Manoj Keshav*

The brain is the organ of perception. The eyes may see something, but it is the brain that gives these sensory stimuli their meaning; two people may be exposed to the same stimulus, but their different personalities and life experiences will determine their perceptions of that sensory stimulus. Ria and Leela both looked at the saffron-clad Hindu spiritual guru. Both of them have never seen this particular guru before in their life. But Ria looked at the guru with reverence and admiration, while Leela felt anger and disgust looking at him. The visual image or the stimulus was the same for both of them, but their perception of that visual image was completely different for both of them.

There are two areas that we can enhance or fine-tune to improve our capabilities. The first is our ability to improve how we receive information through our five input channels: visual (sight), auditory (sound), kinesthetic (touch), olfactory (smell) and gustatory (taste). This ability is sensory acuity. The second is to relook at and rework our perception of life. We don't look at reality just as it is. We look at it through the filters of our beliefs, assumptions, judgments, biases, momentary feelings, moods, etc. To be able to see reality just as it is, we need to work on how we perceive life. In this chapter, we will focus on how we can enhance our sensory acuity.

## How to Develop a New Level of Awareness Through Sensory Acuity?

For some people, the ability of these five senses to receive information is well developed. On the other hand, for some people, the ability to receive information is very poorly developed. When given stale or slightly spoiled food, some people will neither be able to make out the nasty smell nor the disgusting taste. They would just eat the rotten food and won't know the difference.

Not being able to make out if the food has turned bad through smell or taste is not a rare occurrence, and it is becoming more common these days. For most people, the five senses are beginning to rust slowly. It is getting clogged and hazy. The ability to make finer visual, auditory and kinesthetic distinctions is becoming an uncommon ability. The reason is that we have lost touch with our physical reality and are mostly lost in our head.

## Overthinking Everything

What do most people do nowadays? They wake up thinking about something and continue living in their heads, lost in their thoughts, throughout the day. They are lost in thoughts throughout the day irrespective of the time, place and situation. They are lost in thoughts while listening to a client or during a holiday or while holding their loved one's hand. At the end of it all, most people spend most of their energy on compulsive thinking and daydreaming. This process is called **overthinking everything**.

People often advise their fellow beings not to eat excessively, sleep excessively or speak excessively, but very rarely does someone advise not to think excessively. Making a mountain out of a molehill is an idiom referring to an over-reactive, histrionic behavior where a person makes too much of a minor issue. And it looks like the state of humanity is currently stuck in this 'automatic, over-reactive, thinking too much' mode.

To be able to feel the breeze while standing in the balcony, to taste the flavors of juicy fruits, to explore and feel the grass barefoot, to be drawn to the fragrance of a flower in a garden—all these natural functions now seem to be a thing of the past. For the modern human, these natural things are quite alien. To worry about the future, regret the past, get paranoid over nothing, lose sleep due to anxiety or simply brood over nothing seem to be the existential reality for most of humanity.

## Alcoholic Vs. Mindoholic: What's the Difference?

An alcoholic is a man or a woman who suffers from alcoholism; they have a distinct physical desire to consume alcohol beyond their capacity to control it, regardless of common sense.

According to Alcoholics Anonymous UK, who have no unique definition for alcoholism, "It may be described as a physical compulsion, together with a mental obsession. Apart from having an enormous craving for alcohol, an alcoholic often yields to that craving at the worst possible times. The alcoholic knows neither when nor how to stop drinking."

Similarly, 'mindoholic' is the distinct mental obsession with consuming thoughts beyond one's capacity to control it, regardless of common sense. Mindoholic can be described as a psychological compulsion to think repetitive and unproductive thoughts throughout the day. Apart from having an enormous craving for thinking, a mindoholic person often yields to that craving at regular times and the worst possible times. The mindoholic knows neither when nor how to stop thinking.

It is not about you using the mind the right way or the wrong way. In reality, the mind is using us, just how the drink takes over the alcoholic and not the other way around. An alcoholic believes he has a justified reason to drink when he has none. Mindoholics believe they are using the mind, but it is just the other way around.

### Living in the Fantasy World in Our Head

*Jai is in a meeting at the corporate headquarters. He is physically at the meeting, but mentally something else is going on. He is incessantly talking or muttering to himself, but to people sitting next to him, he looks normal. They don't know what is going on in his head. Jai appears deeply involved in the meeting, but inside his head, analysis after analysis is going on. At times, this analysis occurs in the form of speculation or judgment. At other times, this analysis appears as comparisons or complaints. At other moments, it can be in the form of fantasy, obsession or paranoia. But if this constant need for mental analysis continues beyond a point, the right word for it is paralysis. It is typically at this time that Jai's shoulder freezes, jaw muscles get tensed up and breathing becomes erratic.*

> *Jai wants the meeting to get over, and he wants to get out, but the meeting continues; Jai feels suffocated and has no idea what is being discussed. His mind goes everywhere and nowhere, and the mental paralysis keeps him stuck. The other members still have no idea what is going on in Jai's mind. They can only see Jai's smiling face and Jai's head nodding by which they conclude that Jai is a very attentive and committed professional. Similarly, Jai has no idea what is going in others' mind. All he can see are smiling and nodding faces. "They all look so attentive and committed," thinks Jai.*
>
> *The watchman looks through the window and sees everybody in the meeting smiling and nodding. "They all look so happy," thinks the watchman. Soon, the thoughts engulf him, and the watchman finds himself lost in the fantasy world of daydreams. To an onlooker, the watchman looks so attentive and committed.*
>
> – Manoj Keshav

## Is Thinking Our Strength or Weakness?

Our ability to think is our greatest strength, but excessive and compulsive thinking has cut us off from reality—the here and now. What is the point of ordering the best ice cream or dish on the menu and not savoring it because your mind is somewhere else? What is the point of going on a holiday and spending the whole time thinking about work or office tasks? What is the point of talking to the customer while worrying about your kids and later at home worrying about customers while having dinner with kids?

Rivers are getting polluted, our sky is getting polluted, our soil is getting polluted and even space is getting polluted. The root cause of all these environmental pollutions is because our mind is polluted due to excessive and compulsive thinking. No animal or plant has polluted the planet earth the way we have because no animal or plant thinks as compulsively as we do. Thoughts of anger, greed, fear, jealousy, suspicion, scarcity, paranoia, etc., are the root cause of all the ill that we see around us. The human mind is filled with repetitive, useless or harmful thoughts. Continuously worrying and being anxious all the time has become the normal state for most people. In other words, overthinking everything is the root cause of all human pain on planet earth.

We don't have to let go of our thinking ability and become an animal or a plant. The ability to think is our greatest strength. If only we could use our thinking skills for the betterment of ourselves and the planet earth. Instead, we are misusing our thinking ability. Just like an alcoholic, we are addicted to our thinking so much so that our mind has become a tormentor in our head, and it continuously worries and blocks us from experiencing joy and peace. How to stop thinking excessively? In fact, if we can reduce the quantity of our thinking, the quality of our thoughts will automatically go up. How to reduce the quantity of thoughts? How to get in touch with life in the here and now? NLP sensory acuity exercises fine-tune our five senses, which then enables us to get in touch with life in the present moment.

## How to Fine-Tune all Your Five Senses?

The French scientist Jean-Baptiste de Lamarck (1744–1829) is noted for the Law of Use and Disuse that states, "The parts of an organism's body that are used become more developed, the parts that are not used become smaller and may disappear."

Not using our five senses to their fullest ability may not lead to their disappearance, but their ability could reduce over the years. Having a fine sense of smell, taste, sight, hearing and touch enhances every life experience. For most people, all five senses begin to dull with disuse, but there are ways you can sharpen them.

When a sensory system has been activated, the other senses do not assume the role of an uninvolved spectator. Multiple human senses work together as a team to produce a perception. Imagine a very crucial moment like crossing a busy road. If our senses worked independently of each other, each standing in a queue to deliver fragmented information to the brain, that would be a disaster. Instead, multiple inputs from different brain circuits are processed to generate a single unified experience.

Enhancing sensory acuity involves noticing, in the environment, things that we did not notice before. It is about being totally aware of the present moment and stretching our ability to notice the finer aspects and making subtler distinctions.

**Here is how the 'Enhancing Sensory Acuity' exercises can take you to a new level of awareness:**

## 1. Olfactory/Sense of Smell

The olfactory system gives humans their sense of smell by collecting odorants from the environment and transducing them into neural signals. This sensory system uses the molecular chemical compound in substances or odorants (odorant is any substance that has a distinctive smell) to discern information about the environment.

The primary sensory organ responsible for the human's sense of smell is the nasal cavity, which contains olfactory receptors that perform the transduction of odors into neural impulses.

- **20-minute practice technique:** Spend 20 minutes consciously smelling everything that you come across. For example, when you pick up the newspaper, see if you can smell it. You don't have to bring the newspaper close to your nose. Just read the newspaper the way you always do but take in the smell. Different newspapers smell different. Later, when you pick up your coffee cup, smell the coffee. Do different brands of coffee smell different? Or are they all the same?

When you walk from your bedroom to the kitchen, is there a difference in the odors? Can you make out from the smell in the kitchen what could have happened in the kitchen a while ago?

Can you make out if a dish is cooked correctly just by the smell? Can you close your eyes and just by sniffing make out if a cake's flavor is chocolate, strawberry, vanilla or Black Forest?

As you get better at distinguishing smells, start working with smells that are more difficult to tell apart like strawberry, cherry and raspberry or lemon, lime and grapefruit. If you are walking on the road, just by the aroma, can you figure out the shops that you passed by? Did you pass by a bakery? A vegetable shop? A restaurant? It's fun doing this exercise, and you can enhance your ability to smell if you practice this exercise consciously every day for 20 minutes.

- **Describe smells out loud:** When you identify and describe a smell out loud, your ability to perceive it is sharpened. Make a habit of talking about smells as you experience them. Describe them out loud using specific language, the way a wine connoisseur would talk about the characteristics of different wines.

Make a point of noticing and talking about everyday smells. For example, describe the nuances of your dinner's scent: "I can smell the earthy ground corn in these tortillas, the sweet and spicy tang of the chicken filling, the fresh soapy scent of the cilantro and the floral citrus burst of the lime."

Neuroanatomical research of the brain suggests that the sense of smell is far more critical for healthy human functioning than previously realized. Smell receptors have direct connections with the cerebral cortex without initially passing through various subcortical relay stations, as is found in all other senses.

Smell data are then sent to 20 different parts of the brain, including areas involved in memory, emotional reactivity and motivation. Examples exist wherein the sense of smell in animals overrides the strength of their other senses.

If we can work on our sense of smell and stretch our ability to distinguish various types of smell, we can have a better sense of smell. Blind people become able to recognize family and friends by smell, not because they have a better sense of smell, but because they must depend more on this sense.

With practice, one can identify people from different cultures by smell because our diets influence our body odors and different cultures have different diets. Research shows each human has their own distinct odor. Like fingerprints, every person has their own distinct odor. Also, scientific research shows some odor receptors are also expressed in human sperm. These enable sperms to swim toward certain chemicals that propel them toward the egg.

Research indicates that we humans can recognize our own t-shirts by smell. Research also suggests that women have a better sense of smell than men.

Research indicates a relationship between sexual behavior and smell; it has been identified in animals ranging from insects to non-human primates. Chemical odor called pheromones are produced and released by females of many species to attract males during the breeding season. Sexual behavior is abolished in rats following removal of olfactory bulbs. The control of the sexual behavior of humans is far more complex than that of lower animals, but it appears that 25% of people who become anosmic (loss of the sense of smell) lose their sex drive.

A relationship between smell and human memory has also been documented. Some individuals have powerful olfactory triggers, whereby a particular odor can help them recall in vivid detail an event from the past. Recent evidence suggests that a decline in smell sensitivity correlates with the onset of memory impairment in people with Alzheimer's disease.

Reduced sense of smell can lead to carelessness with personal hygiene due to reduced ability to smell body odor, loss of pleasure in eating, less joy in daily life because of decreased ability to smell flowers, fresh bread and other pleasant odors and a greater risk of sickness or injury as a result of reduced sensitivity to the smell of smoke, gas, hazardous chemicals or spoiled food.

Smell (olfactory), along with taste, represents the chemical senses in humans. Unlike the other senses, smell stimuli do not have unique names, as colors or taste do, but are likened to other things (e.g., flowery, fruity) or other experiences (e.g., burned). We can identify 10,000 different odors.

An individual human smell-receptor is as sensitive as an individual dog's smell-receptor. Dogs, however, have 1000 times more receptors than we do.

Aromatherapy is a form of holistic therapy that believes certain odors can cure certain health problems. Although most of the claims of aromatherapy remain untested, some laboratory evidence shows that motivation and emotion may be responsive to different odors. For example, the odor of green apples has been shown to lower blood pressure and promote relaxation. The odor of lavender has been demonstrated to raise the basal metabolic rate, which facilitates concentration and increases alertness.

The ability of humans to detect faint odors of chemicals in the air is impressive, typically characterized in units of parts per billion. For chemical t-butyl mercaptan, which companies add to odorless methane so we can detect a gas leak in our homes, we can detect a mere 0.3 parts per billion.

Taste and smell are closely related. You can try an experiment by tasting a food item first by holding your nose and then tasting the same food without holding your nose. During the second time, the experience of smell will not change, but somehow you will feel as if your tongue is working better.

## 2. Taste

Humans are born with some basic flavor preferences. A newborn infant will make a happy, cooing face if a drop of sugar solution is placed on his or her tongue and will crinkle up his or her face when given lemon juice. Humans, along with few other species like horses and monkeys, are born with a preference for the taste of sweet. We humans also have an inborn preference for salt. Bitter and sour are acquired tastes.

Taste works very much like olfaction, except with much fewer types of receptors—just bitter, sour, salty, sweet and umami (savory). Most people use the word 'taste' when they really mean flavor. Taste refers to sweet, sour, salty, bitter or umami; flavor includes the smell, texture, temperature and color of food.

Many food dishes are combinations of three or more primary tastes. Ketchup, for example, is surprisingly complex, with tastes of umami (tomatoes), sourness (vinegar), sweetness (sugar) and saltiness (salt).

**Bitter:** A poison alarm, bitterness is a distinctive bad taste accompanied by a reflexive 'yuck' expression on the face. Hundreds of substances, mostly found in plants, taste bitter. But a little bitterness makes food interesting—and healthy. Antioxidants, which aid metabolism and help the body ward off cancer, account for much of the bitter taste of kale, dark chocolate and coffee.

**Salty:** Our brains are programmed so that a little salt tastes good and a lot tastes bad. This ensures we consume just enough to maintain the salt balance our bodies need to function. But beware—your palate can adapt to crave a lot of salt, as in the case of people who eat the typical American diet. Good news: If you cut back on salt, your taste buds can adapt to be satisfied with less.

**Sour:** The mouth-puckering sensation is caused by acids in lemons, yogurt, sourdough bread and other food. Scientists aren't sure how exactly it works, or even its precise biological purpose, but many suspect that sourness originally signaled that the food was decomposing and was potentially unsafe to eat.

**Sweet:** The most elemental of taste pleasures, sweetness signals the presence of sugars, the foundation of the food chain and a source of energy. Today, though, our sweet tooth is overstimulated by an avalanche of sugar in our diet.

**Umami:** Japanese for 'delicious taste,' umami is produced by certain amino acids. It's best described as 'savory'—a taste rich in flavor. Examples of umami food include seared and cured meats, aged cheeses, fish sauce, green tea, soy sauce and cooked tomatoes.

## *The Umami Story*

*A Japanese chemist named Kikunae Ikeda was enjoying a bowl of dashi, a classic Japanese soup made from seaweed. He sensed that he was tasting something beyond the sweet, sour, salty and bitter category. He was intrigued and decided to find out. He wrote, "Common to asparagus, tomatoes, cheese and meat but...not one of the four well-known tastes." Ikeda went into his lab and found the unknown ingredient. He wrote in a journal for Chemical Society of Tokyo that it is glutamic acid, but he decided to rename it. He called it* **umami***, which means 'delicious' or 'yummy' in Japanese.*

*Glutamate is found in most living things, but when they die, when organic matter breaks down, the glutamate molecule breaks apart. This can happen on a stove when you cook meat, over time when you age a parmesan cheese, by fermentation (as in soy sauce) or as a tomato ripens under the sun. When glutamate becomes L-glutamate, that's when things get 'delicious.' L-glutamate, said Ikeda, is a fifth taste.*

*It turns out, almost 100 years after Ikeda wrote his article, a new generation of scientists took a closer look at the human tongue and discovered, just as Ikeda had insisted, that yes, there is a fifth taste. Humans do have receptors for L-glutamate, and when something is really, really yummy in a non-sweet, sour, bitter or salty way, that's what you're tasting. In 2002, this became the new view. It's in the textbooks now, and scientists decided to call this 'new' taste, in Ikeda's honor, 'umami.'*

## **Taste Aversions**

Your reaction to a particular taste is based, in part, on your prior experiences with similar flavors. Have prior exposures been pleasant or revolting? Taste aversions—an intense dislike for food, but not one based on an innate biological preference—typically stem from prior bad experiences with food. Sometimes, a single exposure that results in foodborne illness (and usually an unpleasant night near the bathroom) is all it takes for your brain to create the negative association.

The food that triggers the illness is correctly identified only part of the time. Typically, the blame is pinned on the most unfamiliar thing in a meal (this is known as sauce béarnaise syndrome). Sometimes, the illness isn't even food-related, but a negative association is still learned and becomes tied to the suspected culprit. This type of conditioned taste aversion is known as the Garcia Effect. As further proof that we're at the mercy of our subconscious, consider this: Even when we know we've misidentified the cause of an illness, an incorrectly associated food aversion will still stick.

## Mindful Eating

Most people eat when they are not hungry and drink when they are not thirsty. And when they eat, their mind is engaged in daydreaming, processing stressful thoughts, watching TV or engaging in conversations. That is, the body is involved in the act of eating while the mind is somewhere else. Mindful eating is to become aware of physical hunger and to relish eating nourishing food. Mindful eating is to enjoy every bite with all your senses, especially your sense of taste and smell.

Mindful eating also involves becoming aware of our emotions. Is there stress in the body? Are you feeling sad and lonely? Are you worrying about your tomorrow? Fear, anger, sadness, anxiety, stress or negative emotions can trigger a craving for food or snacks which can activate the pleasure areas of our brain and help us ease the pain and relax. Easing pain and discomfort by eating—and in most cases, overeating—is a daily occurrence for a lot of people.

Bringing awareness to our emotions and learning healthy ways to activate the pleasure areas of our brain (like playing a game that you love or watching a comedy show on TV) can help us relax and say no to overeating or unnecessary eating.

Maintain a journal of how your emotional states and thoughts affect your body and how this affects your choice of when, where and what to eat. This will help you uncover deeper reasons for overeating.

In the beginning, don't try to eat your whole meal with mindful, complete awareness as it might be difficult. Start slowly, a moment of silence before a meal and then mindfully take the first three bites. Chew slowly as you take in those bites and then give a word to your experience. With regular practice, you will be able to have your whole meal with mindfulness.

## 3. Sight (Visual)

The human visual system responds to that portion of the electromagnetic energy spectrum ranging from 400 nanometers (nm) to 700 nm, known as the visible spectrum or light.

This is a small portion of the full spectrum of electromagnetic radiation, which ranges from 1nm (x-rays) to 100 m (radio broadcast waves).

Humans and primates, in general, are extremely visual creatures. Some estimates indicate that as many as 80% of the neurons in the human cortex respond to visual stimuli.

"Attention is an essential component of visual perception," says Takeo Watanabe, a professor at Brown University. One of the best ways to enhance our visual ability is to improve our attentional function.

Though 20/20 vision is sometimes called 'perfect vision,' people can actually do much better than that. Baseball players tend to have extraordinary vision; in fact, one of the greatest baseball players in history, Babe Ruth, was thought to have 20/8 vision. That type of super sight plays an important role in helping players figure out where the ball is going and can provide a critical edge while playing.

The following exercises are designed to help cultivate a heightened awareness and appreciation of a moment in life. The exercises, done daily and consistently, can improve your visual acuity tremendously.

## 20-Minute Visual Observation Exercise

Plan this exercise for about 20 minutes. Say you are about to brush your teeth, as you pick up the toothbrush, mindfully observe the toothbrush. What color is the toothbrush? In case your toothbrush is red in color, try to make out what shade of red color it is. Is it a scarlet red or like red wine? Perhaps a brick red or tomato red or an apple red? Look closely…what color is your toothbrush? What shape is it? Does it look new or old? If it looks new, what made you conclude it is new? If it looks old, what made you conclude it is old? How do the bristles look? Do all the bristles look alike? Do the bristles appear soft? Or extra soft? Or do they look firm and strong? Look at every aspect of the toothbrush. Where is the toothbrush brand inscribed? Can you guess the font in which the brand is inscribed? For example, if it is Pepsodent, is it written in capital letters or small letters? Is it in italics or bold? And as you brush, keep focusing visually on what you see around. How is the tap? Does it look old or does it look new? How does the mirror in the bathroom look? Does it have a frame? If so, is the frame metal or made of plastic? For 20 minutes, mindfully observe everything around you. It is a very powerful exercise. If you can do that every day, it can dramatically increase your ability to make finer distinctions visually.

## Zoom in–Zoom Out Technique

Look at an object. It could be your wallet, watch, pen or your mobile; choose any object in front of you. Now zoom in to the object about 10 times the size of that object. If it is a pen, make it a very big pen in your mind's eye. A pen that is as big as the Eiffel Tower in Paris. Then look at the details of the visualized pen and see if it matches the real pen that is in front of you.

Then zoom out of that object and make it look like a microscopic object. How does it look? This technique will sharpen your visual acuity.

## Draw the Object Technique

Look at the object and then close your eyes. Now visualize the object so that you can draw that object mentally. For example, if it is your wallet, then look at the wallet, close your eyes and visualize the wallet in detail so that you can draw the wallet in your head. While visualizing if you don't have all the details, then open your eyes and look at the wallet again. Now close your eyes and see if you have all the details to draw the object. This exercise can greatly enhance visual memory and acuity.

## Alien Technique

Sherlock Holmes is a master when it comes to observing details.

*When Holmes first met Dr. Watson, his soon-to-be partner in solving crimes, the detective made a certain and offhand claim: "You have been in Afghanistan, I perceive."*

*Watson's reply: "How on Earth did you know that?"*

*Holmes, naturally, deduced it: "I knew you came from Afghanistan…"*

*The train of reasoning ran, 'Here is a gentleman of a medical type, but with the air of a military man. Clearly an army doctor, then. He has just come from the tropics, for his face is dark, and this is not the natural tint of his skin, for his wrists are fair. He has undergone hardship and sickness, as his haggard face says clearly. His left arm has been injured. He holds it in a stiff and unnatural manner. Where in the tropics could an English army doctor have seen much hardship and got his arm wounded? Clearly in Afghanistan.'*

Imagine you are an alien that has twice the observation power compared to Sherlock Holmes. Now imagine your ability to observe details and connect the dots are far higher than ordinary humans. Be in this state of mind for about 20 minutes. Tell yourself, "I have this extraordinary observation skill." Observe everything around you with this heightened state of awareness. Regular practice will ensure your observation skills and visual acuity improve.

## 4. Auditory/Hearing

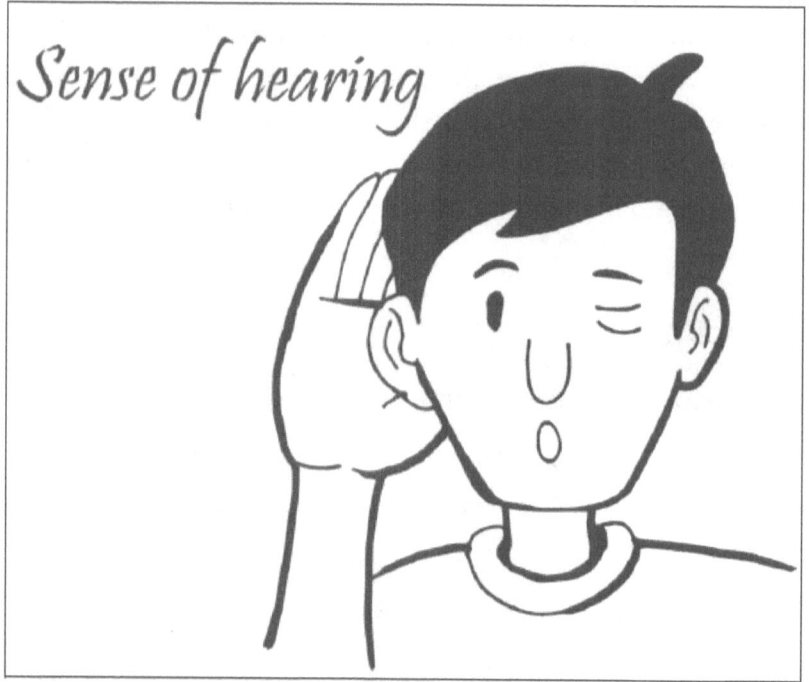

Our world is enriched by the sounds that surround us: a great song on the radio, the accelerating sound of a bike, a bird singing, a child laughing, sound of waves when you are sitting on a beach. Sounds make everything come alive. Imagine a dog barking without any sound. Imagine rain or a waterfall without the accompanying sound.

Sound also alerts us to potential danger. A baby crying, a telephone ringing and the blare of fire alarm are a few instances that bring out the importance of hearing.

The ear detects primarily three attributes of sound: its pitch (frequency), its loudness (amplitude) and its location in space. Pitch is determined by the frequency of vibration of the eardrum. The human ear can perceive frequencies from (approximately) 20 to 20,000 cycles per second. The unit of measurement for frequency is Hertz (Hz).

Loudness is determined by the amplitude of the in and out movement of the eardrum. The amplitude of sounds is measured in decibels (dB). The sound of rustling leaves is about 20 dB. An ordinary conversation between two people is roughly 60 dB. The point where sound becomes painfully loud is around 120 dB.

We are able to localize the source of sound in space because we have two ears. Two factors are key to localize the source of a sound. Firstly, the sound will be slightly louder in one ear than the other. Second, and most importantly, it will arrive at one ear slightly earlier than it arrives at the other. Nerve cells in the brain compare the time of arrival of a sound at the two ears and calculate the location in space of the source. Sound sources along the body's midline axis are the hardest to localize.

Mozart could hear a piece once and play it perfectly from memory alone. The blind frequently identify everyday sounds with great clarity. Some doctors can listen to the heartbeat and know what the patient is suffering from. Some mechanics can listen to a car engine and know exactly where the problem is. And there are tribal people living in the jungle who can listen to Mother Nature and know when it is going to rain, when a storm is about to come or when a snake or tiger is nearby.

Hearing isn't like other senses; if a light is too bright, we can always close our eyes or turn away, but our hearing is always 'on,' even when we are asleep.

## Enhancing Auditory Acuity

### Mindful Listening

By listening with conscious awareness and by trying to make finer auditory distinctions, you can enhance your auditory acuity. The brain centers that govern hearing will develop if you consistently practice mindful hearing. Because you have ears and you are listening all the time, mindful hearing may sound like a joke to you. Just because we have muscles, it does not mean we are strong. Exercise is required to develop our muscles. Similarly, just because we have ears, it does not mean that our auditory acuity is excellent. Exercise is required to develop our auditory acuity.

The greatest obstacle to mindful hearing is the habit of daydreaming and our mind's wandering into the past or future. When we are with a customer, we think about the boss. When we are with the boss, we think about our spouse or family. When we are with our spouse or family, we think about our to-do list. Presence (being completely aware and present in the here and now) is the rarest state that people experience. Our mind has become a chatterbox filled with too much noise. You need to be in the now in order to listen. Stop and notice some of the sounds around you now. Perhaps the sound of the AC or fan humming away, chirping of a bird, a car passing by, the hum of the refrigerator, the sound of your breath…be fully present and just listen.

Practice mindful listening every day for 20 minutes. Let the sounds you hear by the doorway lead you into total presence. Listen intently, but without straining. When you pick up the newspaper and open it, listen to the sound that the newspaper makes. When you open the cap of the toothpaste, listen to the sound; when you open the tap, listen to the sound that the tap makes and then listen when the water flows through the tap. Be in the now. Keep doing what you need to do, but keep your conscious attention on the sound. When you put on your shirt, listen to the sound. When you open the drawer, listen to the sound; when you type on your laptop, listen to the sound; when you open the door, listen to the sound. Be fully present. Can you hear your own heartbeat? Be still and just listen.

1. **Listening Without Judgment:** When you listen to others, you also need to be listening without judgment, without your own agenda and without planning what you will say next. Poor listeners are frequently unable to separate their own needs and interests from those

of others. Everything they hear, they compare that with themselves. Somebody speaks about their car, automatically they compare that information with their own car. Somebody speaks about the place they went for a holiday, they compare that information with their own life.

Mindful listening is being fully present in what another person is saying, not just their words, not just the tone, pitch and volume of their speech, but to listen to their feelings, needs and purpose. Listening fully to another person does not mean you agree or validate everything they say, it just means you are being there for them to express themselves. Mindful listening encourages others to feel understood and to speak more openly and honestly.

2. Practice Identifying the Source of Sounds. Close your eyes and ask a friend to walk to a certain spot in a large room or an open space. Ask them to stand about 20 to 30 feet away. Have a partner make a sound using a bell or horn and then point to where you think the sound came from. Have your friend change their direction and distance each time.

3. Stretch Your Auditory Capability: For this exercise, stand in a room with your eyes closed. Have a partner do different things involving sounds for identification: switching on a light, turning off the AC, opening a briefcase, rearranging the books on a shelf, dropping a paper clip, walking with different types of shoes. As your friend is doing these things, your job is to be fully present and identify the various sounds. As you improve your ability to listen and make out what's happening, ask your friend to make it more challenging, like turning the pages of a book, sipping a coffee, writing on a piece of paper, walking barefoot, etc.

4. Coin Test: Ask your friend to drop a coin on the floor. With your eyes closed, can you figure out the denomination of the coin? Ask your friend to drop coins of various denomination. With total presence, can you detect the different denominations that were dropped?

5. Symphony Instrument Exercise: Listen to an audio recording of a symphony and listen to each instrument being played. Then listen to it in entirety. Again, listen to each instrument being played.

6. Floor test: When you are in a lift, can you make out, just by listening, which floor you are in?

7. Road Vehicle Test: If you are sitting on a bench next to a road, can you just listen to the sound of a vehicle and figure out what vehicle just passed by? Later, can you also detect the model/brand? Was it a Honda car? Or an Audi Q7?

8. Sound of cooking test: In the kitchen, when you cooking, can you, by sound alone, figure out if it is properly cooked or not?

9. Sound of Breath Test: Can you listen to the sound of your own breath or the sound of another person breathing?

Practice mindful listening every day, at least, for 20 minutes. With consistent practice, your auditory acuity will improve drastically.

## 5. Kinesthetic (Touch)

It is said that seeing is believing, but one might add that touching is being absolutely sure. There is something fundamental and direct about touch perception.

According to Dictionary.com, the term 'kinaesthetic' was coined by British neurologist Henry Charlton Bastian. The term comes from the Greek words '*Kinein*' (which means 'to move') and '*aesthesis*' (which means 'sensation').

**Kinesthesia in medicine:** This is the sense that detects bodily position, weight or movement of the muscles, tendons and joints; the sensation of moving in space. Kinesthesia happens when the brain gets feedback from muscles and ligaments about how the body is moving (Vocabulary.com).

In NLP there is External Kinesthetic Acuity and Internal Kinesthetic Acuity.

## External Kinesthetic Acuity

Becoming aware of the ouch as you hold sand in your hand while sitting on a beach, feeling the wind on your skin as you stand on the balcony, feeling the water on your skin as you take a shower, feeling the sun on your skin as you go out for a walk—all of these are external kinesthetic experiences.

It is the skin senses or cutaneous system which provides us with information about events on the surface of the body rather than about events at a distance, as in the case of vision or hearing. The most commonly experienced skin sensations are warm, cold, moisture (dry/wet), pressure and vibration.

## Is Skin the Best-Tailored Suit to Fit Our Body?

The skin is the largest sense organ of the body, containing millions of receptors. The human skin accounts for 12–15% of the weight in the average adult human body, constituting the largest of all bodily organs. The skin is a tight-fitting elastic spacesuit, not only serving 24/7 as a reliable defense barrier but also doubling as a highly sensitive information gathering data recorder.

Superbly tailored to fit our body, the skin cloaks the muscles, body tissues, bodily fluids and internal organs, shielding them from injury and innumerable attacks by dangerous microscopic insects and bugs.

Foreign objects, toxins, air, fluids and living organisms can seldom penetrate the boundary of the human body's watertight cover. Even a tiny intrusion, like that of a mosquito bite, is reported immediately, which coordinates a typically aggressive response to the security breach.

## Do People Die of Touch Starvation?

Touch is a significant part of interpersonal relationships. Shaking hands, kissing, holding hands and hugging are common practices in different life situations.

In the 1960s, psychologist Harry Harlow demonstrated that infant monkeys deprived of touch simulation from parents and siblings exhibited gross abnormalities. In extreme cases, the behavioral abnormalities were irreversible.

The observations made of children raised in orphanages in different countries indicate that physical contact with caregivers is necessary for normal development. Healthy social and cognitive development of a child can be impaired if the child does not receive sufficient affectionate touch and cuddling. Scientific evidence suggests that infants who do not receive warm affectionate touch from their parents or caregivers during the first year of life are restricted in the ability to develop trust. There was also a study conducted that revealed that lack of physical touch in the initial months can lead to long-term ailments, including poor immunity, insufficient resistance and increased vulnerability to mental illnesses.

Touch is a fundamental aspect of human nature. Even fleeting forms of touch may have a powerful impact on our emotional and social functioning. The emotional impact of touch is ingrained in our biology. Touch releases oxytocin, a hormone that decreases stress-related hormones.

In an experiment, a couple who engaged in warm touch exercise, during which they touched each other's neck, shoulders and hands, had more oxytocin in their salvia than couples who did not engage in this exercise. (Holt-Lunstad, Birmingham, & Light, 2008). Likewise, women who report frequent partner hugs display higher levels of oxytocin in their blood than women who report few partner hugs. (Light, Grewen, & Amico, 2005). Research also shows that people in deep comas show beneficial heart rate changes when their hands are held. People may not die of touch starvation, but touch is a fundamental need for our well-being.

## Mindful Touch Exploration

For 20 minutes, bring your attention to touch sensation. For example, when you pick up the newspaper, can you, for a moment, close your eyes and feel the paper with your hands? Is it rough? Is it smooth? Is it thin? Very thin? Is it warm/wet/ dry? Can you differentiate 'Times of India' newspaper and 'The Economic Times' newspaper by touch? When you walk on the floor barefoot, how does it feel? Is the floor warm/cold/rough/smooth? When you wash your hands, feel the sensation of the water. Does your skin enjoy the sensation of water or does it feel uncomfortable because the water is too cold or too hot?

Experience the world through touch. See if you can differentiate various currency notes through touch. See if you can read the personality of a person after a handshake. Was that person's hand sweaty? Firm? Rough? Too cold? Warm? Even though a handshake is for a few seconds, there is so much one can decipher about another person by bringing attention to the feel of the handshake. Experience the world through your hands. Experience the world through your feet. Experience the world through your body. How does it feel when you are in a swimming pool? How does your skin feel when you are lying down on the grass in a park? How does it feel when you run a marathon and your t-shirt is drenched in sweat? How does it feel when you affectionately hug another person? Practice mindful touch exploration for 20 minutes every day.

## Are Our Senses on Guard Even as We Slumber?

You are in deep sleep. A tiny little insect, whose weight can be measured in milligrams, crawls over your skin. Although the pressure exerted by this tiny insect's footsteps is next to nothing, it is sufficient enough to trigger a sensory warning alarm, and you suddenly awaken to find yourself hunting for the potentially dangerous trespasser. The senses are on guard even as we slumber.

Our hair is connected to touch receptors and play a central role in information gathering. When a strand of hair is slightly bent or pulled, we are alerted by the sensory receptors lodged at the base of each individual hair. An external object may be closing in on us, possibly in an attack mode. The term hair-triggering response is not a metaphor; rather, it serves as a physiological signal designed to assure our safety and survival.

Mindful touch exploration is to touch with full awareness. It enhances one's ability to make finer distinctions through touch.

# Kinesthetic Internal Awareness

## Vestibular Perception

The auditory system responds to movement at a distance from the body. The cutaneous system (skin senses) responds to movement on the surface of the body. The vestibular system responds to movement of the whole body.

## Proprioception

Vestibular perception is about perceiving the current position, orientation and movement of your whole body. Proprioception is about perceiving the position of individual body parts based on touch receptors and actions of the motor system. The vestibular system tells you how you move and when you move. It keeps you from falling over, determining when you are leaning forward, back, left or right.

Proprioception is the sense of where your individual body parts are located. Some of that information can come in through your eyes. There are many different types of receptors involved in proprioception. Specialized neurons are present in the muscles and the tendons that sense tension as well as angles of each joint. The skin itself contains touch receptors that can be used to infer how much a particular part of your body, such as a limb, is extended.

The proprioception sense sends to the brain continuous sensory feedback from receptors located not only in muscles but also in the tendons, ligaments and joints. This sense is crucial for the ability to perform daily activities, such as sitting, standing, walking and climbing stairs, where coordination of muscle groups is necessary and cooperation between body parts is required to maintain the fluidity of motion.

## Somatic Sense

Somatic sense includes experiencing the sensation of our body, our muscles (are they relaxed or tight?) and how we feel inside. Somatic sense includes visceral sense, which is literally the gut feeling. (Viscera are the internal organs such as stomach and intestine.) Visceral sense is the subjective perception of the sensations of the internal organs. Somatic sense generates much of the feeling component of emotions. Most emotions have a physical component. For example, when we are nervous, we may feel a knot in our stomach; when we are angry, we may experience a rise in our heart rate; when we are embarrassed, we may feel our face blush. Somatic sense also signals hunger, fullness and tummy upsets.

Body awareness is the sense that we have of our own body. It is an understanding of the parts that make up one's body, where they are located, how they feel and even what they can do.

## Practicing Internal Body Mindfulness

**Where in the body technique:** Any time you are stressed or feeling frustrated, angry or sad, ask yourself: Where in the body is the negative emotion?

For example, if you are feeling frustrated, ask yourself: Where is this frustration in my body? Is this frustration in my eyes? Or is it my stomach or in my chest? Can I feel the frustration in my hands, in my throat? How is my body? Does this frustration tighten my muscles? Does it have an impact on how I breathe? Am I breathing faster? Slower? Have I stopped breathing?

This is a powerful exercise. Anytime you feel a negative emotion, the first thing that you can do is to feel the emotion in the body physically. Locate where in the body you feel it and allow yourself to physically experience what you feel.

Even for positive emotions, you can practice this technique. When you are happy, ask: Where is this happiness in my body? Is it my eyes, or is it on my cheeks? Can I feel this happiness in my feet, in my hands, in my stomach or in my chest? How is my body? Is it light? Or is it heavy? How is my breathing? Faster? Slower?

Bring your whole attention to the body so that you can ground your happiness within your body. Body awareness brings healing. It helps you to get in touch with reality. Your body never lies. It helps you to manage your emotions. Body awareness helps to release negative emotions of the past. When you regularly practice body mindfulness through this technique, psychosomatic ailments and symptoms will reduce. This is how powerful body mindfulness is.

Through both external and internal kinesthetic awareness, one can enhance the quality of perception and quality of life. Enhancing sensory acuity allows you to cut through the cobweb of unnecessary thinking and become more alive and present. It enhances your quality of thinking, improves health and helps in self-actualization. Deliberate and consistent practice is the key to success.

# Chapter 4
## Anchoring

*John's wife's favorite place to relax was to sit on an old rugged wooden bench on the beach and look far into the sea. John, sitting next to his wife, wondered how his wife is able to relax when he could never do it. He had his problems in the office. His mind would always be in the office. He could hardly concentrate on what his wife was saying. The vast sea, the cool breeze and the beautiful sky didn't seem to exist for John. As a mental patient would shiver in agony when given an electric shock, his mind continuously rattled with problems at the office. "How do I relax?" wondered John. His wife had now closed her eyes. She was sitting with her spine straight like a tree, legs crossed like a Buddha. She would now meditate for about 10 minutes. John would continue thinking about his problems at the office. But today, John decided, for a change, why not meditate. He closed his eyes and soon realized his mind was like a storm; it was very uncomfortable. He didn't want to think of his office as the storm would rage more ferociously in his mind. So, he thought of an angel.*

*An image of an angel came to his mind. She appeared in front of him and handed him something. She disappeared, and John's mind went blank. He opened his eyes and looked into his hands; there was a bit of a paper. He looked at his wife. She was still meditating. He opened the paper. In it was written: "Use NLP anchor to calm down." Did the angel really put this in his hand? Did his wife do it? Suddenly, he didn't want to know how the bit of paper came to his hand. He just knew his life was going to change.*

According to the Oxford English Dictionary, an anchor is:

1. a heavy object attached to a cable or chain and used to moor a ship to the sea bottom, typically having a metal shank with a pair of curved, barbed flukes at one end.

E.g., The boat, no longer held fast by its anchor, swung wildly.

2. a person or thing which provides stability or confidence in an otherwise uncertain situation.

E.g., The European Community is the economic anchor of the new Europe.

3. an anchorman or anchorwoman in radio or television

E.g., He signed off after 19 years as CBS news anchor.

4. secure firmly in position.

The tail is used as a hook with which the fish anchors itself.

5. provide a firm basis or foundation.

E.g., It is important that policy be anchored to some acceptable theoretical basis.

Just like the way a ship is latched or secured to the shore with the help of an anchor, through NLP we can latch on to an inner state of calm confidence to face the difficult weathers and situations of life through using NLP anchors. For example, when an individual, while driving with all the necessary legal papers and driving license, experiences waves of fear every time he spots traffic police, he can trigger an internal response of calmness through an NLP anchor when he spots the police. A student who breaks into a sweat and gets nervous during an exam can trigger an anchor of confidence to deal with her anxiety right before the exam. A man who returns home with an agitated mind due to stress at work can get into a state of ease and relaxation as he enters his home by triggering an NLP anchor.

We can latch on to confidence, joy, calmness, a state of affection and love in spite of changing external circumstances and provocations by NLP anchors. We can be what we want to be at any point through NLP anchors. Storm and wind can toss around a boat that is not anchored, damage and shred it to pieces. A boat that is anchored remains unscathed during the storm.

NLP anchors act like an umbrella. When it rains, an umbrella comes in handy and keeps us dry and warm. When a situation or person creates an atmosphere where there is the possibility of slipping into an unresourceful state (rain), all that we need to do is trigger an appropriate NLP anchor (open up the umbrella).

**NLP anchoring is a process of welding together an 'internal' or 'external' trigger to an internal state.**

### The Saint and the Magic Ring

*During the time when the recession was at its peak, Sanjay decided to give up everything; not that he had much choice. His company had already asked him to resign. They didn't even have enough funds to pay the employees their salary. His girlfriend had left him for a guy who had a secure job with the government. The bank that loaned him money to buy a car had seized his car as he couldn't keep up with the monthly installment payment. His credit cards had maxed out. Feeling depressed, angry and lonely, he decided to quit everything. He decided to go to a forest and live a natural life, like animals; hunt like them or be hunted. Anyway, life would be better in the woods than in a city zoo.*

*Months passed by in the forest, but his depression, anger and loneliness only increased. He couldn't sleep. He ate leaves and sometimes meat cooked in fire. He feared snakes, tigers and foxes. At times, Sanjay would scream continuously out of fear and frustration.*

*One day, it began to rain and it seemed to continue for days. Sanjay had to look for a cave or natural housing of some kind. After days of searching around like a madman, he finally found a deep cave. As he took slow steps further within, he saw a faint light. To his surprise, Sanjay found a man at* the rear end. It was an elderly saint humming a tune, with a lamp, laptop and an iPhone X next to him.

Sanjay was surprised. He said, "Hi, saint," to the saint. The saint gave him a smile. The saint said, "Hi. I am no saint. I am a retired IT consultant. I am here in the forest to spend my last days meditating and being with Mother Nature."

"Someone who is meditating full-time in a forest is a saint to me," replied Sanjay.

The man replied, "Well, then you can call me a saint. Now, come here. Take this ring; it is a magic ring. It is called the NLP anchor ring. It has a small button on the side. Every time you are feeling down, all you have to do is press the button. And you will have the confidence to do whatever you want. The ring will never fail; it always works. Now wear the ring."

Sanjay didn't know what to say. He hadn't come to this ex-IT consultant for a solution. He was only looking for a cave to stay. Anyhow, he wore the ring. The saint said, "Good, now that you are wearing the ring, think of a time when you were genuinely confident, when you were brimming with confidence."

Sanjay thought of the time he participated in a college debate. He was truly confident during the debate. He remembered getting a lot of applause for his exceptional performance.

The saint continued, "Now allow that confidence to radiate inside you. Allow your eyes to sparkle with that unshakable confidence. And as your face glows, allow the inner radiance to spread through your muscles and into every cell. And as you experience this peak state of confidence, press the button on the ring."

Sanjay reaches out and presses the button on the ring, and as he presses the button, the ring gently squeezes his finger.

The saint continued, "As you feel the pressure of the ring, allow the magic of the ring to turn your confidence within you to get entrenched *deeply, so deeply that nothing can shake it." Sanjay felt so wonderful, so confident, that it felt like a divine light was radiating from within. He felt secure, complete and truly positive. "Now take your hands off the ring and open your eyes."*

*"How do you feel?" asked the saint.*

*"I feel on top of the world. I feel wonderful," replied Sanjay.*

*"Wait for the rain to stop and leave the forest to go back to the place you came from. Anytime you feel down, press the button on the ring and allow the magic to take over you," said the saint.*

*"How does this magic ring work, saint?" asked Sanjay.*

*"If you want to understand the science behind it, buy a good book on NLP and read about the NLP anchoring process thoroughly or attend an NLP workshop. And remember, it is not the ring, but the NLP anchoring process that's doing the magic," said the saint.*

*"What's NLP? And what's NLP anchoring process? Never mind. The inner shift that I have experienced is what is really important," thought Sanjay.*

*Sanjay felt a sense of gratitude toward this modern saint. He promised he would return every year just to see him. He walked back to the city, and he knew he will move forward in life with confidence. And if he slips, he has the NLP anchor ring with him.*

– **Manoj Keshav**

Thoughts, behaviors and emotions can be seen as the three resources we have. When these three resources are aligned together, there is tremendous power in a person. But when one of the resources is not aligned with the other 2, the person no longer has access to the power within. It is like one of the wheels of a tricycle is stuck and won't rotate; if one wheel gets stuck, the whole tricycle gets stuck. Similarly, if one of the resources that we have moves in the opposite direction or gets stuck, we lose our inner power; the whole person gets stuck. Behavior cannot exist without emotions. A confident handshake involves an internal state of confidence intertwined with the behavior of extending the hand and giving a handshake. A nervous handshake is a handshake that is powered by nervousness. Emotion impacts behavior. And thoughts and emotions affect each other as well. Happy thoughts cause happy feelings, and depressing thoughts cause unhappy feelings.

*Raj, as a 6-year-old boy, was beaten up by another 6-year-old. Raj couldn't fight back as the other boy was much taller and heavier, with an aggressive look in his eyes. Raj felt tiny in front of this bully. Although he was beaten up only once, he developed a fear of big guys. Now, as an adult, when he meets a taller and heavily built man, his knee would go weak and his voice would tremble. His power would leave him, and his eyes would convey fear. Unless Raj decides that the emotions associated with big men are unhealthy and that he needs to do something about it, he will remain stuck. Anchoring can help Raj step out of this unresourceful state. All that he would need to do is to trigger an NLP anchor of confidence to feel powerful when he comes across a bigger man.*

## What is the Key Skill Every Individual Needs to Learn?

Our emotional state can make us or break us. Excellence cannot be achieved with guilt, fear, shame, stress, fear and negativity. What we need is confidence, inspiration, passion and joy in what we do and courage. Learning to stay anchored in the face of provocation, disturbance and threat is the key skill every individual needs to learn.

Leadership programs emphasize vision. A vision that does not create warmth in the heart, that does not inspire, is a vision without a soul. Most of the vision statements of organizations look like computer program codes; there is no life in it. It is the emotions that bring alive a vision.

Leadership programs emphasize execution. Execution without passion is like a dead man trying to complete a task. On a Monday morning, if you look around, you'll find many office-goers who inch toward their office like they are dead inside; alive in the body but dead in spirit. No wonder morale and productivity are so low in so many organizations. And instead of reaching out to the heart, instead of transforming the inner states, most organizations believe it is the 'processes' that need to change.

Different situations require different emotional states. A state of relaxation would be most helpful while on holiday; a state of concentration would be appropriate while trying to thread a needle; a state of confidence while going through a job interview and a state of courage while fighting in a war.

## Can We Choose an Emotional State?

Most people believe that they cannot choose their emotional state. They believe that it just happens. "I am a short-tempered guy; I am a sensitive person, I just cannot sleep if someone criticizes me. I cannot stand my mother-in-law shouting at me, I just burst into tears every time it happens."

However, people do have the ability to choose an emotional state and hold on to it in spite of external circumstances or other people's behavior. NLP anchoring can help in choosing or holding on to a resourceful emotional state when required.

## What is an Anchor? What is the Difference between Anchors and NLP Anchors?

An anchor is a stimulus or a trigger; it may be a sound, an image, a touch, a smell or a taste that triggers a consistent response. We can choose the resourceful state that we want and stay 'anchored' in that state and not get drifted away by our own fear, lethargy, guilt, shame or anger.

## What are Anchors?

> **A Remembered Picture**

For Radhesh, an image of the Hindu god Hanuman, who is representative of courage, power and faith, puts him in a resourceful state. Anytime he is scared, like while walking alone on a dark street, remembering the picture of Hanuman in his mind fills him with courage, power and faith. His chest expands, his breath becomes deeper and energy fills his muscles.

A visual anchor is a sight and the resulting consistent response. For example, the sight of an army soldier, the national flag, lipstick, Gandhi's statute or a birthday cake will create a consistent response that differs for each person. The visual pictures could be external, or these pictures could be internal in our mind. These internal pictures, too, create a consistent response when we recall them.

> **A Touch**

Jane loves to read books, especially inspiring books like the autobiographies of Hellen Keller, Martin Luther King, Steve Jobs, etc. Every time she reads a passage that inspires her and moves her heart, she crosses her heart with the index finger of her left hand. Now if she wants to get inspired, all she has to do is to cross her heart with the index finger of her left hand.

Kinesthetic anchors fire off with touch. The touch could be external, like when someone or something touches our body, or it could be when we touch ourselves in a nurturing or inspiring way. For example, when you take off your shoes and walk barefoot on a beach, which makes you feel happy and relaxed, you will associate the touch of sand with warm emotions. If the cool of the steel strap of a wristwatch that you got for an achievement makes you feel proud, every time you feel the steel strap of that watch against your wrist, the sense of pride will be triggered.

> **A Voice**

For Stephen, who once stayed in a small flat close to a church, the sound of a church bell is a 'call' to close his eyes and think of Christ for a few moments. Now even after he has moved from the house, whenever he hears the sound of a bell, Stephen's whole body and inner state transform into a deeply prayerful, spiritual state.

Auditory anchors fire off with a sound. Examples are a specific ringtone of a mobile, the doorbell, the creaking noise when someone opens the door or the siren of an ambulance.

## ➤ A Taste

Ranbir, a professional boxer, had the habit of having a bite of chocolate just before a fight. As Ranbir walks toward the ring with the chocolate melting in his mouth, and his taste buds savor the taste, he screams and jumps with aggression, prepping himself to be in a state where he is ready to fight.

Today, even when is at home, all alone with no intention to fight, just taking a bite of chocolate kicks off his aggression, and his every muscle and bone gets ready for a good fight.

Gustatory anchors fire off when a particular taste hits out taste buds. Examples are a specific brand of pickle that reminds you of your mom, a cough syrup that evokes your childhood memories, a particular flavor of ice cream that evokes a romantic response, etc.

## ➤ A Smell

She never knew this handsome young man would sweep her off her feet. She was madly in love. Every time she went out with him, when she held his hand and looked into his eyes, her heart leaped with joy. The most alluring part of the moment was his perfume. She would snuggle into his arms and take in the scent, and it would fill her entire body with a feeling of warmth, security and pleasure.

Later, when he was away for higher studies, she caught the smell of the same perfume in a perfume shop; it triggered the feelings she had with her man, and her body responded with feelings of love and warmth.

Olfactory anchors fire when a certain smell of a person or object enters your nose. Freshly baked bread, onions, perfume, a piece of fruit, the smell of camphor, etc., are examples.

All of us have anchors in us. For the vast majority of people, these anchors get created in us unconsciously. The sight of the national flag fills our heart with patriotism. The smell near a crowded railway station causes our nose to shrink, our throat to constrict and we experience disgust.

## Can We Consciously Create Resourceful Anchors?

Learning to consciously create resourceful anchors is the heart of this chapter.

### Single Robust vs. Repetition Robust

### Single Robust

A single event in life can create a robust association. Jim, while learning to swim, unknowingly moves toward the deeper side of the pool. When he decides to stand where he is, his legs can't reach the floor. He panics and finds himself struggling to stay on the surface as he frantically moves his hands and kicks his legs hard underwater. Due to the overwhelming fear, he finds himself being pulled down, and he chokes on some water. He barely takes a breath before his mouth goes under the water. His coach spots him and pulls him to safety.

This single event has such a dramatic impact on Jim that he stays away from swimming for the rest of his life.

Anchors can get created through a single life experience.

### Repetition Robust

There are times a single event may not create a strong association. But when the events get repeated again and again, a strong association could get created. Meera finally gets her driving license and decides to drive to the office for the first time. That day, on the way back home, she spots a speed bump a little too late. Before she could slow down, she hits it harder than expected. She loses control and grazes a taxi parked on the side. It ends with a big row between the taxi driver and her, with a crowd around them. Luckily, there is only a very minor scratch visible on the taxi. Meera settles it by giving some cash to the taxi driver to fix it.

Meera's spirit is not dampened by this incident. But after a week, she hits a tree. No bruises on her, but the car has to go through some repairs.

The very next week, she rams the car into a lamp post; again, no injuries although the car requires repairs. After the 6$^{th}$ accident, she gives up driving for the rest of her life.

Although all of them were minor accidents, the consistency with which these accidents took place week after week created a robust association in Meera.

These anchors or associations are created only through repeated and consistent experience of a stimulus over a period of time.

## What is NLP Anchoring?

### NLP Anchoring Defined

NLP anchoring is **intentionally** inserting a stimulus (visual, auditory, kinesthetic, olfactory or gustatory) when a person is fully in touch with a specific experience.

### Example

- Think of a humorous event or events in your life when you had deep, belly laughter; moments when something hilarious happened and you doubled over with laughter and felt happy and light. When you do recall this happy state, and re-experience it at the moment, touch a specific spot on your forearm with your index finger. (Here we are intentionally inserting a kinesthetic touch stimulus. This process of deliberately inserting a stimulus is called NLP anchoring process.)

- Again, think of the funny/happy moment and when you feel the same emotional state within, touch the same spot on your forearm with your index finger.

- After repeating this anchoring process a few times, take a break and then without thinking of any specific events, just touch the specific spot on your forearm with your index finger. If NLP anchoring has taken effect, it will evoke in you a happy state similar to the earlier event.

Note: Earlier, you thought of a happy/funny incident and then touched the forearm with your index finger. After the NLP anchoring process has taken effect, touching the forearm with your index finger evokes a happy/hilarious feeling within you. How is this useful? Anytime you want to feel happy, all you have to do is touch the specific spot of your forearm with your index finger and there you go…feeling happy!

The inserted stimulus is referred to as the 'NLP anchor.' The anchor then can be used to trigger the experience again and again.

## Why Do We Need NLP Anchors?

The process of anchoring is designed to associate a stimulus to a particular response on purpose. A state of confidence, a state of calmness, a state of congruence, etc., can be felt in seconds just by firing an anchor.

For example, Jim is a devout Christian. Every time he enters the church on the hilltop close to his house, he experiences a sense of calmness. If Jim touches a specific spot on his elbow and applies a little pressure with his thumb and repeats this process every time, he experiences calmness. Over a period of time, the specific touch and pressure will get paired with a state of calmness.

Once it is anchored successfully, whether Jim is at home or on the streets, if he wants a state of calmness, all he needs to do is touch that specific spot on his elbow and apply the same pressure with his thumb.

There are times a single anchoring is enough to produce results, and sometimes repeated anchoring is required to produce consistent results.

# Self-Anchoring

I. **The first step would be to identify an unresourceful state that you often find yourself in.**

### Examples

1. When someone criticizes you, you get angry or very defensive or maybe you start crying.
2. When someone raises their voice and speaks to you loudly or harshly, you react by screaming or perhaps you get scared.

3. When you have to stand in a queue, and the queue is moving forward very slowly, you get bored and irritated, stressed out or angry.

4. During a job interview or when you walk into your boss's cabin, you may become nervous and your voice loses its power and clarity.

5. When your child is not co-operating with you, you may lose your temper and shout or even beat your child.

**II. Once you have decided which unresourceful state you would like to change in a real-life situation, decide which resourceful state you would like to replace it within the same life situation.**

People learn breathing techniques and meditation, which they usually practice in the comfort of their home. But when faced with a difficult or tricky situation, the techniques that worked at home don't seem that helpful. Anchoring helps people to access resourceful states during tough situations in life.

**Examples**

1. During criticism, you may like to be in a state of open-mindedness so that you can listen to the criticism and examine the merit of it. You can learn from it if it is constructive criticism and move on in life rather than becoming overly defensive and losing sleep over it. It is one thing to say 'let me have an open mind' and another thing to be open-minded while listening to criticism. Anchoring can help you trigger that state of open-mindedness.

2. When someone shouts at you, you may like to be in a state of empathy, where you can understand why the person is shouting and connect with what the person is feeling. For example, if someone yells at his/her partner as soon as they get back from work, the partner can listen with an open heart instead of getting defensive. Screaming back will only make things worse.

3. If you are waiting in a queue, there is not much you can do by feeling irritated and annoyed, except causing yourself ill health through stress

and high BP. Instead, you can use the time to feel peaceful and tranquil by triggering an anchor.

4. When you walk in for a job interview or into your boss's cabin, instead of experiencing nervousness, you may like to feel confident. NLP anchoring can help you with this.

5. When you are teaching your little child, instead of impatience and anger, which in the long run can distance you from your child, you may like a creative state of mind. You can think of different innovative methods to sustain the interest of the child and teach the child in a way that the child finds it interesting. NLP anchors can help you trigger that creative state.

## III. Self-Anchoring Process

There are two ways to create anchors. One is through repetition: pairing an internal state to an image, sound or touch repeatedly. The other is through a single intense association. That is, when a person is feeling a particular state intensely (feeling really powerful or confident or a very deep state of relaxation), an NLP anchor is introduced. The NLP anchor or stimulus could be a specific touch, sound or visual image.

### Steps

1. **Prepare:** Switch off your mobile and ensure you are in a place where you won't be disturbed. Sit comfortably on a chair and allow yourself to relax.

2. **Choose a Resourceful State:** One that you would like to experience. It could be a state of confidence, state of peace and tranquility, state of rapt attention or maybe a creative state.

3. **Choose an Anchor:** An anchor could be a visual sight, a specific sound or a touch.

Visual sight or image: An image of a beautiful lake, a beautiful flower, a diamond, a lion, dove, rainbow, sunrise, etc., are examples. You can choose your own unique image, which has a personal meaning and can be visualized in your mind. Of course, actual objects like a ring or a precious stone, too, can be visual external anchors.

**Sound:** Birds chirping, the sound of a waterfall, waves, a little child's laughter, chants such as OM, etc., are examples. These sounds can be recalled in your mind or played back through a device.

**Touch:** Touching and applying pressure with the thumb and index finger on one of the earlobes or touching the wrist of the left hand at a specific spot with the thumb of the right hand are examples. The touch should be unique and shouldn't be like a regular touch (like touching the chin while thinking).

4. **Associate the NLP Anchor With the Resourceful State:** Create that resourceful state (like confidence or tranquility) by recalling an event in your life when you experienced that resourceful state. Use visualization to experience the resourceful state intensely within. When you fully experience that resourceful state and you feel great within, introduce the NLP anchor (like a specific touch or sound).

For example: Let's say you want to feel confident, rather than nervous, during a job interview. The desired state is that of confidence. Let's assume the stimulus or anchor chosen is physical touch: touching the tip of the ring finger of the left hand with the thumb of the right hand.

To start the process, you must first get into a state of confidence. Imagine a time in your life when you were highly confident. Step into that situation and feel the event as if it is happening now.

Allow the confidence to radiate within you. Let the confidence shine through your eyes, move through your veins and allow it to envelop you completely. As you feel this confidence filling you within and moving toward its peak, press your left ring finger with your right thumb. Once satisfied that you have pressed your ring finger for a sufficient time while you were experiencing the intense state of confidence, pull back your hand and release the touch.

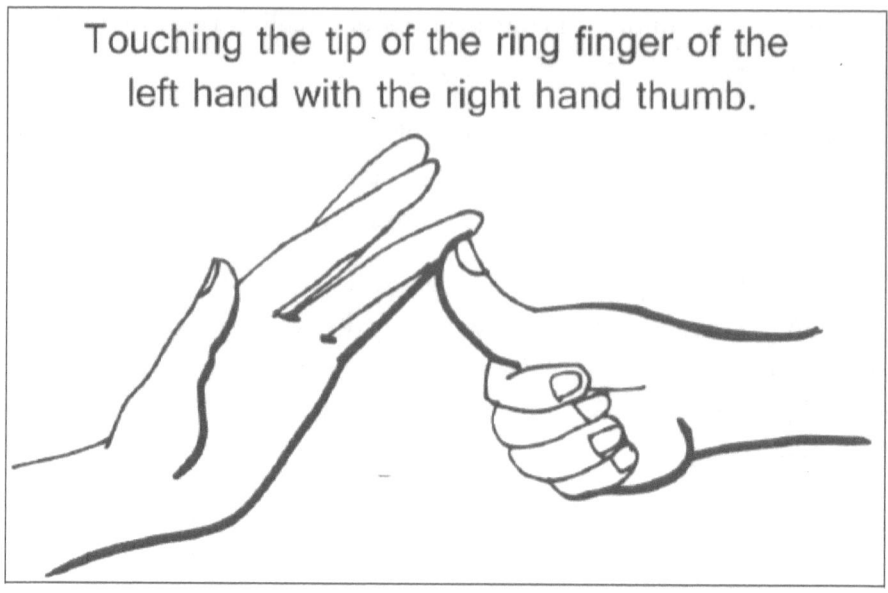

Touching the tip of the ring finger of the left hand with the right hand thumb.

5. **Break State:** Now come back to the present. Think of how many windows are there in your home or try to recall your mobile number backward. This helps create an important phase called the break state.

6. **Repeat the Anchoring Process:** Through visualization, experience that resourceful state again and when you feel it intensely, introduce the NLP anchor again (touching the left ring finger with your right thumb).

7. **Repeat the Process of Anchoring a Few More Times:** Anchoring—break state—Anchoring—break state—Anchoring—break state.

8. **Test the Anchor:** Think of a general topic like the weather or politics, and while doing so, press your left ring finger with your right thumb exactly the way you did while anchoring. This is called firing the anchor.

If a state of confidence is activated inside you, then the process was successful, and the anchors are now in place and working well. If you don't experience a state of confidence, the process is likely to have not been established successfully. Hence, it would be advisable to start from the 1st step and go through the same process with added intensity.

9. **Future event:** If the process has been successful, then think of a future situation where you would like to experience this state of confidence. Imagine yourself in a situation where you would typically be nervous and fire the anchor. How is the response inside? Does the anchor trigger a state of confidence within? If yes, then you have completed the self-anchoring process.

# Preconditions for Successful Anchoring

Anchoring is successful only under certain conditions. The key factors that influence the outcome of anchoring are:

**1. The Resourceful State Needs to Be Pure And Intense**

The resourceful state that ought to be experienced within needs to be experienced in an intense state. For example, if the resourceful state that is sought is confidence, then a below average state of confidence may lead to the failure of the anchoring process. On the other hand, an intensely felt state of confidence leads to successful anchoring.

If a person recalls the desired state (confidence) in a detached manner, the person may not feel it intensely. This would lead to the failure of the anchoring process. It would be ideal if a person can recall a time when he felt intensely resourceful in an associated state. This precondition of intensity is essential to the success of the anchoring process.

Intensity can also be felt for a mixed-up state (e.g., you might feel confidence along with fear). It needs to be noted that the intensity of a pure resourceful state (pure confidence or peace, etc.) needs to be used for the anchoring process.

**2. The Uniqueness of the Anchor is Crucial to the Success of the Anchoring Process**

We are constantly interacting with the environment and forming associations unconsciously.

*For example: As a little boy, Albert clasped hands whenever he felt scared. Sometimes, he would wake up in the night all alone in his tiny bedroom, too frightened to step out and knock on his parents' bedroom. Albert would clasp his hands and would lie down till sleep envelops him. When he was 12 years old, his best friend left for another school. Every time he thought of his best friend, he would clasp his hands.*

*When he was 13, Albert had to play a role in a school drama. His role included playing a shy character who would clasp his hands every time he spoke. At 14, a new teacher taught a class in a way that impressed him. Every time this new teacher wanted to emphasize a point, he would clasp his hands. Soon, Albert too started clasping his hands every time he emphasized a point to his friends or parents. As you can see, for Albert there are many associations associated with the clasping of hands. Hence, to use the clasping of hands as an anchor would not be appropriate.*

Anchors will be powerful when they are unique. Shaking hands, touching our chin, slapping the back of our head every time we make a mistake are all common gestures drenched with too many associations.

Anchors need to be very unique, distinct and reproducible. For example, pressing the middle of the ring finger with the other hand's thumb and index finger; the pressure ought to be the same. If it is an auditory anchor, then the volume and tonality need to be reproduced precisely.

## 3. The Timing of Pairing the Stimulus and Response

The law of association states that memories of events, objects, people, ideas and so on are linked through:

1. A continuity in space;

2. Contiguity in time.

Hence, events occurring in the same place or at the same time become associated with each other. Contiguity is a view that we form a relationship through mere contact in time (we learn that two things are associated because they occur together in time). For example, we learn that when we cut the birthday cake on birthdays, people will sing the birthday song.

So, time is crucial to the anchoring process. Here, the two things that must occur together in time are the intense resourceful state and the stimulus (could be touch, sound, image, etc.). The best timing to introduce the anchor would be the time when the inner resourceful state (e.g., confidence) is reaching close to the peak and still intensifying. Once the resourceful state has peaked or is dropping down from the peak, it would not be an ideal time to introduce the stimulus. Hence, calibration is crucial to identify when the resourceful state is moving closer to the peak.

### 4. Conducive Environment

An atmosphere free of external noise or disturbance is essential for the success of the anchoring process. If during the anchoring process, an ambulance passes by with blaring siren, it would be a bottleneck to the anchoring process. Due to the loud ambulance siren, either the internal state would get disturbed or the ambulance siren would get imprinted as the stimulus.

Hence, a safe, silent and relaxed atmosphere is required for the anchoring process. Even an uncomfortable chair that squeaks and moans would be an obstacle to the process. Jewelry or accessories that make noise can cause a distraction in the anchoring process. Even chewing gum or munching on something during the process can interfere with the results. All care should be taken to create a conducive environment.

**5. Easily Reproducible**

The distinct and unique stimulus needs to be reproduced exactly. If the stimulus is pressing the wrist with the thumb finger, then every time the exact same spot on the wrist must be pressed precisely the same way. Even the pressure ought to be the same. If a slightly different part of the wrist is pressed every time, the anchoring process will fail. Care should be taken to introduce the stimulus in exactly the same spot, the same way.

# NLP Anchors are of Three Types:

## 1. Stacked Anchors

**Similar states that are anchored to the same trigger to create a more powerful 'composite' state are called stacked anchors.**

**Stack:** A pile of objects, typically one that is neatly arranged. E.g., A stack of stones or books laid on top of each other.

There are two ways you can do this:

**Stacking in anchoring involves the same stimulus with multiple internal resourceful states.**

Here, internal resourceful states that are similar (like calm, relaxed and creative) are anchored to the same stimulus.

Assuming you get stressed while driving through heavy traffic, instead of stress, you would prefer calmness. You can create an anchor of calmness through the basic anchoring process. So, when you are at home, let us say you take yourself to a state of calmness and every time you are deeply calm, you touch a specific spot on your wrist (let's call that specific spot 'Spot X') with the index finger. In stacking, you would go further. Apart from calmness, you may want to be relaxed. You may also want to be in a creative state because you want to use your driving time to brainstorm and come up with creative ideas for your work and life.

So, after you have set the anchor for calmness, you take yourself to a deep state of relaxation and you touch 'Spot X' with your index finger the same way with the same pressure. Once this is set, you take yourself to a creative state and touch the same 'Spot X' with the index finger the same way.

This way, you have stacked calmness, relaxation and creative state on to the same stimulus. While driving, once you fire the anchor—i.e., touch the 'Spot X' with your index finger—you would find yourself in a calm, relaxed and creative state. Driving would not only be a pleasure but also productive.

**Stacking: Multiple stimuli—same internal resourceful state.**

**Here, the same internal state (like the state of peace) is anchored to multiple stimuli. (e.g., touch, word, image, etc.)**

Let's say waiting in the airport makes you restless. You would prefer to relax and be at peace when you wait in an airport. So, you anchor a state of peace by touching a specific spot on your wrist when you are in a state of deep peace. Then you anchor the word 'cool breeze' to a state of deep peace. Then you anchor the image of 'Buddha meditating' to deep peace.

Now when you want that state of deep peace, you fire the anchors: touching your wrist, uttering the words 'cool breeze' and visualizing the image of the meditating Buddha. All the anchors would take you to a very deep state of peace. Waiting in the airport would become equivalent to meditative peace.

## 2. Chaining Anchors

The word 'chaining' was used by eminent psychologist B F Skinner. He stated that 'chaining' is a behavior technic that involves breaking a task down into smaller components. The simplest or first task in the process is taught first. Once that task has been learned, the next task can be taught. This continues until the entire sequence is successfully chained together.

The technic of chaining anchors is useful when you would like to move from an unresourceful state to a resourceful state in a series of steps than in one go. The primary reason for choosing a series of steps is the complexity or difficulty in experiencing a shift from one state to the extreme opposite in one go. Also, because of the logical chain, your brain is much more likely to accept the changes, too.

> *Example*
>
> *Rajesh works for a software development company. He is a fresh recruit and has been with the company for the last 12 days. He was invited to attend one of the company's regular meetings. There were about 20 people in the conference hall, and everyone in the room was far more experienced than him. As the meeting proceeded, Rajesh felt a glow inside his mind; an idea had come to him. His face lit up. Very spontaneously, he got up and shared the idea with everyone present there in an enthusiastic manner. As soon he finished, there was silence. It was not just silence, there was anger. Everybody was looking at him with a cold, angry stare.*
>
> *Rajesh felt uncomfortable and sat down. The silence continued for some time, and then the meeting continued as if Rajesh never spoke.*
>
> *Later, Rajesh's boss called him to his cabin and shouted at him for his 'inappropriate behavior.' He was told never to behave that way, or he will be thrown out of the company.*
>
> *That was 14 years ago. Rajesh changed many companies. His current boss is open-minded, and he works for an organization that doesn't*

*believe in strict hierarchy; ideas are welcome from juniors and seniors alike. But Rajesh feels a constriction in his throat in every meeting. He feels withdrawn and anxious whenever he feels like sharing an idea in a meeting. So, he remains silent during the meetings, and this has been his way for the last 14 years. This behavior cost him many promotions and salary hikes. Now for Rajesh to shift from an anxious state to a creative and enthusiastic state in one go could be a difficult task. It would be better to lay down a series of steps to move from the current state to the desired state.*

*Rajesh could move from a state of anxiety to a relaxed state; from a relaxed state to an energetic state; from an energetic state to a creative state and from a creative state to a communicative state (a state where he can express himself spontaneously).*

## Chaining Anchors: The Process

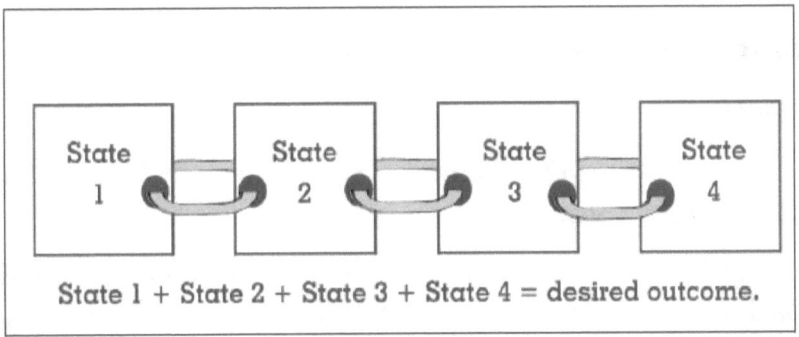

State 1 + State 2 + State 3 + State 4 = desired outcome.

1. **Identify an Unresourceful State** that you want to work on. Choose an unresourceful state that is complex enough and intense enough that it requires a series of anchoring to reach a resourceful state.

2. **Plan the Number of Steps** (i.e., the number of states)

   *In the above example, five steps are required to be chained together.*

   *Anxiety ⇨ Relaxed State ⇨ Energetic State ⇨ Creative State ⇨ Communicative State*

Take time to think through the steps and map out a sketch that leads you to the desired state.

3. **Elicit the First State Within and Anchor it.** Elicit the unresourceful state. Here you need to experience the unresourceful state fully. This can be achieved by thinking about the situation that triggers an unresourceful state within. Go through the unresourceful state and when it is intense, anchor it (visual, kinesthetic or auditory).

*For example:*

> **Anxiety** ⇨ *Relaxed State* ⇨ *Energetic State* ⇨ *Creative State* ⇨ *Communicative State*
>
> *In the case of Rajesh, he can imagine himself speaking in a corporate meeting. This thought of speaking in a meeting will trigger the unresourceful state of anxiety. As Rajesh experiences this anxiety state, he anchors it by touching and pressing the knuckle of the little finger of his left hand for two seconds.*

4. **Break State:** Think of your birthday in reverse order.

5. **Elicit the second stage state within and anchor it.**

*For example:*

> *Anxiety* ⇨ **Relaxed State** ⇨ *Energetic State* ⇨ *Creative State* ⇨ *Communicative State*
>
> *For Rajesh, the second stage state is a state of relaxation. Now Rajesh thinks of a time he felt relaxed. He thinks of the time he spent sitting next to a beautiful lake in a hill resort. This makes his body relax. He anchors this state by touching and pressing the knuckle of the ring finger of his left hand for two seconds.*

6. **Break State:** Think of your ATM pin in reverse order.

7. **Elicit the third stage within and anchor it.**

*For example:*

> *Anxiety* ⇨ *Relaxed State* ⇨ **Energetic State** ⇨ *Creative State* ⇨ *Communicative State*

*Now Rajesh thinks of a time he felt energetic. He thinks of a picnic he went on with his friends and how energetic he felt through the picnic. As he thinks of this experience, he moves into a state of energy. As the energy peaks, he anchors this state by touching and pressing the knuckle of the middle finger of his left hand for* two *seconds.*

8. **Break State:** Think of all the windows in your house and identify which is the smallest window.

9. **Elicit the Fourth State Within and Anchor it.**

*For example:*

> *Anxiety* ⇨ *Relaxed State* ⇨ *Energetic State* ⇨ **Creative State** ⇨ *Communicative State*
>
> *Now Rajesh is asked to think of a time he felt very creative. He thinks of his college project where he was at his creative best. Ideas just flowed through his mind, and he felt certain and strong in his capacity to express himself. As Rajesh experiences this creative state, he anchors it by touching and pressing the knuckle of the index finger of his left hand for* two *seconds.*

10. **Break State:** Add 22+ 31 + 67 = ?

11. **Elicit the fifth state within and anchor it.** (Note: In this example, there are five stages. In your case, the number of stages may be less or more.)

*For example:*

> *Anxiety* ⇨ *Relaxed State* ⇨ *Energetic State* ⇨ *Creative State* ⇨ **Communicative State**
>
> *Now Rajesh thinks of a time he felt communicative. He remembers the school oratory competitions in which he won first place. He recalls how spontaneously he spoke. Now the knuckle of the thumb is touched and pressed for* two *seconds for the purpose of anchoring.*

12. **Break State:** Subtract 17 − 32 = ?

13. **Testing:** Test the anchors to make sure they all work, ensuring to break state between each one. If any one state is not anchored properly, then the process of anchoring that state needs to be undertaken again.

**Chaining:** Chain each state together by:

- Fire Anchor 1, and when it is at its peak, fire Anchor 2 and release Anchor 1

- When Anchor 2 reaches its peak, fire Anchor 3 and release Anchor 2

- When Anchor 3 reaches its peak, fire Anchor 4 and release Anchor 3

- When Anchor 4 reaches its peak, fire Anchor 5 and release Anchor 4 and hold on to the final Anchor for about 5 seconds

## *Example*

- *Fire the first anchor. Here Rajesh presses his little (pinky) finger's knuckle. As Rajesh is experiencing that state of anxiety, the second anchor is fired simultaneously. This is done by pressing the knuckle of the ring finger. Now Rajesh presses both the pinky and the ring finger's knuckles simultaneously.*

- *As Rajesh is experiencing the second anchor, the first anchor is removed. Here he has moved from the anxious state to a relaxed state. As Rajesh is experiencing the second state intensely, his middle finger knuckle is pressed to fire the anchor of the energetic state.*

- *And as he is experiencing the energetic state, he lets go of the ring finger. When the energetic state becomes intense, he fires the anchor in the index finger, allowing him to experience the creative state.*

- *And as he is experiencing the creative state, he lets go of the middle finger. When the creative state becomes intense, he fires the anchor in the thumb, triggering him to experience the communicative state.*

- *As he is experiencing the communicative state, he lets go of the index finger. He stays a little longer (about five seconds) in the communicative state before letting go of his thumb.*

**14. Testing:** Ask yourself how you feel. If you are feeling resourceful and are experiencing the final state intensely, you have completed the chaining process successfully. Otherwise, you need to do the exercise again.

*Example: Rajesh checks within, and he feels he is in a very confident and communicative state.*

**15. Future Pace:** Make yourself think of a time in the future when you will be in a similar situation but will act differently in an empowered way. How's your behavior and what do you find yourself feeling?

*Example: Rajesh imagines he is in a meeting, and he is sharing his ideas enthusiastically and spontaneously.*

## 3. Collapsing Anchors

Collapsing anchors is an effective way to lessen or change an unwanted internal state. This is achieved through integrating or fusing together an unresourceful state and a resourceful state. There are times when all that we want is to lessen a painful feeling to a level where it is manageable.

For example, we may not want to replace the fear of height with confidence. Perhaps we would like to replace the fear of public speaking with a state of confidence. But a little fear of height can warn us when we are on the edge of a building and keep us from harm. Hence, it's good to not do away with the fear completely. But if the fear is so much that we cannot even step into the balcony or terrace, then we need to lessen the fear. This technic of collapsing anchors would be the apt way to do that.

Alloys are made by mixing two or more elements. Adding a small amount of non-metallic carbon to iron produces an alloy called steel. While collapsing anchors, a new internal state is created by mixing an unresourceful state and a resourceful state. The resulting new state is different from the original unresourceful state and the original resourceful state; it is a unique state with its own aroma. Since the unresourceful state was fused with a resourceful state, the resulting new state would definitely lessen the intensity or do away with the unresourceful state.

## Collapsing Anchors: The Process

1. **Choose an Unresourceful State** that you want to change or lessen the intensity of.

*For example, every time you read or hear news about environmental degradation, you might experience intense anger within, and you find it hard to calm down for another day or two. Your work suffers, and you are not able to relate to people during this angry phase. You are not doing anything to solve the environmental degradation problem other than getting intensely angry.*

You may want to lessen the intensity of the anger so that you don't lose your clarity of thought and decision-making.

2. **Associate with This Unresourceful State** and allow the unpleasant state to be felt within you. As you experience this unpleasant state, anchor it.

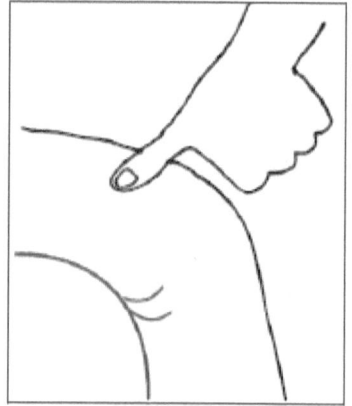

*For example: As you are experiencing this unresourceful state by thinking of environmental degradation, press with your left thumb against a muscular region of your left leg near the knee.*

Repeat this process a couple of times. Test the anchor and see if it works. As in, see if you associate the feeling with the tactile stimulus by your knee.

3. **Break state:** Think of something different and mundane, like guessing how many windows are there in your home or office floor or how many seeds are likely to be there in a watermelon.

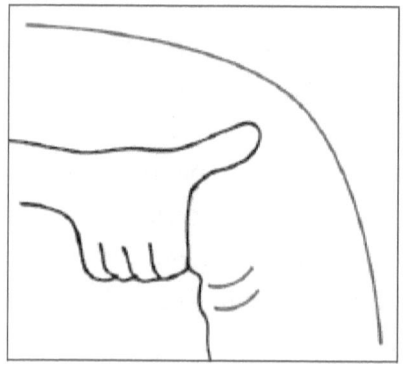

4. **Now choose a resourceful state:** A state of insight, power, inspired state, influence, creative state, enlightened state, peaceful state, etc.

*In the case of the example regarding intense anger due to the subject of environmental degradation, let us take the state of power. This state enables you with the power to lead, the power to initiate and the power to positively influence and contribute toward environmental well-being. Think of a time when you felt powerful and took charge; a time when you took initiative and influenced people around you.*

*Once you experience that state of power, associate with it. When you experience this sense of power fully within you, with your right thumb, touch a different spot (not too far from the first anchor spot) near your left knee and anchor this state. Test the anchor.*

5. **Break State:** Think of something different, like how much is 20 + 1864?

6. **Test First Anchor:** The unresourceful state

7. **Break State**

8. **Test Second Anchor:** Resourceful state

9. **Break State**

Note: If the anchors don't work, you need to redo the anchoring process till both the anchors work fine.

Once Step 9 is completed, both the anchors will be established and working fine.

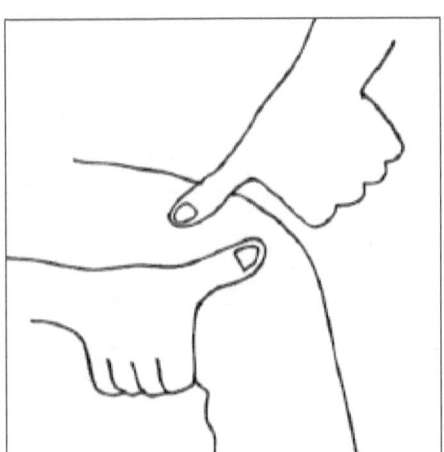

10. Now fire both the anchors simultaneously. As the two states fuse together, you will be left wondering what's going on. Allow the two states to integrate. The resulting state will be either a less intense unresourceful state, a neutral state or a resourceful state.

If the resulting state is a less intense unresourceful state and you would like to further reduce the intensity of the unresourceful state, then make the resourceful state more powerful and repeat Step 10.

*In our example of environmental degradation, when you fire both the unresourceful state (anger) and the resourceful anchor (power), the resulting state could be less anger or a kind of neutral state or a state of power.*

*If you are satisfied with less anger, then you move forward to Step 11. If you want to further reduce anger or change anger to power, then make the resourceful state's power stronger and repeat Step 10.*

11. **Future Pace:** Think of a similar situation that might occur in the future where you experienced an unresourceful state in the past. Take your attention within and take stock of your inner state as you think of this future situation. If the collapsing anchor technic has worked for you, then you will experience the new integrated state instead of the old unresourceful state.

*In our example, when you think of a future situation—for example, reading an article about environmental degradation—what do you see happening within you? Does it trigger the old agitation and anger or does it bring up the new integrated state? If you experience the new integrated state, the collapsing anchor process has worked for you.*

### God is Peace

*Rushmi has been married now for 10 years. She is deeply religious, and prayer is a way of life for her. She is a great devotee of Lord Krishna. She can see in her mind Lord Krishna playing the flute, wearing a peacock-feathered crown. She feels pure love and divine joy emanating from Krishna's beautiful face.*

*She feels peace, clarity and joy whenever she thinks of Him. For Rushmi, Krishna is the source of all knowledge, the divine God and the symbol of eternal peace.*

Her husband Rajesh is an atheist; he doesn't believe in any god. He often makes fun of Rushmi and her faith in her God, Krishna. Rajesh works for a large software company, and he is so busy at work that he has neither time nor any inclination for religion, God or religious beliefs. He believes in hard work. He is delighted with his spectacular career success. He has climbed the ladder to become the CEO of the firm and is highly respected in the industry.

Rajesh is invited as a keynote speaker at an IT conference in London. As he reaches the conference hall, he comes to know that one of the keynote speakers is a spiritual guru. He doesn't like it. "What is the need for this stupid godman in a tech conference like this?" The conference moves on. There is a huge crowd around the spiritual guru and many of them are touching the feet of the guru. Rajesh finds the whole scene disgusting.

In the afternoon, after lunch, Rajesh is surprised when the spiritual guru comes and sits next to him. The guru asks Rajesh, "What is your strength?" Rajesh finds himself speechless. The guru asks again, "What is your strength? What quality do you admire in yourself the most?" "I am a peaceful person, especially during a crisis," Rajesh replies. "In fact, the bigger the crisis, the deeper the peace I experience. And the decisions that I make from the depth of the peace within, most often, are the best decisions," Rajesh adds.

The guru looks at him for some time. Rajesh feels the silence the guru emanates. "You have the blessing of God, whether you like it or not. God is peace. When you face a crisis, what do you do first?" Without waiting for an answer, the guru leaves.

Rajesh sits there thinking, "What do I do first?" He sits there for a long time, pondering, "What do I do first?" Suddenly, it dawns on Rajesh that whenever he feels weak and low in the face of crisis, the first thing he does is to think of his wife Rushmi. The moment the picture of his wife's face comes *to his mind, his whole body experiences a shift. The calm, glowing, serene face of his wife never fails to move him into a more profound state of peace.*

*Rajesh breaks himself out of his thoughts. "What? My wife is the reason for the depth of peace I experience during a crisis? Oh! I never knew that. God is peace. What did the man mean by that? What did the spiritual guru mean when he said I have the blessing of God? Thinking of my wife's face does make me experience peace. God is peace. Hmmm." Rajesh continues musing over the guruji's comments.*

– **Manoj Keshav**

# Chapter 5
# Circle of Excellence

Circle of excellence is an anchoring process that can help us experience a state of excellence within and around us. The term 'circle' refers to space. The term 'excellence' refers to a state that surpasses the ordinary. Excellence refers to transcendence or pre-eminence; to be exceptionally good.

Michael Jordon is considered one of the greatest athletes of all time. Michael Jordon wouldn't have achieved an extraordinary record if he couldn't have created a state of excellence within him as he played basketball. His body, mind and spirit moved into a state of peak performance on the court. It's as if there is a circle around him: the circle of excellence.

## Karna's Story

Karna is one of the most intriguing characters of *Mahabharata*, the longest Indian epic written around two millennia ago. Karna was the son of Kunti and the Sun God. Being the son of the mighty Sun God, he was born with a *kavach* and a *kundal*, armors that would make him invincible.

Karna wanted to learn the *Brahmastra* mantra from a great teacher called Parashuram. The mantra is a set of sacred words and sounds that when uttered gives a certain sense of inner peace and power. The *Brahmastra* is considered the deadliest weapon. It was said that there was neither a counterattack nor a defense strategy that could stop it. The *Brahmastra* never missed its mark and had to be used with very specific intent against an individual or army as the target would face complete annihilation.

Although Karna wanted to learn the *Brahmastra* mantra from Parashuram, there was a hitch. Parashuram would only teach the mantra to a member of the priestly clan. Karna belonged to the warrior clan. So, Karna disguised himself and lied to Parashuram that he belonged to the priestly clan and appealed to him to accept him as his disciple.

Later, Parashuram comes to know the truth, and he curses Karna that he would forget all that he had learned at a critical juncture. Parashuram's curse led to Karna's defeat at the Kurukshetra battle.

At the most critical moment during the battle, Karna forgets all that he had learned from Parashuram. Isn't that the case for many people? Not that these people are cursed like Karna. But the fact remains that during a critical moment in life, many people lose their inner stillness and creative power, which leads them to perform far below their capabilities.

**During life's crucial moments, are we at our best or at our worst?**

For example, a highly talented and skilled professional doesn't get through a job interview because fear and nervousness make him feel his worst during interviews. Critical information refuses to come to his mind. The right words fail to come forth, his face would freeze in anxiety and smile would become *Mission Impossible*. These are the times we want to be at our best, but we end up at our worst like Karna.

The circle of excellence is a wonderful NLP anchoring process that can help you move into the zone of excellence.

## Circle of Excellence: The Process

1. Stand in a place where there is empty space in front of you. The space should be big enough to draw an imaginary circle on the floor and big enough to step in.

2. Take a few deep breaths and allow your body to relax.

3. Now draw an imaginary circle in front of you. Give the borders a color that you like. Now throw, sprinkle or pour some color inside the circle.

Pick a color you like. Add the color not just onto the floor but to the entire circular space in the air like a big imaginary round egg into which you will soon be stepping.

You can add multiple colors or just a single color. The net result should be a circle with your favorite color/colors. At the end of this step, your circle would look colorful, beautiful and inspiring to you.

4. Add some music to the circle if you wish to. It could be the pleasant sound of a flute playing from inside the circle. It could be a calming OM sound emanating from the center of the circle. It could be the pleasant sound of birds chirping or the soothing sound of a water stream. Or it could be anything else that you find relaxing and inspiring.

5. Now add resources like creativity, enthusiasm, laughter, joy, peace, a state of health, a congruent state of oneness, lightness, calmness, love, togetherness, etc. Choose the resource that you'd like to have within and want to channel through you. Add all these resources into the circle until it comes alive with the resources, colors and sounds.

6. When you are ready, step into the circle. Close your eyes. Feel the resources floating in the circle around you, flowing into you through the soles of your feet, into the muscles, fibers and cells of your body, all the way to the top of your head. Feel yourself being filled with all those wonderful resources like love, joy, peace, etc. Feel the color and listen to the pleasant sound as you stand inside the circle. Allow yourself to soak in as many resources as possible, and when you feel satisfied, step out of the circle.

7. Break state: Think of something mundane and random like how many kilometers you think you drove last year.

8. Look at the circle of excellence in front of you—so beautiful, colorful, enriching and inspiring. Look at how it glows with all the resources you need. Step in again and allow all the resources to flow into you once again. Feel the change happening within you as these resources flow into you. Stay within the circle till you are satisfied. When you're satisfied, step out of the circle.

9. Break state: Mentally calculate what 3 × 44 is.

10. Repeat Steps 8 and 9 a few more times till you feel that the anchor is strong enough such that the moment you step into the circle, you shift into a highly resourceful state.

11. Now think of a situation in which you felt unresourceful when you wanted to be your best. Once the incident comes to your mind, step into the circle and allow the sound, the colors and the resources to flow into you.

    As you stay within the color, be aware of the colors, the soothing sound and the wonderful resources that are flowing into you. Once you feel like you have soaked in all these inspiring resources and you are content and satisfied, step out of the circle.

12. **Break state:** Think of how many steps there are in your apartment.

13. **Future state:** Think of the same situation that you will encounter in the future. As you visualize the future scenario in your mind, step into the circle. Allow the resources to flow into you. Keep your focus on the colors, the soothing sounds and the resources that are flowing into you. Take your time. When you are satisfied, step out of the circle.

If you feel resourceful, confident, relaxed and filled with resources like confidence, peace, etc., at the end of the circle of excellence process, then it has worked for you. If not, you can go back to Step 3 and 4 and make your circle of excellence more powerful. The more inspiring and powerful the circle of excellence is, the better it will work for you.

### Spreading the Net of Excellence

*Revathi felt wonderful after the circle of excellence exercise. She had sprayed tranquility, serenity and a state of relaxation inside the circle. She had felt light and at the same time, deeply peaceful inside the circle. Her whole body experienced a state of relaxation. Her circle was rich with the color of purple, the relaxing music of a piano and a gentle, cool mist all over.*

*A couple of days later, she had to go to school for a parent-teacher meeting. Revathi was very nervous. Her son did pretty okay in school, but he was not among the top achievers in his class. She feared that there would be complaints against him. As she walked into the hall where her son's teacher was seated, she found many parents present in the hall. She was asked to wait for her turn. As she waited, her nervousness increased, her heartbeat went up and her muscles tightened.*

*It seemed like an eternal wait. And then she heard her son's name being called. As she got up, she found her knees weak, and she experienced waves of anxiety engulf her.*

*As she walked slowly, she reached into to her handbag and pulled out a rolled-up imaginary circle of excellence. She spread the circle of excellence in front of her as a fisherman would cast out the fishing net.*

*She could see the purple, hear the relaxing music and feel the cool mist inside the circle. She stepped into the circle of excellence. And she immediately felt her whole body relax, and her mind was calm and still. As she stepped out of it, her thoughts became clear: Her boy did well, and there was nothing to worry about. Even if the teacher had something to say, she knew that she was proud of her son and will have an objective conversation with the teacher. There was no reason to be nervous.*

*The whole experience took only a few seconds.*

*"You look so bright and radiant. And your smile, it is so beautiful, Mrs. Revathi," said the teacher.*

— **Manoj Keshav**

# Chapter 6
# Swish: Reprogramming Habits

*"All our life, so far it has definite form, is but a mass of habits."*

**– William James**

We are what we repeatedly do; our patterns and habits are who we are. Contrary to what we believe, it is not that we do what we want to do. We do what we have always been doing repeatedly. After making a New Year resolution, maybe for a few days, an individual does what he or she really wants to do, but eventually, he or she would give into his or her habits.

Are we free human beings or are we slaves? We are slaves—slaves to our habits and patterns. And this is true for most people. Only a few realize that they can choose their habits and patterns. Those men and women who create habits they want are the ones who are genuinely free. Rest of us are slaves. Rest of us can never do what we want to do. It's the habits that rule over us.

## Swish Vs. Anchoring

Anchoring is a conscious process to create a stimulus-response association. In Ivan Pavlov's world, every time the dog heard the bell, the dog salivated. In NLP world, every time you fired your NLP anchor for confidence, confidence flowed in.

Swish is not about creating completely new associations but replacing old and unhealthy associations with new, healthy associations. The swish was developed by Richard Bandler in the early 1980s and is a powerful NLP process for change.

## The Golden Rule of Habit Change

*"You cannot extinguish a bad habit, you can only change it."*

**– Charles Duhigg,**
*The Power of Habit: Why We Do What We Do in Life and Business*

*"Turkey mothers are good mothers—loving, watchful, cleaning and huddling the young beneath them. But there is something odd about their method. Virtually all of this mothering is triggered by one thing: the "cheep-cheep" sound of young turkey chicks. If a chick makes the "cheep-cheep" noise, its mother will care for it; if not, the mother will ignore or sometimes kill it."*

**– Robert Cialdini,**
*Influence: The Psychology of Persuasion*

Quoting M.W. Fox's experiment involving mother turkeys, Cialdini—in his book *Influence*—illustrates how the mother turkey gets aggressive when a polecat, a natural enemy, approaches. Mother turkey starts off squawking, pecking and clawing with rage when the polecat approaches her or her babies.

M.W. Fox's experiment found that even a stuffed model of the polecat, when drawn by a string toward a mother turkey, received an immediate and furious attack. However, when the same stuffed replica carried inside it a small recorder that played the "cheep-cheep" sound of baby turkeys, the mother not only accepted the oncoming polecat but gathered it under her. When the tape recorder was turned off, the polecat model again drew a vicious attack from the mother turkey.

"How ridiculous a female turkey seems under these circumstances? She will embrace a natural enemy just because it goes "cheep-cheep," and she will mistreat or murder one of her own chicks just because it does not make the sound. She seems like a machine whose maternal instincts are under the automatic control of that single sound. Ethologists would tell us that this sort of thing is far from unique to the turkey. They have begun to identify regular, blindly mechanical patterns of action in a wide variety of species." (Cialdini, 2009)

Just as the 'cheep-cheep' sound triggers maternal instincts in mother turkeys, I believe a specific sound, image, touch, smell or a taste can trigger simple to complex reactions in us, too. A trigger can set off a smoking ritual, another trigger can set off the rage button in you and yet another trigger can set off the depression button.

The super key to change a habit is to identify the trigger. In most cases, you will find a single trigger can set off an entire chain of complex habits. There are also habits that have multiple triggers, and in this case, identifying them would be necessary to bring about a successful and sustainable change.

When we get into a lift, we would prefer to press a single button to reach our destination floor. We wouldn't want a complex array of buttons; one button to say, "Yes, I am ready," another button to say, "Now the lift can close." And yet another button to say, "Check if everything is in order."

A complex system kicks off in the lift when we press one button; so do reactions stir in our unconscious. It does not want to process too much information, conduct a brainstorming session, weigh the pros and cons, etc. The unconscious kicks off a chain of habit with just a single trigger (just like the 'cheep-cheep' sound).

Swish is one of the most important and powerful processes in NLP to bring about change. Swish sets up a new behavior for the same old trigger. Swish is also a powerful pattern interrupter.

A pattern interrupt is a disruption, often unexpected, in the flow or sequence of a habit or thought. The unconscious mind's strength lies in running preprogrammed patterns and habits. Its weakness lies in taking a conscious decision. Decision-making is the forte of the conscious mind and herein lies the power of the pattern interrupter. When you interrupt a pattern, the unconscious mind trips into a tailspin and enters a 'confusion' mode. It then waits for the conscious mind for instructions or decisions. It is at this time you can insert new, desirable changes in the unconscious mind.

The swish can be used to change any response or behavioral pattern that is self-defeating or unhealthy.

**Examples**

1. Snacking, even if you are not hungry: This extra eating can flood the body with extra calories and unhealthy ingredients, which can further cause serious and chronic health problems like diabetes, heart problems and acidity.

2. Smoking addiction: Behind every cigarette pack is the message 'Smoking Kills,' but people still persist with the habit. Habits, no matter how strong they are, can be transformed.

3. Indulging in junk food: Fast food is rich in trans-fat, sugar and artificial preservatives. But a life dependent on constant fast food will add to your waistline and cause serious health problems.

4. Nail-biting: This habit of using your teeth to cut your nail, just to pass the time or due to extreme nervousness, can cause germs to enter your body.

5. Picking at your skin: If there is a flaw on your face, you must resist continually picking on it. If you constantly keep worrying about acne by touching it, it will grow more. Besides, it will lead to scars and inflammation.

6. Nose picking: After touching several things, taking the same fingers into your nose is an unhealthy habit.

7. Feeling intimidated: When someone who stares at you, speaks harshly or loudly or is physically larger than you, approaches you, it makes your knees lose power.

8. Being oversensitive to criticism. Whether criticism is patently false or has some truth in it, whether it is intended to be hurtful or helpful, it can wound the psyche. Still, a healthy response would be to consider the criticism of others, integrate what may be true or helpful and recover from the hurt feelings that are sometimes unavoidable. Oversensitivity, extreme defensiveness, sleepless nights, anger, shame or a psychosomatic illness may indicate that there is a self-defeating pattern at work, and it needs to be transformed.

9. Feeling irrational jealousy: Jealousy which stems from one's own insecurity can be a toxic emotion—a poisonous cocktail of possessiveness, envy and mistrust. Left like that, it can ruin your relationships.

Apart from the above list, you can pick any emotional–behavioral pattern that is self-defeating and that which often repeats itself to work through the swish process.

## The Swish Process

### Stage I

**Finding the Trigger**

**Getting the Cue Picture (Trigger)**

1. Sit comfortably in a chair and relax. Think of a time and place when you experienced the undesirable response or pattern that you want to change. Once you recollect the incident, time and place when you experienced the unwanted response, take a deep breath.

2. Now get into the undesirable response. Allow yourself to experience it fully by seeing what you saw then, feeling what you felt then and hearing what you heard at that point in time. Now go back in time, 10 seconds at a time. Keep going back in time until there is no undesirable response inside. Now ask yourself what is it that you see in front of you—outside of you—with your own eyes that trigger

off the unwanted response. The main goal is to find the very first thing that sets off the chain reaction of events that leads you to the unwanted habit or pattern. If it is a sound or smell or any other non-visual sensation, make a visual picture that you associate with that sensation.

*For example, let's imagine Sanju has picked his smoking habit as the undesirable response or pattern that he wants to change. He needs to think of a specific time he smoked in the recent past. It could be last night, this morning or maybe a week ago. Once he gets a specific incident, time and place, he needs to allow himself to experience what he experienced just before he picked up the cigarette. Let's assume the incident happened yesterday. So, Sanju needs to recall what he saw, felt and heard while smoking.*

*After this, he needs to go back 10 seconds at a time, notice what he was seeing, feeling and hearing just before he lit the cigarette. Then, he has to go another 10 seconds back, when he had the urge to smoke, and notice what he was seeing, feeling and hearing at that point in time. Next, he will need to rewind another 10 seconds, when he didn't have the urge to smoke, and notice what he was seeing, feeling and hearing then. The key is to find the very first thing that sets off the urge to smoke.*

*Note: In case of smoking, there may be multiple triggers; hence, sometimes each trigger needs to be worked on. In some cases, working on one or few triggers is good enough for total transformation as the brain would generalize the response and bring about the necessary changes within.*

3. You may have to go a little forward in your mind, or a bit backward, till you get the trigger. The trigger may not necessarily be external. It can also be internal like a thought or an emotion that occurred. Explore internally and externally till you identify the trigger. How do you know it is the trigger? The trigger would set off the pattern immediately.

*For example: In Sanju's case, there is a point in time when he didn't have the urge to smoke, and the next moment he gets the urge to smoke. He needs to keep replaying the scene forward and backward till he finds the moment when the trigger hits him and shifts him from a moment of no urge to a moment of* urge to smoke. Let's say it is the visual sight of a tea shop that caused the urge to smoke in this particular incident. (Note that smoking generally has multiple triggers.)

Let's take another example a person who comes home and gets down to snacking immediately. He might identify that the sight of the refrigerator is the trigger. When this gentleman entered his home, he didn't have the urge to snack, but as soon as he looked at the refrigerator, the urge to snack gets triggered. For another person, it may not be the sight of the refrigerator, but the smell of cookies that triggers off the urge to snack.

Note: Stage 1 of the swish process (getting the cue picture) is all about identifying the trigger that kick-starts an unwanted habit or pattern.

## Stage II

### Once You Have the Cue Picture (Trigger)

1. **Notice the Details:** How far is the 'visual picture of the trigger' in front of you? How bright is it? How big is it?

    > For example, for Sanju, the urge to smoke got triggered when he looked at a tea shop. It is the visual image of the tea shop that was the trigger. He needs to keep that picture of the tea shop in his mind and answer the questions: How far is the image of the tea shop in my mind? How bright is the picture of the tea shop? And how big?

2. **Make the Trigger as Powerful and Strong as You Can:** Make it brighter—keep increasing the brightness of it. Check if increasing brightness makes the trigger stronger. Bring it closer—keep bringing it closer and closer. Check if bringing the picture closer makes it stronger. Make it bigger—keep making the picture larger and larger. Check if making the picture bigger makes it stronger. As you make the cue image brighter, bigger and closer, the cue image will be at its strongest and most powerful state for most people. The key point is to make adjustments in the visual picture of the trigger so that it is at its

strongest. At this stage, you need to open your eyes and visualize the cue picture in front of you.

*For example, Sanju needs to make the tea shop more attractive and more tempting by working on that picture of the tea shop. By bringing it closer and making it brighter and bigger, if the urge to smoke increases, then that's exactly what needs to be done. The key point is to make the trigger its strongest version.*

3. **Let the Image of the Trigger Go Away—far away:** Now with rocket speed, send off the cue picture (trigger) far into space. See the cue picture becoming smaller, blurrier and fading into the distance.

   *For example, here Sanju sees the picture of the tea shop moving away from him far into the distance. The more it moves away, the smaller the picture becomes. Finally, it becomes a dot and then fades into space.*

4. **Repeat Step 3 a Couple of Times:** Check if it is all gone or if there are any feelings left.

5. **Double Check:** If required, move physically or kick off any remaining feelings into the distance. You can scream or shout if you feel like it to kick off any negative feelings still present.

6. **Break State:** Think of your mobile number backward or the top three songs of last year. You may also take a small walk or stretch yourself.

## Stage III

### Steps to Create a Desired 'Highly Resourceful You' State

1. Sit in a chair, close your eyes and relax. Take a couple of deep breaths. Now take your time and create an image of your future self out there in front of you (dissociated), the way you would look and feel when you have already overcome the pattern or response that you want to change. *For example, for a smoker, he would look and feel relaxed when*

*he passes by a group of smokers. There is no urge in him to smoke in spite of the smell of smoke around him.*

2. Make the future self-image more and more powerful by giving resources that would make a difference—resources like calmness, self-discipline, self-love, joy, confidence, high self-esteem, radiance, sense of humor, etc. See these resources in your future self in front of you and see how the body of the 'future self' reflects these qualities. For example, when you give a lot of joy to the image of your future self, see your eyes sparkling with joy and your face brimming with joy. See your breath deepen as the body feels the joy. See how the whole body of your future self is radiating joy. It is very important to see these resources wonderfully transforming the body.

3. Now stand up and move into that space where your future self is and stand in that space. Soak in all the resources, and let it flow over and

through you. Once you experience a sense of completion, come back to your chair and sit down.

4. **Ratcheting:** This refers to the situation when a car jack is used; when the lever is lowered, the jack goes up, but when the lever is raised, nothing happens. Similarly, one can ratchet the positivity in the future self-image.

> Now create an image of the future self (dissociated) that is stronger and more powerful than before. Give more resources to it. This time, the future self is a little more joyful, the state of peace slightly deeper and the radiance on the face slightly brighter. Keep giving resources or enhance the existing resources. Once you feel the future self is now far more powerful than the earlier future self, step into that space and soak in all the resources. Say to yourself, "I feel good about myself. I feel wonderful. I love myself." Let the resources flow into every part of your body and mind. Stay in that space till you are satisfied.

5. Now come back to the chair and see the 'future self'—highly resourceful you (dissociated)—in front of you that is even more powerful by seeing the 'future self' with even more resources.

Repeat Steps 4 and 5 till you have a highly robust future self, a future self that has immense power, a future self that you are magnetically drawn to.

Make sure to leave the future self-image dissociated at the end of the process to attract resources in the future.

## Stage IV

### The Swish

6. Now close your eyes, take the image of your future self (highly resourceful you) and make it into a small radiant dot at a distant point. Allow the radiant dot to come closer, and as it comes closer, notice how it gets larger and larger until it becomes the original life-size it was

with all the brightness, color and resources. Once you see this highly resourceful you, open your eyes.

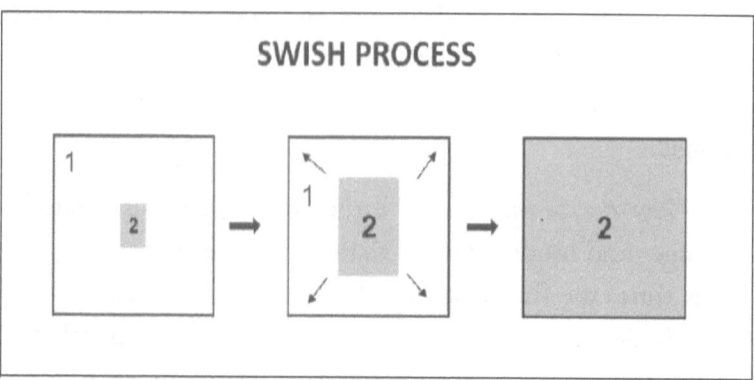

Repeat Step 6 till it is anchored properly. (Repeat as many times as necessary.)

7. Bring the cue picture (trigger), which was thrown off into the distance, back to the position and state of immense power to the left or right.

8. **Swish:** Close your eyes and look at the cue picture (trigger). Let it shrink and recede to a distant point and simultaneously see the small radiant dot of the highly resourceful you at a distance; it is slowly coming closer, becoming larger and brighter and ends up as the life-size original highly resourceful you. Get inspired by seeing the picture of this highly resourceful you—your future self-image. This can be accompanied by a 'swiiisssssh' sound, but it is not necessary. The whole process should take two seconds just like how the 'swiiiissssssh' sound takes just two seconds.

9. **Break State:** Blank all images in the mind screen and open your eyes. Take a deep breath.

10. Repeat Steps 8 and 9 as many times as necessary. Note: Step 9 is critical. This is to prevent the states from looping.

11. **Testing:** Bring the cue picture in front and check what the internal response is. If the response is a resourceful response, then the swish process has worked.

12. **Ecology Check:** Check to see if any part of you objects to this new behavior. If there is any objection, find out the positive intention of the objection and then redo the swish process. If you sense an all-clear signal, then proceed to Step 12.

13. **Future Pace:** Think of a future event when you are likely to encounter the cue picture (trigger) in real life and think of how you would respond. Would a new response be triggered or will the old response resurface? If a new you is what you see, then the swish strategy has transformed your self-defeating response.

* * *

The key to great living is not in replacing unhealthy patterns with healthy patterns. The real key is knowing that we have the power to choose our habits and patterns. Being self-aware and conscious of whether your emotional–behavioral patterns are serving you or turning out to be hurdles in an ever-changing environment is the key to success. Our greatest strength, in due course of time, can become our greatest weakness. For Blackberry, the keypad was their greatest strength. The same keypad became, at a later point in time, their greatest weakness.

Hence, this regular checking in to be aware of our inner patterns and habits as an ongoing process and making changes when needed is the way to change repetitive patterns. Swish helps us interrupt a stubborn pattern and allows us to replace it with a new pattern. And when this new behavior becomes a liability in the days to come, we know we can change that, too; therein lies our power.

Also note that for swish to have succeeded, it is crucial that the highly resourceful state is truly powerful. Every effort should be made to make this state very potent and compelling—a state that is truly inspiring; it energizes you and uplifts you. Once you have created such a rousing, stimulating and encouraging highly resourceful state, the swish is sure to work miracles.

You usually won't know how you would respond the next time you encounter the trigger. The swish pattern creates a powerful, motivating and resourceful self-image of who you want to be. This motivating state organizes and directs the unconscious to figure out a new, healthy response to the trigger.

The swish pattern leaves it to the unconscious mind to creatively deal with it. And when you do encounter the trigger and respond to that in a resourceful way, you can experience the magic of NLP unfolding right in front of you.

The swish pattern can also be done with the auditory system. Instead of a cue picture, it could be a cue sound (trigger), and the resourceful state would be an inspiring and powerful self-image and/or voice.

* * *

### The Strange Locket

*Rohan felt sad for the man who fell while trying to get on a bus. The bus conductor didn't bother to get down and help the elderly man. He just blew the whistle, and the bus moved on. Rohan ran up to the man and helped him sit up. He took his water bottle from his school bag and gave it to him. The old man drank a little water and wiped the dirt off his forehead. He stood up slowly with the boy's help. "I slipped," said the old man. "I am ok. Thank you, my son. Now go on. Don't be late to school," he said as he patted Rohan's back with appreciation.*

*"Where are you heading to?" asked Rohan.*

*"To Chennai."*

*"Chennai? That was the last bus to Chennai from this stop. The next bus is not until tomorrow morning. What will you do the whole day and night, uncle?"*

*The old man scratched his head. He had just enough money for the bus. He didn't have any more for another night stay.*

*The boy read the old man's worried face. He took his hand and said, "Come with me, uncle. My home is close by." He took the old man to his* home. He introduced the old man to his mom and said, "He is my friend who will leave for Chennai tomorrow. He will be staying the night with us." Rohan's mom gave him a radiant smile. "Please come in. It would be a pleasure to have you with us. Please consider this as your own home."

Rohan rushed off to school. As soon he finished school, he rushed home. He found the old man resting in the guest bedroom. Later that evening, Rohan introduced him to all his friends. He was very friendly and cordial with all his friends.

That night, Rohan heard a knock on his door. He looked at the clock. It was 4.00 a.m. It was too early for him to get up, but he went and opened the door. The old man was standing there with a small box. Rohan ushered him in. The old man opened the box and took out a thin chain with a locket made of ordinary steel. He put the chain on Rohan's neck. "I don't know if I would get to speak to you later. You may have to rush to school. I wanted to present this locket to you."

"I was a soldier in the army and have been in many wars including World War II. There were many Indians who fought for the British during World War II. Later, I fought for my country and have won many medals and honors.

The reason for all my glory lies in this locket. It has the power of the universe. Whenever I felt weak or fearful, I prayed. And the universal confidence flowed in me through the locket. Keep it, my boy.

Whenever you feel weak or when your knees tremble in fear, pray to the cosmic force, and the universal confidence will flow unto you through the locket. Just expand your chest and nostrils while praying so that the energy flows in. I have been carrying this treasure for too long, not knowing to whom to hand it over. I feel relieved now. Now it is in the right hand. My dear son, you would use this for the well-being of humanity."

That day the old man left for Chennai. Rohan would grow up to empower thousands of people. Rohan became highly successful and became a role model for many. But sometimes Rohan does wonder why his old *friend gave him an imaginary locket and chain. He had opened an empty box and spoke of a chain and locket, and he had put that imaginary chain and locket on his neck. Purely out of respect, he didn't say anything although Rohan felt that his old friend was out of his mind. Rohan could neither see nor feel a chain and locket on his neck.*

*But somehow, every time he felt weak and fearful, he expanded his chest and nostrils and breathed in confidence through the imaginary locket. It always worked. He always felt flushed with confidence. He always felt the connection to the cosmic force. Never mind whether there is a real locket on his neck or not, his old friend is the reason for his extraordinary success.*

*He had searched the entire city of Chennai for the old man. He couldn't trace him. Never mind. His blessing and gift of confidence are always with him.*

– **Manoj Keshav**

# Chapter 7
# Clearing Confusion With Visual Squash

## Squash

The dictionary meaning of squash is, "to crush or squeeze something into small or restricted space." For example, *"She squashed some of her clothes inside the bag."*

In NLP, squash is a process to integrate conflicting parts within us in a way that helps us find new solutions or directions.

We often notice conflicts and wars that happen around us. Groups clashing, nations at war, etc. What we fail to see are the wars or conflicts that occur within us. Sometimes we experience dilemma over small things in life, but at other times, we experience being torn apart for significant decisions in life.

Let's look at a small example of conflict within. A part of us wants us to go to the party, and a part of us wants to stay back and finish our pending work. The dilemma to do this or that can be time-consuming and stressful at times.

Swish is about interrupting a pattern and enabling ourselves to choose healthier responses. The squash process works by resolving opposing views or polarities, which tend to make us immobile. We might end up feeling torn and unable to make a decision. NLP squash helps us feel integrated amidst such conflicting interests within us. The concept of visual squash does not decide whether option 1 or option 2 is better. It helps integrate qualities and capacities of both the sides. The visual squash method combines visual and kinesthetic senses. It is a variant of the collapsing anchors technique.

## The Visual Squash Process

1. Stretch your hands with the palms facing upward. Visualize the two opposing views or polarities and place one on each hand. Let us call one side of the conflict option 1 and the other side option 2. Let's assume you have option 1 on your left hand and option 2 on the right hand.

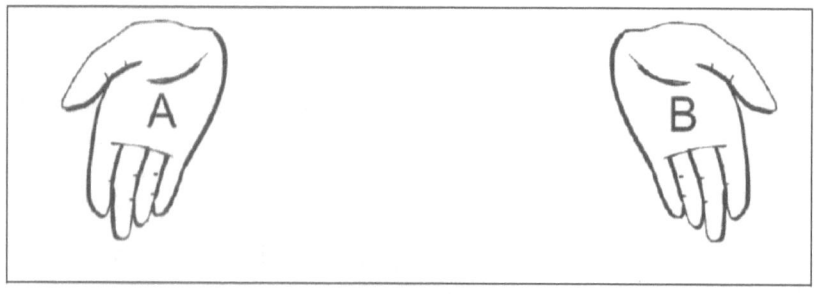

2. Look at the left hand and see option 1. See what that part of you looks like, hear its tone of voice and feel it. Once you connect to this part of you, which is on your left hand, ask, "What's your positive intention?" or "In what way are you helping me?" Once you get a positive intention, shift your attention to the right hand and look at option 2. See what this part of you looks like, sounds like and feels like. Again, ask for the positive intention from this part of you. Wait till you receive an answer.

3. The next step is to establish communication between both these parts of you. Allow the first part of you (option 1) on the left hand face the other part of you (option 2). Let them face each other and appreciate each other's positive intention. Let each of them know how the other part is playing a valuable function.

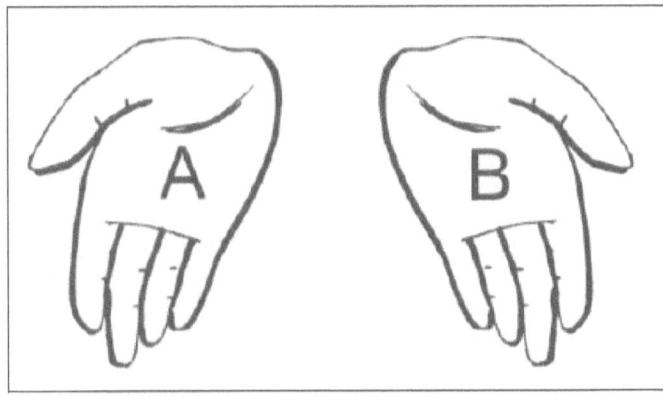

4. Once you have established communication, the next step is to integrate the polarities. Slowly bring your hands together at a pace that feels right, and when the hands are close together, gently squash the two options into each other, allowing them to integrate with each other. As both the options integrate, your body might experience a shift. You might experience new feelings, a release of tension stored within and a change in your breathing pattern. Allow the body to settle down. Now open your hands and see what this new option looks like, sounds like and feels like. This new and integrated option (option 3) will have the valuable elements from both the earlier options and assimilated itself to form an entirely new solution.

The whole process brings you into a state of congruence, clarity and power to move forward.

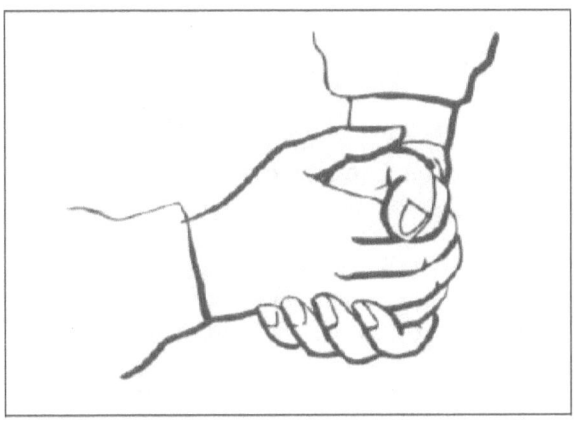

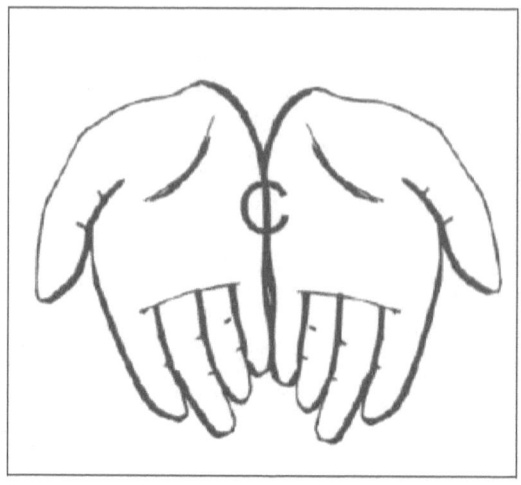

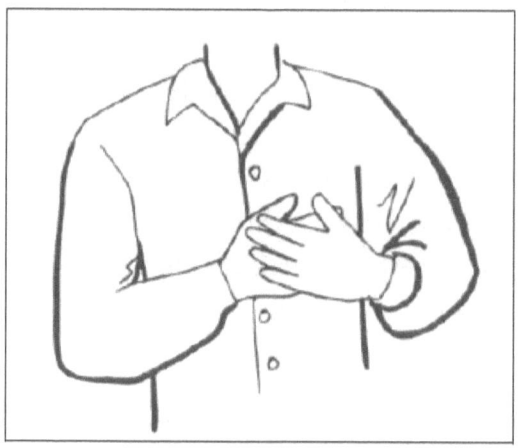

\* \* \*

### King Chakravarthy's Dilemma

*King Chakravarthy was in a quandary. He was pacing up and down in his colossal golden palace. Defending the kingdom from attacks had become his first priority for the last four years. There had been some attack or the other every now and then. His army had been succeeding against every attempt by an enemy group, but in the process, many soldiers had laid down their lives.*

*For the last two years, the king had been recruiting farmers into the army by giving them thorough training. This brought the size of his army back to its original size. But this had left agriculture in a dire state. Food shortage had led to the spread of fear throughout the kingdom.*

*"What to do?" King Chakravarthy's dilemma looked unsolvable to him. Without sufficient soldiers, the kingdom was under direct threat from the army. Without farmers working in the field, the kingdom would slowly deteriorate. King Chakravarthy decided to visit his father to figure out a solution. He visited Sarvorar Garden, where the late king, his father, was buried.*

*Once the soldiers retreated and let King Chakravarthy have some time alone, he knelt down and prayed to his father's soul. A golden circle appeared and a voice said, "Yes, my son. What happened?" After offering his prayers with folded hands, the king narrated his predicament.*

*His father's voice beamed from the center of the golden yellow light and instructed him to break a small branch from a tree and bring it to him. The king did as he was told. The branch looked like a stick in the hands of the king; a stick with many leaves on it.*

*The voice of his father then guided him, "What part of the branch represents the farmer and what part represents the soldiers?" The king thought for a moment. He looked at the branch; it looked like a stick. Yes, he could fight with this branch as if it was a stick. Yes, the branch was, no doubt, a weapon. The king kept looking at the branch. He focused on the leaves now, and the entire branch now seemed to be symbolic of agriculture. Looking up, he replied, "I don't know. The branch and its strength represent a weapon in the hand of a soldier; at the same time, the branch with its leaves represents agriculture."*

*"Well done, my son," the voice replied. Remember that your father's and all your great grandfathers' blessings are always with you." With this, the golden yellow circle disappeared.*

*The king realized that his father's presence had disappeared. He was puzzled. What did his father mean when he said 'Well done, my son'? He stood there for a long time looking at the branch and then the king's face brightened. He returned to the palace feeling confident.*

*A soldier who was looking at the king from a distance never understood why the king visited his father's grave. But one thing he did notice was that after every visit, the king returned stronger and more clear-headed.*

*The next day, the king announced the solution: All farmers had to be soldiers for six months and be farmers for the next six months. He also ordered all his soldiers to learn to farm and be farmers for six months and soldiers for the next six months. Now, every soldier was a farmer and a soldier. When required, he could deploy more farmers on the field, and when needed, he could deploy them on the battleground. The branch represented both the solider and the farmer.*

*The kingdom grew stronger and more prosperous. The king was admired far and wide for his confidence and intelligence. Only the king knew that his confidence came from the knowledge that whenever he found himself in inner conflict, his father's voice would squash all his dilemmas into solutions.*

— **Manoj Keshav**

# Chapter 8
# Outcome Frames

*"If you don't know where you are going, you will probably end up somewhere else."*

**– Laurence J. Peter**

The trouble with not having an outcome mindset is that you will run all over the football ground, throughout the match, without scoring a single goal. Having clarity on the outcomes you want in life is the key to success. Imagine constructing a house without an outcome in mind. The secret of getting what you want is knowing what you want. "All successful people have a goal. No one can get anywhere unless he knows where he wants to go and what he wants to be or do," says Norman Vincent Peale.

What do you want? If the outcome is clear and precise, your thoughts, energy, intelligence and every fiber of your being will shift in the direction of your outcome. Clarity of outcome brings power within. You start moving in that direction, grabbing every opportunity on the way and turning your dreams into reality.

Most of us believe everything that others tell us about what we can/can't do, without questioning their beliefs.

*"Don't ever let someone tell you that you can't do something. Not even me. You got a dream, you gotta protect it. When people can't do something themselves, they're gonna tell you that you can't do it. You want something, go get it. Period."*

**– Chris Gardner,**
*The Pursuit of Happyness*

When an archer is asked to shoot anywhere, he or she will be confused. Give the archer a target and challenge him or her to hit the bullseye and everything changes. The whole body, mind and energy come in unison to achieve the outcome. It is important to decide what we are going to make of our lives.

> *"It is better to be at the bottom of the ladder you want to climb than at the top of the one you don't."*
>
> **– Stephen Kellogg.**

### I know what I don't want. Would that be enough?

Some people have clarity about what they don't want. When asked about their goals, most people talk in terms of what they don't want, rather than what they want. This, too, they realize only after things go wrong. And a lot of their precious time and energy goes into figuring out 'why' they have what they don't want. Once they have clarity that they don't want what they have, they move out of the mess, only to move into another thing that they don't want. Not knowing what you want makes you go from one mess to another. Your whole life is likely to focus on getting out of one crisis after another.

In NLP, outcome thinking is a way to think in terms of what you want, instead of what you don't want. Outcome thinking involves imagining what you really want by stepping forward in time and experiencing the same.

"Don't do this and don't do that," is what people tell others most of the time. "How do you do a don't? All I know is I feel I won't when I am told to do a don't," goes a line a children's song by Ruth Bebermeyer, which is often quoted by Marshall B. Rosenberg while teaching nonviolent communication through his workshops. Speaking positively by avoiding to speak in terms of 'don'ts' is a concept that we need to keep in mind while communicating with others. It is also something that we need to keep in mind while communicating with ourselves. How can your brain do a don't? Don't think of a pink elephant. Well, is that possible? All that your subconscious mind is going to feel is 'won't' when told to do a 'don't.'

Outcome and goals are not things that can be bought in a shop. "Many people fail in life, not due to a lack of ability or brains or even courage, but simply because they have never organized their energies around a goal," says Elbert Hubbard. There are times when a person feels aimless in life, especially when things go wrong continuously. There are also times when a person no longer wants to set goals after failing to achieve previously set goals. The reason for not achieving goals is mostly due to not having a complete understanding of the process of goal setting.

## Abstract vs. Concrete Outcome

People often express their goals in abstract and symbolic terms rather than concrete and sensory terms. Abstract language is not a language your subconscious mind understands; hence, they don't inspire us. We conceive the abstract through our mental processes and perceive the concrete through our senses.

Language may be our most powerful tool. We use words to communicate our own feelings, needs and desires through speaking or writing. Words are the best verbal or written representation of our experience. However, they are not the **experience.** Words inform us, inspire us and enlighten us. Words can also confuse us, misdirect us and complicate simple things. Words can be bridges, but they can also be walls.

The word 'freedom' seems familiar, but it is an abstract word. When somebody says, "I want freedom," what is it that he or she really wants? Financial security? A divorce? A holiday? Clearing debts? Learning to drive? Looser pants? The meaning of the word 'freedom' can be interpreted in a 1000 different ways. Does this mean we shouldn't use abstract terms? No. We need abstract words but not for goal setting. Abstract language creates more walls than bridges in your journey toward your goals.

Concrete terms refer to objects or events that are available to the senses. This is the exact opposite of abstract terms, which label things that are not available to the senses. Examples of concrete terms include water, a slice of cake, a wedding ring and a red rose. Because these terms refer to objects or events that we can see, hear, feel, smell or taste, their meaning is easily comprehensible. While abstract terms like 'responsibility' differ in meaning from person to person, concrete terms like 'a red rose' stay pretty much the same irrespective of circumstances and culture.

The phrase 'I want success' is abstract. Success means different things to different people.

I want to own my own apartment in Mumbai. (The word apartment is concrete)

I want to drive my own Range Rover. (Range Rover is concrete)

I want to go on a holiday to Paris. (Holiday in Paris is concrete)

I want to climb Mount Everest (Climbing Mount Everest is concrete)

All these are examples of concrete language or sensory language. Can you see that concrete terms are clearer and more interesting than abstract terms?

We experience the world first and most vividly through our senses. From the beginning, we sense hot, cold, sharp, soft, warm, mummy, daddy, chocolate, nose, hand, etc., through our physical senses. If you find yourself bored or confused while listening to a speaker, chances are that you are lost in generalizations or abstractions. Your understanding improves once the speaker offers specifics in sensory language with examples.

### Oh, God! What Happened?

*Unnikrishnan managed to complete his graduation despite been born in a small town in southern India. His parents passed away when he was in school. He had worked in a restaurant in the evening and gone to school during the day. It was difficult. After his graduation, he wanted to go abroad and make a lot of money. He decided to go to Dubai, known for its opportunities and luxurious life.*

*In the beginning, it was difficult. Unnikrishnan found himself working in a restaurant in Dubai. It was not much different from what he was doing in his small town, just that the restaurant was much bigger and fancier. But he decided to work hard, and every night, he dreamed of becoming one of the wealthiest men in Dubai. Years went by, and through tremendous hard work and commitment, he opened a restaurant himself. Fast forward another decade and he owned a chain of restaurants. He later diversified and got into many businesses. Whichever sector he entered, he did well. In fact, he found himself growing exponentially. In 30 years, Unnikrishnan became one of the wealthiest and most successful businessmen in the Middle East.*

*One day, he looked at his gray hair and knew his time was limited. He was in his mid-60s, and he wanted to retire. He didn't want to run around or be stressed out. He wanted to go back to his native town in South India. He wanted to relax and spend the rest of his time in peace. He wanted to walk around the place where he had spent his childhood. And he wanted to die in the land he was born in, not in this foreign country. Suddenly, it dawned on him that he didn't have a home in his native town. He had inherited his parents' land. All that was needed now was to build a lovely home. But he didn't want to build just another house; he wanted a masterpiece. He wanted his home to be unique. He wanted his home to remind him how successful he had become. He was going to spend his last days in this house, so it had to be the work of a genius.*

*There were many architects and builders in his hometown. But they would build just another house, which would look like any other house in the town. Maybe they would build a bigger or fancier home, but none of those local builders would be able to build a masterpiece. "Where can I find the world's best architects for my home?" He thought of New York, London, Hong Kong, Tokyo and many other cities. And the name 'Dubai' flashed in his mind.*

*"Home to some of the most amazing futuristic buildings in the world, Dubai has the world's tallest building, the tallest hotel, the largest shopping mall and the iconic Palm and World Islands. Why do I need to go anywhere? This is the city where I can find the best architects. I have millions and millions of dirhams in the bank. Why should I compromise? I need to build a home which I am going to relish for the rest of my life."*

*Unnikrishnan decided to approach builders in Dubai. It would cost him a lot more, but money was no problem; he wanted the best. A few builders politely told him that they would not be able to take up the project as it was in another country. But one firm took it up when Unnikrishnan told them that he would pay far more than the market price.*

*This firm assembled their best architects to design this unique house for their special client. Unnikrishnan gave them the details of his land—its measurement, plot size, etc.—and told them multiple times that he wanted something original, something truly unique; he wanted a masterpiece. His house should not look like any other house. The team of engineers and architects took it up as a challenge and decide to give their all.*

*They showed him one design after another, but he rejected all of them. "I've seen this house in the south of France." "Ah! This one—I have seen in California. I want something original. I want a masterpiece." The team dove deeper into creative ideas and spent hours on brainstorming original ideas. After weeks of great effort, they came up with yet another design. They invited Unnikrishnan and showed him the model house. Unnikrishnan kept staring at the 3D model from different angles. His silence baffled the engineers and architects, who were waiting for his reaction. Finally, Unnikrishnan's silence turned into a smile and soon his face was so radiant and joyful as though he had won a billion-dollar lottery. He hugged everyone on the team, and his eyes were filled with tears. With a slight tremble in his voice, he said, "I am so happy. This is exactly what I wanted. This is a masterpiece. This is original. This is unique. Congratulations, guys. Great work!"*

*Unnikrishnan sat with the team, detailing every aspect of his house for the next few days. Finally, Unnikrishnan was fully satisfied with the design of his home. He felt on top of the world. He felt that this was the most important project of his life. He had not thought of anything else the last few months. He then asked the firm to go to his native town in India and construct the house for him.*

*The CEO of the firm told him that he would send two senior engineers to oversee the construction. Unnikrishnan was furious. "Why only two engineers? I don't want any local folks to be part of this project. They are not familiar with the latest technologies. They will ruin the plan. I want only experts to work on my dream home. What is the point of coming up with a masterpiece design and having some local workers spoiling it? Every person who works for this project needs to go from Dubai, and everyone needs to be an experienced professional. Is that clear?" The CEO was surprised.*

"Why would they travel all the way and work out of a small town in India?" asked the CEO. "Because they will make more money there than in Dubai. I am willing to pay them more than what they get here in Dubai. The whole team of workers and engineers must go from here and only experienced folks; every one of them. And you will make more money doing this project than doing a similar project in Dubai. Do we have a deal?"

"Of course. If these engineers are going to make more money there, who would say no? It's a deal. Done. We will update you every week on the progress," said the CEO as he shook hands with his client.

The whole team went to Unnikrishnan's native town and started the project. They keep updating Unnikrishnan every Monday. Weeks turn into months, and the project was finally completed. The project head informed Unnikrishnan over a call. "Sir, the project is fully completed. It has come out incredible. To be frank, when we all came to this small town, we were frustrated. But now we are so excited. Sir, I have more than 27 years of experience as a civil engineer. I have constructed many houses in Singapore and the Middle East. I must honestly tell you that your house is a masterpiece. Passers-by stop to take a good look and even take photos of it. It's breathtakingly beautiful, if I may say so myself. You should come down soon to see your dream home, sir."

Unnikrishnan was super excited and started right away. Throughout his flight, he kept visualizing his house. He had seen drawings of it, but he wondered how much more magnificent it would look in real life. As soon as he landed in Cochin Airport, he took a taxi to his hometown.

After four hours, he reached his place and saw the whole team of engineers and workers in their uniform, waiting on the road to receive him. The chief engineer welcomed him with a garland and pointed to the newly constructed building. Seeing the house, Unnikrishnan stated sweating profusely, and then he seemed to breathe hard before he collapsed on the road. The chief engineer was shocked. He had read somewhere that some people when they are very happy can also get a heart attack. Once they

> *revived him from his spell, Unnikrishnan gained back his consciousness and looked at the house. The chief engineer prodded, "Sir, what happened? Are you ok? Are you happy with your house? The house is exactly how you wanted it. We have built the house flawlessly. What happened? Are you ok? You look so depressed."*
>
> *"Yes, the house is exactly how I wanted it. But you have constructed the house in the neighboring plot. My house is standing on a plot that belongs to the government. My plot is the adjacent one. Oh, god!" he said and fainted again.*
>
> – Manoj Keshav

If the vision is flawed, if the plot on which you are constructing your life is wrong, then everything will go wrong. Excellence in execution cannot compensate for weakness in goal setting. Setting a clear outcome is one of the most important elements in NLP, whether it is for change or achieving something new in life. Whether it is therapy or a coaching session, whether it is life or a small project, it is essential to set a clear outcome.

The outcome frame is a set of questions that orient your thinking in a way that maximizes the possibility of achieving what you really want. If you are stuck and don't see a way out, the outcome frame can help you discover choices and new possibilities. Outcome frames not only help you set a clear direction but also motivate you to move in that direction.

Rather than analyzing why a problem exists, the outcome frame organizes energies and intelligence around what is wanted and how to achieve it. Every human being has unlimited resources and capabilities. Scientists are baffled by studying a single human cell and its capabilities to do trillions of things flawlessly. The human brain is a miracle. We appreciate a diamond. We appreciate a sunset or sunrise. We appreciate a waterfall. But very few people appreciate the extraordinary intelligence every human is gifted by nature. We human beings are far more precious than the world's most expensive diamond. Very few people realize their full potential. The outcome frame helps a person tap into their own potential and lead a life that he or she truly desires.

## The Blame Frame

Compare and contrast is one of the best ways to comprehend new concepts. Let us understand the concept of outcome frame by comparing it with the blame frame.

Do the following exercise:

1. Think of something that is a problem or a 'stuck state' in your life right now.
2. Keep that problem in mind and ask yourself, "What's wrong?"
3. How does this problem limit you?
4. Why do you have this problem? What caused it?
5. Whose fault is it that you have this problem?
6. Which is the worst time you experienced because of this problem?

## The Outcome Frame

Take a deep breath; if needed, go for a small walk or stand up and do some stretching. Now, let's try the outcome frame.

1. Think of something that is a problem or a stuck state in your life right now. (Preferably think of the same problem that you thought of while doing the blame frame exercise.)
2. What do you want?
3. When do you want it?
4. How will you know that you have achieved this outcome?

5. When you get what you want, what else will improve in your life?
6. What resources do you have to help you achieve your outcome? (Resources include time, energy, creativity, experience, intuition, inner resources, courage, etc.)
7. How can you best utilize the resources that you have?
8. What are you going to do now to get what you want in life?

Now that you have answered these questions, take a deep breath and notice your feelings.

How did you feel when you went through the blame frame, and how different was it when you went through the outcome frame? The blame frame questions make you feel stressed out and drained of energy, whereas the outcome frame energizes you, leads you to the future and opens up new options to achieve what you want.

## Let's Examine Each Of These Questions

### What Do You Want?

When you are swayed by your emotions, there is a tendency to flow in the direction of your feelings. A person who is irritated tends to stay there or may get progressively more irritated as the day progresses. A person who is sad and depressed may flow with that emotion and remain sad and depressed for a while; even self-awareness may not take that person out of those negative emotions. The person may also use insights of self-awareness to experience more of negative emotions. For example, an irritated person, once he or she becomes aware of the irritation within, may now get more annoyed for being irritated in the first place.

Asking the question 'What's wrong?' makes you feel worse. The answer to 'What's wrong?' lets you know what you do not want. And when you reflect on all that you do not want, you are going to feel even worse. Many people believe that if you feel extremely terrible about something, you will change. It is not so in reality. When a student gets low marks, she might feel bad, but that does not improve the score next time. The question 'What do you want?' breaks this vicious cycle. It motivates you to look ahead and visualize what you really want. And when you reflect on all that you really want, you are going to feel optimistic, confident and inspired.

### *An example of what happens to the question 'What's wrong?'*

> **Therapist:** *So, what's wrong?*
>
> **Wife:** *Everything. He is the most selfish person I have seen. He is self-centered, egoistic and doesn't care about me.*
>
> **Husband:** *She is exaggerating; complaining and nagging is part of her character.*
>
> **Therapist:** *Tell me more.*
>
> **Wife:** *Last night, he came home at 12.30. He didn't even inform me that he was going to come so late. He never communicates. He has some insecurity within him just like his father.*
>
> **Husband:** *She is the one who does not know what communication is. There is a difference between nagging and communicating. She will never know that. It is probably because she doesn't use her brain to understand it. And I don't blame her for that; it's in her DNA. Her father, grandfather...all are like that.*

### *An example of what can happen in the same scenario with the question 'What do you want?'*

> **Therapist:** *What do you want?*
>
> **Wife:** *I want him to communicate more with me. I want him to care for me and keep me informed when he is going to be late from his office.*

> *Husband: I want her to understand the pressure I face in my office. Sometimes, I am in a meeting, and the meeting drags on for hours. It is difficult to attend calls in front of my seniors and talk.*
>
> *Therapist: Tell me more about what you want.*
>
> *Wife: I understand his office pressure. Just that I miss him so much. I want him to make it up to me by talking to me more often and taking me out on weekends.*
>
> Husband. Of course, I will. I want to come home on time and spend time with you, rather than sit through those meetings late in the evening. Just that I want to keep the job. (He gets up to hug his wife.)

## 1. When Do You Want It?

Imagine booking a flight without knowing when the flight will take off. Imagine scheduling an appointment without knowing the date and time. Imagine picking up a newspaper that does not mention dates and time. Imagine picking up a loaf of bread in a supermarket, which does not have the manufacturing date or expiry date. Even while booking a movie ticket, the time and date are crucial.

When it comes to changes that we want to bring about, some changes can be done in a second. If that is so, why take more time? Of course, certain outcomes take more time and effort, but it is essential that you estimate the time that is required to do the job.

The question 'When do you want it?' jolts a person out of wishful thinking to ground reality. It is now no more a wish or a desire; it is now something that is tangible and needs to be achieved within a specific time period.

> *Therapist:* So, both of you want to be understood by each other. What else do you want?
>
> *Wife:* Spending more time together and communicating more often.
>
> *Husband:* If she understands what I am going through in the office, that would be enough.
>
> *Therapist:* What about spending more time together and communicating more often?
>
> *Husband:* Yes. Even I want to spend more time together and communicate more often. Just that, on some days, I am too preoccupied with work. Except on those stressful days, I would like to spend more time with my sweetheart.
>
> *Wife:* If you talk to me about what's happening in the office, only then will I be able to understand what you are going through at work.
>
> *Therapist:* So, what do both of you want?
>
> *Husband:* More communication and more connection.
>
> *Wife:* Yes, more communication and more connection.
>
> *Therapist:* So, when do you want it?
>
> *Husband:* Now onward.
>
> *Wife:* From now.

## 2. How Will You Know That You Have Achieved The Outcome?

To answer this question, you need to imagine that you have already attained the outcome you want. In such a scenario, see what you will be seeing, hear what you will be hearing and notice the feeling within. This question leads a person from abstract dreams to a clear outcome. What will you see once you have achieved the outcome? What will you hear once you have achieved your goals? What would you feel once you have achieved the results you want in life? The question encourages a person to think in concrete and sensory language.

> ***Therapist:*** *How will both of you know that you have achieved the outcome?*
>
> ***Husband:*** *What will I see once we achieve the outcome of more communication and better connection? I see my wife's happy face. I see her listening to me with rapt attention. I see her listening to all that is going on with me. I see that she is talking and sharing all that is going on with her. I see her opening the door with a smile on the days I get home late. I see us hugging more often. I see us both holding hands and spending more time together.*
>
> *What will I hear? I hear her affectionate voice. I hear her whispering 'I love you.' I hear soft music playing in the background as we spend time together. I hear the sound of waves as we walk together on the beach.*
>
> *What do I feel once I have achieved the outcome? I feel more loved and more connected. I feel more complete and happy.*
>
> ***Wife:*** *What will I see once we achieve the outcome? I see a smiling hubby when I open the door. I see us sitting, having coffee and talking with each other. I see us both going for walks and talking to each other. I see myself waking up happy and going through the day feeling refreshed and alive.*
>
> *What will I hear? I hear my hubby's roar of laughter. I hear his deep, peaceful breaths while he is sleeping. I hear his appreciative and caring words.*
>
> *How will I feel? I will feel love, happiness and excitement within me. Yes, I will be happy.*

## 3. When You Get What You Want, What Else In Your Life Will Improve?

This question gets a person to move out of the box and think more broadly. The answer to this question can play a powerful motivating force to go after the outcome. The person will also be able to see how everything is interconnected. Life is not compartmentalized; everything affects everything.

> *Therapist:* When you get what you want, what else in your life will improve?
> *Husband:* My health will improve. After our fights, my stress goes high. I become more irritable. Sometimes, I end up with a headache. Once we have more communication and more connection, I will be a lot less stressful. Coming home will be a stress buster for me. So, my health will definitely improve. She spoke about going for a walk together, that will improve my health as well.
> *Wife:* Yes, mine too. I find it difficult to sleep after a fight with my husband. Once we have more communication and feel more connected, I am sure I will have better sleep. Overall, I will be healthier. I will also speak to my friends and parents more affectionately. So, my relationship with others will improve as well.
> *Husband:* I think my performance at work will improve, too. And so will my relationship with my in-laws.

## 4. What Resources Do You Have That Will Help You Achieve Your Outcome?

To achieve our goals and realize our outcome, we need to harness and mobilize our resources. To start a business, we need money, contacts, etc. Those are external resources. Creativity, communication skills, problem-solving skills, resilience, discipline, etc., are internal resources. The sheer number of people who have started from nothing and reached great heights in life goes to show that if we mobilize our internal resources toward a clearly defined outcome, then we are unstoppable.

> **Husband:** *I can take the initiative to communicate and keep my wife informed of what's happening, especially in the office. I can be more empathetic when she is in a bad mood. I can exercise my creativity to give her pleasant surprises so that she does not get bored by the same routine week after week.*
>
> **Wife:** *Love, forgiveness, caring, empathy, listening without judgment are the resources I would like to tap into to feel more connected to my husband.*

### 5. How Can You Best Utilize The Resources That You Have?

Resources don't get utilized by themselves. An active effort is required to use the God-given resources to live a fuller and happier life.

> **Wife:** *I have learned the art of visualization. Every day, I will visualize that I am a loving, caring, empathetic, non-judgmental person with excellent listening skills.*
>
> **Husband:** *Visualization sounds great. I will allocate time to communicate with my wife on my daily schedule till it becomes a way of life. I will also plan weekend getaways and holidays much in advance. Yep, planning and visualization should help.*

### 6. What Are You Going To Do NOW To Get What You Want In Life?

"From tomorrow, I am going to be a different person."

"I will start eating healthy Monday onward."

"I will exercise every day from Jan 1st."

All these statements strengthen our procrastination muscles. 'What can I do NOW?' is the best question you can ask yourself. It pulls you out from inaction and makes you take a step forward right now.

> **Husband:** *I would like to give a hug to my wife right now.*
> **Wife:** *Me, too.*
> *They both get up and hug each other.*

# Chapter 9
# Advance Listening Skills with Metamodel

> *The Merriam Webster dictionary defines the word 'meta' as beyond; above; higher level.*
>
> *Example: "A movie about making a movie is just so meta, especially when the actors criticize the acting."*
>
> ***The metamodel*** *is a model of a model. Meta-modeling is the process of generating such metamodels. A model is an abstraction of a phenomenon in the real world; a metamodel is yet another abstraction, highlighting properties of the model itself.*

*"Language...has created the word 'loneliness' to express the pain of being alone. And it has created the word 'solitude' to express the glory of being alone."*

– **Paul Tillich**

Other than human beings, no other species has such articulate languages. No other species can speak a language with such speed and precision while following complicated underlying rules and structure that all languages have. Animals use gestures and sounds—but no way do they equal our language system that consists of words, nouns, verbs, etc.

Although language is one of the most significant and momentous works of the human species, it is also a poor representation of our experience.

> **Expression of an Experience**
>
> *Vishal entered the Communication Skills Workshop organized in his college. He was slightly nervous as he knew he would be required to speak and participate in the workshop. None of the participating students were from his class, and he knew nobody.*
>
> *Vishal's fear vanished as he found himself participating in various games and activities conducted by the trainer. It was then that the trainer called out to Vishal and requested him to share a happy or memorable incident. It was easy for Vishal to think of a memorable incident. He had gone to a hill resort recently and had a wonderful time.*
>
> *So, Vishal stood up and with gleaming eyes said, "It was an awesome experience. I went to this hill resort and had such a wonderful time. Oh! The weather was awesome. Food was mouth-watering. It was pure fun. Well, that's it. I mean, it was awesome. Thank you."*
>
> *Vishal sat down. The trainer walked up to the whiteboard and asked the crowd, "All those who thought Vishal went alone to the resort, raise your hand, please." A few hands went up.*
>
> *"How many thought he went with his family to that hill resort?" Many more hands went up. "How many thought he went with his friends?" Many other hands went up.*
>
> *"How many thought of chicken and seafood when Vishal described mouth-watering food?" Many hands went up.*
>
> *"How many thought of vegetarian food when Vishal described mouth-watering food?" Again, quite a lot of hands went up.*
>
> *"How many thought the hill resort was in India?" Some hands went up.*
>
> *"How many thought it was abroad?" Many hands went up.*

> *Well, you all see…when Vishal spoke, we created pictures in our mind which are far from reality. Vishal's experience can never be fully shared through words and sentences. The map can never equate itself with the territory. Language does help us navigate through life; at the same time, language is a very poor representation of an experience.*
>
> — **Manoj Keshav**

Language is a very poor representation of an experience. When a person says, "I had a wonderful holiday. It was a beautiful hill resort. It's an amazing place." Listening to these words, some people would conclude that this person went with his family to a hill resort and had a good time. There are also people who would conclude that this person went with his friends to a hill resort and had a wonderful time. There are also people who would conclude that this person went to a meditation and yoga camp in the hill resort and felt rejuvenated. There are also people who think that he went alone to a hill resort and admired the birds, trees and animals because, for them, being with nature is amazing.

There are thousands of ways to interpret the statement 'I had a wonderful holiday. It was a beautiful hill resort. It's an amazing place.' This statement is not the experience. The statement is a representation of the experience. In fact, this statement is a very poor representation of the experience. The entirety of this person's experience can never be fully expressed in language.

When we listen to people, we are listening to words and sentences, which are not their experience. We hear these words and make pictures in our mind. The pictures that we make in our mind may not match the pictures in the speaker's mind.

## NLP Metamodel

The breakthrough metamodel was published in 1975 by Richard Bandler and John Grinder in their book *The Structure of Magic: A book about Language and Therapy,* Vol 1. Metamodel is an important topic in NLP, and it helps us become better listeners. It helps us to understand what's going on within a person.

## Words Are Representations. What Does That Mean?

2 kids sitting in a garden keep looking at a beautiful red rose. After a while, both of them decide to draw the rose. Both of them engage in drawing with great involvement and enthusiasm. When they finish it, they compare it with each other and think their own drawing is better than the other's. They wanted to know whose picture looked the most like the real rose. When the kids showed their pictures to their parents, the adults could not make out that the drawings were that of a rose. Somebody said the drawing looks like the planet Mars and another thought it looks like a red football.

The drawing is a representation of the flower. A good artist can create a better representation of the flower, and someone who does not know to draw might create an inadequate representation of the flower. In either case, it is a representation of the flower and not the flower itself.

We go through an experience, and we create a representation of it in our mind. Just like no artist can draw a flower the exact same way, no two people going through the same experience will describe the experience using the same words and sentences. No matter how good a person's language is, the language is a representation and not the reality itself.

## Should We Listen to a Person's Experience or the Underlying Structure of How He or She Creates the Representations of All Their Experiences?

Effective therapists don't just go about asking for more information about the representation, but they look for the underlying structure of how an individual creates their model. Just like how an artist does not only teach her students how to draw a specific object, like a flower, but also teaches the process and techniques required for drawing all shapes and forms. Similarly, it is not the experience that we need to change but our methodology of creating a representation of our experiences. A good artist's work will be appreciated no matter what he creates. Similarly, it is not what we experience but how we represent what we experience that enriches our life.

There is structure to the way we represent our experience and the way we create models of our world. The moment we work on our structure, the moment we enhance it, our experiences will become richer, and we will produce better results in life. It is like the moment an artist improves his skills, every drawing that he would draw henceforth would be more precious and more profound.

The components that go into a building construction would be cement, bricks, steel, etc. Similarly, one of the key elements that go into building an individual's model of the world is language. Our choices of words and our pattern of sentence-making play a crucial role in the way our model of the world gets created.

By studying the language an individual uses, we can uncover the blocks and limitations that a person has set up within himself or herself. By considering the choices of words and phrases a person uses, we can get a glimpse of his or her model of the world. We get to know if the person has a model that limits choices or a productive model that shows up choices.

The metamodel helps us identify the deletions, distortions and generalization that people make while they share their thoughts.

## I. Gathering Information

When a patient goes to a doctor and says she is not well, the first thing the doctor would do is to ask more questions because 'I am not well' is too vague to diagnose.

When a citizen goes to a police officer and says, "I have been cheated," the first thing the police officer would do is to ask questions because 'I have been cheated' is too vague to figure out what went wrong.

When a prospective home buyer goes to a real estate consultant and says, "I am interested in buying a house," the first thing the consultant would do is to ask more questions about the budget, what kind of house, the location, etc. The statement 'I am interested in buying a house' is too vague for a consultant to offer his suggestions.

When a kid comes and tells her dad, "I don't like school," the father might get angry and tell the child how important it is to go to school. For an NLP practitioner, the statement 'I don't like school' is too vague to diagnose the problem. The first thing an NLP practitioner would do is to ask more questions.

When the boss says, "I don't like you," in a harsh tone, the employee would fall into silence. For an NLP practitioner, the statement 'I don't like you' is too vague to diagnose the problem. The first thing an NLP practitioner would do is to ask more questions.

When a wife says, "The biggest mistake of my life is marrying you," the husband would fly into a rage and shout back, "The biggest mistake of my life is not divorcing you." The argument would go on past midnight. For an NLP practitioner, the statement 'The biggest mistake of my life is marrying you' is too vague and the first thing she would do would be to ask more questions.

Gathering information is very crucial to solving problems. Imagine a doctor who doesn't listen to what you say, doesn't carry out any examination or tests and prescribes medicines based on his or her mood. Would you go to a doctor like that?

## I Just Don't like You

*Joseph got ready for the interview. It was crucial that he cleared this interview. He was in a dire financial state. He knew he could not be without a job. There was no place to go to borrow more money. He had been without a job for the last five months. During this time, what kept Joseph going was the NLP practitioner course that he had enrolled in. He had been learning new skills and not wasting his time sitting at home without a job.*

*As he reached the office, he took a deep breath and stepped in. His heart sank when he looked at the large number of people waiting for the interview. "So many have turned up for just one vacancy," thought Joseph. Anyhow, instead of worrying, he decided to relax and wait for his turn.*

*When his turn came, he took a deep breath and stepped inside. It was a spacious conference room. There were three interviewers. Joseph greeted them with a smile and said, "Good morning." No one replied to his greeting. The serious-looking interviewer seated in the middle scanned Joseph from head and toe and with a stern voice said, "Please sit down."*

*Joseph took a deep breath and sat down. The man continued, "Your name is Joseph. I see. Let me be very frank with you, Joseph. I just don't like you."*

*Joseph instantly became curious. To him, 'I just don't like you' was too vague. So, he asked, "Is it that you don't like my look or the way I greeted you? If I may ask, can you please tell me what specifically you didn't like in me?"*

*The man gave Joseph a hard, long look. There was silence. Joseph's face reflected curiosity. The man continued, "Do you not know basic corporate etiquette? You are wearing black shoes with a brown belt. The right thing to do is to wear matching belt and shoes."*

> *Joseph, knowing now what the real problem was, replied, "I didn't know that. Thanks for bringing it to my attention. I have learned something new."*
>
> *All three interviewers looked at each other. The man continued, "Joseph, can you tell us about your educational background?"*
>
> *3 days later, Joseph received an email confirming that he was selected for the job. His pay package was slightly more than what he was expecting. He re-read the confirmation email many times. Finally, when he got up to tell his family that he got a job, his eyes were filled with happy tears; he was glad he got this job. He also felt wonderful that he had handled the interview well, thanks to the training that taught him to dig for more information before coming to a conclusion.*
>
> – Manoj Keshav

According to A. Korzybski, a Polish American scientist remembered for his theory of general semantics, "Map is not the territory it represents, but, if correct, it has a similar structure to the territory, which accounts for its usefulness."

Language is not the experience, but it is a representation of an experience. Comprehending another person's experience is useful. During this process of comprehension, if we jump to conclusions, we might end up drawing a wrong conclusion. It would be like a nurse who puts a bandage on the left wrist when the wound is on the right.

Hence, it is crucial to dig deeper when a person gives very little information or when the information is vague. The best way to dig deeper for more information is to ask questions.

Generally, what most people communicate is just the tip of an iceberg. The iceberg here represents their experience. The listener usually fills in the gap with their own experience.

**Example**

Tom is not well. So, he won't join us for the party.

One listener here visualizes Tom in bed, taking medicines, coughing and trying to sleep.

Another listener might visualize Tom vomiting and panting.

Yet another listener might visualize Tom depressed, sad, sitting in a corner and brooding.

None of these listeners may be aware that the images they are creating in their mind are fictitious and not real.

'Not well' can be constructed as a physical injury, mental sickness, hospital emergency, depression, excuse, etc.

It would be best if, instead of filling in the gaps with our imagination, we ask more questions and get a clearer view of things.

If we are interviewing a successful person, we might create a code assuming this is what makes the person succeed; not the true secret behind their success. People usually listen to just a little information, and they fill in the rest by themselves, believing the picture they created in their head is something the speaker experienced. In fact, 80% of the whole picture could be your fabrication, and you may not even know that you have fabricated the information to fill in the missing pieces.

Information gathering is getting close to reality or the truth. Information gathering is to understand. Information gathering is to identify the problem accurately. Just like an ophthalmologist takes his time to understand and diagnose the problem before prescribing reading glasses or medicines, it is essential to have all the inputs before making a decision.

There are five parts in the category of gathering information:

1. Simple deletion
2. Comparative deletion

3. Lack of referential index

4. Unspecified verbs

5. Nominalizations

## Simple Deletion

A simple deletion is one with missing or incomplete information. To identify simple deletions, ask, **"About whom? Or about what?"**

**Example 1**

1. I am scared.

**Scene 1**

*Rakesh comes out of a movie theater after watching a horror movie. He turns to his friend and says, "Hey Sam, I am scared."*

*Sam says, "Come on, Rakesh. It is just a movie. It is not real. Everything is special effects. Don't get scared of the movie scenes. Even I am scared, but I know the movie is not real. It's ok. Now chill. Come, let's go and have a drink."*

*Rakesh keeps looking at his watch and leaves saying, "You won't understand. I need to hurry. I will catch you later." Sam stands there puzzled as Rakesh gets on his bike and rides away.*

**Scene 2**

*Rakesh comes out of a movie theater after watching a horror movie. He turns to his friend and says, "Hey Sam, I am scared."*

*Sam says, "I see. You do look tensed. What happened? About what or whom are you scared?"*

*Rakesh says, "I didn't tell my parents about the movie. They wouldn't have allowed me to go because of the exams. It's past seven now. They will be worried. I am scared that my dad is going to yell at me."*

Sam replies, "You better hurry now. Hope your dad is ok. Go home and study."

Rakesh says, "Thanks, man. You are great. You understand me well. Catch you later."

Rakesh gets on his bike and rides away. Sam stands there feeling good.

## Example 2

### Scene 1

Sadiq comes out of the meeting and takes off his tie. Instead of sitting down on his chair, he starts pacing up and down. A colleague, who notices that he is upset, offers to buy him coffee. As they both walk toward the coffee shop just outside the office, Sadiq tells his colleague Rahim, "I am mad." Rahim puts his hand on Sadiq's shoulders and says, "What to do? Our company management sucks. Our CEO is a nut case. When he speaks, my mind goes into circles like a whirlpool. The moment you came out of the meeting, I knew that our CEO must have given a long lecture. It is not just you, everyone is annoyed with him."

Sadiq says, "It's not what you think."

Rahim replies, "I know, Sadiq. It's ok. You will be alright after some time."

Sadiq says, "I am getting this goddamn call again. Rahim, you go and have coffee. I got to take this call."

Rahim goes to the coffee shop and keeps wondering whether Sadiq will join him or not.

### Scene 2

Sadiq comes out of the meeting and takes off his tie. Instead of sitting down on his chair, he starts pacing up and down. A colleague, who notices that he is upset, offers to buy him coffee. As they both walk toward the coffee shop just outside the office, Sadiq tells his colleague Rahim, "I am mad." Rahim puts his *hand on Sadiq's shoulders and says, "What happened? You look upset. Who or what is worrying you?"*

*Sadiq replies, "We are changing the interiors of our home, and the guy who has taken the contract kept calling me during the meeting. Can't he take the details once and for all in the beginning? I have so much to do at work, and this guy adds to my stress."*

*Rahim says, "That can be annoying. Now that the meeting is over, why don't you give him the details and ensure all his doubts are cleared once and for all?"*

*Sadiq says, "It's him calling again. You go and have your coffee, Rahim. I will take this call now, and if you are still in the coffee shop, I will join you. Thanks!"*

*Rahim, as he sips his coffee, wonders how much their friendship has evolved since they first began working together.*

## Comparative Deletion

In comparative deletion, the referent to the comparison is not given. For example, comparison words are better, improved, superior, preferred, bigger, finer, greater, larger, more appropriate, more desirable, more fitting, more useful, more valuable, worthier, smaller, tinier, greatest good, longer and brighter.

Corporates use these words extensively to market their product or services. They even add a percentage along with the comparison to make it appear authentic. For example, '20% more nutritious health drink.' Here the product is compared to be more nutritious, and the statistics are supposed to add additional weight, but it doesn't say better when compared to what and in what aspect it is more nutritious. More nutritious when compared to a banana, a bar of chocolate or a watermelon?

To identify comparative deletions, **ask, "Better than what or better than whom?"**

## Example

**Statement:** XYZ paint lasts longer.

**Question:** I see, you have confidence in XYZ paint, and you believe it lasts longer. Does it last longer compared to any specific paint brand or is it that XYZ lasts longer compared to its own earlier products?

**Statement:** My husband has the hardest job.

**Question:** You find your husband's job pretty hard. Hardest compared to your job or are you thinking of some specific job?

**Statement:** Susan is the strongest.

**Question:** Hey! You seem to admire Susan's strength. When you say strongest, is it that you feel she is the strongest woman amidst your friends?

---

### Neha vs. Sneha

*Neha got up in the morning and felt depressed. As she glanced at the clock, she realized that she needed to hurry up for college. She was in no mood to go to college. She had no energy and no motivation. Somehow, she got ready and reached college. Class after class, she felt more and more depressed. She was physically there, but mentally she was deeply immersed in self-pity.*

*When waiting outside the principal's office, Rina noticed Neha's droopy eyes, sagging shoulders and lifeless face. Both of them had to meet the college principal. Rina wanted to participate in the women's hockey team and wanted the principal's signature, while Neha had taken too many leaves and had to meet the principal to avoid disciplinary action.*

**Rina:** *What's the issue, Neha? Why are you so down?*

**Neha:** *It's nothing. It's so boring in college that I just sleep at home. I think I have taken too many leaves. That's why I have been asked to meet the principal.*

*Rina:* No, I am not asking why you are here. Can you share what's wrong? Why are you so down?

*Neha:* Well, I hate college…you see…it's boring.

*Rina:* Come on. Why don't you be more honest? Why this sad look on your face?

*Neha:* Well… I don't know. Do I look so bad?

*Rina:* Did your boyfriend leave you?

*Neha:* Hey! I don't have a boyfriend. Never had.

*Rina:* If you can share what's bothering you, maybe I can help. Or not. But at least you can share your worries and feel lighter.

*Neha:* How can I be happy? I am the ugliest. Just look at me.

*Rina:* Is that the issue? You feel you are the ugliest?

*Neha:* Of course, I am the ugliest.

*Rina:* Neha, you don't like the way you look.

*Neha:* Yes, of course.

*Rina:* Neha, when you say you are the ugliest, can I ask you one thing? Compared to whom are you the ugliest?

*Neha:* Well… I am the ugliest.

*Rina:* You really don't like the way you look. Now, are you using the word 'ugliest' in comparison to someone specific? Compared to whom are you uglier, Neha?

*Neha:* If you see my twin sister, you will know how ugly I am. My twin sister Sneha…she is lovely, so pretty…everybody adores her.

*Rina:* I see…so you feel you are ugly compared to your sister.

*Rina:* Neha, the words you use build your life. When you say you are the ugliest, the very same word creates your life. There may be people who consider you not as pretty as your twin sister, and at the same time, you are also far lovelier and more beautiful compared to her and many others because you have your own kind of beauty. Choose your words wisely, your words transform themselves into your life.

*Neha:* Well, you do have a point, Rina. I think I am exaggerating by choosing to go for the word 'ugliest.' It is just that I keep comparing myself to my sister.

> **Rina:** Your sister is her kind of pretty, and you are your kind of pretty. I have seen Sneha, she definitely is lovely. But look at you! You have such beautiful eyes, such strong arms and a gorgeous smile. And I'm sure you have different abilities than your sister, too.
> **Neha:** Yeah. I love sports and enjoy my body as I run around freely. I guess it's not healthy to compare myself to my own sister. Can I not just drop comparing myself to my sister? Can I not accept the way I am and move on?
> **Rina:** Of course, you can. Maybe this would be the last time you wait in front of the principal's office for the wrong reason.
>
> Rina heard her name being called. She got up and walked into the principal's room. Neha sat there in silence. She felt spaciousness in her mind. It was as if her mind had gone empty. Soon, words would fill her mind, but she knew those words were the ones she would carefully handpick.
>
> – Manoj Keshav

## Lack of Referential Index

In this type of deletion, the person, group or thing referred to is not specified.

**Examples**

- ➢ They don't like me.
- ➢ He was rude to me.
- ➢ They are all playing politics.
- ➢ They don't care.
- ➢ It always ends in a mess.
- ➢ We all agreed to meet on Friday.

To uncover the information missing in the lack of a referential index, ask **'who?'** or **'what specifically?'**

### Scenario 1

**Patient:** It is bothering me, doctor.
**Doctor:** What specifically is bothering you?
**Patient:** My stomach, doctor.
**Doctor:** Point with your finger and show me which part of your stomach is bothering you.

In the above example, the doctor is wise enough to uncover the missing information.

### Scenario 2

**Husband:** They are all playing politics.
**Wife:** I see. (Visualizes her husband's colleagues speaking ill of her husband behind his back.) Unlike the doctor, she does not make any attempt to find out the missing information. The husband has not told her exactly who and how many people are playing politics.)
**Husband:** It is so difficult to work in the office.
**Wife:** You should stop going out on the weekends with your colleagues.
**Husband:** Why? What's wrong?
**Wife:** If they are going to backstab you, you should also draw your line.
**Husband:** Who? My colleagues? Oh, no! They are my buddies. Oh! You mean those playing politics? Actually, it is one of our directors. It is the top management who are fighting. My colleagues are fine. They make my life easier.

Had the conversation not proceeded, the wife could have harbored anger toward her husband's colleagues, and her behavior toward them could have changed. Luckily, the conversation progresses to a point where her misunderstanding is cleared. Like the doctor, it is vital to develop skills to ask for missing information.

## Unspecified Verb

These verbs, because of their vague nature, can be interpreted in different ways by the listener. This leads to confusion or misunderstanding.

### Example

**Mary:** My boss was rude to me.
**Listener A:** Imagines boss shouting loudly at Mary.
**Listener B:** Imagines boss not talking to Mary.
**Listener C:** Imagines boss not using courteous words like 'please' and 'thank you' while speaking to Mary.
**Listener D:** Imagines boss staring at Mary.
**Listener E:** Imagines boss avoiding eye contact with Mary.
**Listener F:** Imagines boss throwing papers at Mary.

The word 'rude' can be interpreted in different ways. To find the missing information, ask '**how specifically?**'

**Listener G:** Mary, you do look upset. What happened? How specifically was your boss rude to you? Did he yell at you?
**Marry:** Oh, no! He never yells. He is a soft-spoken person. It is just that when I gave him the report that he wanted, he didn't appreciate me. Usually, he does. I wonder what happened. I just felt him not acknowledging me was rude.
**Listener G:** Well, maybe you can share your feeling with your boss. Maybe you can ask him what happened. It is better to speak and clear the doubts that we may have in our mind.
**Marry:** Thank you. I feel lighter.

**More Examples**

**Statement:** My dad ignores me.
**Question:** You look wounded. What happened? How specifically did your dad ignore you? Did he stop talking to you?
**Statement:** That customer was so demanding.
**Question:** Was it tough for you to speak to the customer? What did he want? How specifically was he so demanding?
**X's Statement:** Jane keeps bothering me.
**Question:** Jane is bothering you? What happened? How specifically is she bothering you?
**X's Statement:** She wants me to join her for an evening walk. Who has the time?
**A's Statement:** Roy went on begging for an hour.
**Question:** For an hour? What happened? What did he do specifically?
**A's Statement:** He proposed to me in more than 20 different ways today.

# Nominalizations

*"We choose our joys and sorrows long before we experience them."*

– **Kahlil Gibran**

When a person describes an ongoing process as a closed event, he or she is unconsciously distorting the experience. This process of distorting an experience is called nominalization. Nothing remains forever, everything is changing, rising and decaying, appearing and disappearing in this whirlwind of space-time.

According to world-renowned mind-body expert, Dr. Deepak Chopra, the human skin replaces itself once a month, the stomach lining every five days, the liver every six weeks and the skeleton every three months. To the naked eye, these organs look the same from moment to moment, but they are changing all the time. By the end of a year, 98% of the atoms in a human body will have been exchanged for new ones.

## Ongoing Event vs. Static Event

The process is something that's ongoing, just like the body is changing all the time. A finished or static event is something that is not changing—something that is frozen in space and time. Our past events in life cannot be changed. It has already happened, so we cannot now go back in time and change it. But some people see an ongoing event as a closed event or static event. This unconscious distortion takes away the power to do something to change a current event. For these people, a particular ongoing event is frozen in time and space.

### Example

A's (who is going through a divorce) statement: "Divorce is very painful." Here, the word 'divorce' is frozen in time and space. It provides no choice nor an end to the event.

A's statement (as an ongoing process): "Divorcing my wife is painful." The word 'divorcing' provides choice and also gives the impression that it is now ongoing and soon the individual would be out of it or may even reverse the process. **'Divorcing' indicates action, choice, a beginning and an end. 'Divorce' indicates a lack of choice with no beginning and end.**

Reversing nominalization and allowing a person to see an ongoing process as ongoing opens opportunities to change what can still be changed. It widens possibilities and gives ways to cope with stress or pain and enables one to be optimistic knowing that a painful event would pass by.

B's statement: I am in deep frustration.

Here, the word 'frustration' is frozen in time and space. It provides no choice.

Challenging B's statement: How are you frustrating yourself?

This question has the capacity to turn the frozen term 'frustration' to an ongoing 'frustrating.' This provides choices and possibilities in dealing with the frustration.

C's statement: Your **perception** is wrong.

The word 'perception' is frozen in time and space. It gives no room for the other person to change his or her perception.

Revised C's statement as an ongoing process: You are perceiving it wrong.

Here, the word 'perceiving' provides room to change one's way of looking at the issue.

The eminent anthropologist Ernest Becker, the author of *The Revolution in Psychiatry*, said, "Depression results from cognitively arrested alternatives." When an individual cannot see choices, he or she is more likely to sink into depression. 'Cognitively arrested alternatives' means that the mind cannot see choices.

> *"It is our choices…that show what we truly are, far more than our abilities."*
>
> **– J.K. Rowling,**
> Harry Potter and the Chamber of Secrets.

NLP is all about choice. Reversing nominalization provides choice. People feel empowered when they can see choices. Many have pulled themselves into a stuck situation by distorting ongoing events and freezing them in time and space. They can break free of the stuck situation once they see the same event as ongoing.

Nominalizations in spoken language reveal what's going on inside. Reversing nominalizations brings about an inner shift within the individual.

> *King Jayendra was aghast when he learned that his only son had become a monk and had left the kingdom to live a life of meditation and prayer in the Tribhuvan Hills. The king was old and weak and was hoping his son would*

take over the kingdom on his 21st birthday, which was just a few months away.

It was midnight, and the king couldn't sleep. How could he sleep? His only son, the prince, had walked out of this warm, cozy, luxurious palace to the cold, naked and dangerous jungles of the Tribhuvan Hills. He couldn't stand; his legs felt weak. He sat down on his throne. The royal court was empty. The candles flickered ominously.

The king kept thinking and pondering, struggling to take a decision. He didn't realize that Mother Earth had done a complete rotation and the light of dawn had filled the royal court. The queen entered the court with a worried expression. Her eyes widened with fear when she looked at the disheveled king sitting there on the throne with tightened facial muscles and clenched fist.

The queen asked, "I just got up a while ago and got scared when I couldn't find you. Your eyes are so red. Were you here all night?" The king looked at her furiously. "Why can't you be with me and encourage your son to come back? If he doesn't listen to you, then you must break your relationship with him completely," the king thundered.

"Going in search of God is not a bad path. Our son gave up this kingdom to find the kingdom of God. How can I tell him to renounce GOD? GOD is above all."

The king got up and looked like he would explode like a volcano, spewing red-hot lava all around. "You cannot take his side and my side. Either you are with me, or you are with him." The king clapped his hand, and two soldiers appeared immediately. "Take the queen to the decision cell."

The queen was put inside the decision cell. The head of the prison explained, "There are two doors, one is purple and the other is yellow. If you want to be with the king, you need to take the purple door. If you want to be with the prince, you can open the yellow door and come out of this cell. If you cannot take a decision, you are stuck in the cell. The food and the *water can last for a week. Beyond that, not being able to take a decision can be self-destructive."*

*2 nights passed by and the queen couldn't take a decision. She wanted her husband and her son. How could she choose between them?*

*By the third night, the queen was so tired that sleep finally embraced her. In the morning, a man was standing in front of her. He was wearing a white robe. "Your Highness, with due respect, you seem to be stuck here. I am from the future. Can I help?" asked the stranger. The queen replied, "Yes, of course, you can. I am not able to take a decision."*

*"The word decision is a nominalization, your Highness. Why don't you say what you said by using the word 'deciding' instead of decision?"*

*"Deciding…what difference would it make, Mr. Nominalization?" asked the queen. The stranger remained silent. "Ok. Let me say it again. I am deciding…well, how do I say it? Ok. Let's see… I am deciding to do… hmmm… What can I do?" the queen thought. With that, the queen woke up and realized it was a dream. Mr. Nominalization had gone.*

*She took a deep breath and sat up. Hmm. Her gaze fell on her crown that she had kept in the corner after she was brought to the cell. She made up her mind. She started digging with her crown. Two days later, she was out of the cell. She had neither used the purple door nor the yellow door.*

*She went straight to the king. The moment the king came to know of everything the queen had done, he went red with rage. "You broke all the rules," he thundered. But he quickly calmed down. "I appreciate that you could see more than two doors. Hmm… I appreciate your tenacity," said the king to the queen. The queen said, "Come with me if you want your son to take charge of this kingdom." The king felt a little uneasy. Nevertheless, he followed the queen to Tribhuvan Hills.*

*It took a week to locate the prince in the jungles. He was atop a hill, sitting on a rock and in deep meditation. When the prince opened his eyes, he could see his dad and mom and about a dozen soldiers. The prince said at once, "I am not coming back."*

*The queen responded, "No, you don't have to. All I want is for you is to wear the king's crown while you meditate. You stay here. You are doing God's work, and you have spiritual wisdom. All I request is that you wear the king's crown and help the ones who ask you for advice."*

*The prince remained in silence and finally responded, "I will wear the king's crown if you wish, and I will guide those who ask for guidance." The king understood. So, he took his crown and with prayers in his heart, helped the prince wear it. "You are the king, my son, henceforth. People of this kingdom shall come to this sacred mountain to seek your guidance."*

*The kingdom flourished under the prince's guidance. People could see the spiritual aura in the prince and revered and admired him. In due course of time, the king's palace was given to the people of the kingdom, and the king and queen joined the prince in Tribhuvan Hills to pray, meditate and commune with God. There were times the queen thought about the two doors in the cell. She was happy that she was finally able to see more than two doors. Life is all about seeing choices.*

*— Manoj Keshav*

## II. Expanding Limits

Without conscious awareness, we put limits on ourselves. Over a period of time, these limits feel like a cage. No animal or human being will feel happy being constrained in a cage. None of us want to be physically restricted in a cage. But many of us restrict ourselves in our mind. Yes, cages offer us safety, but cages provide no expansion of the mind, no growth and no freshness.

The three distinctions given below identify the limits of the speaker's model of the world. It shows how we can challenge these limits. The result is an expansion of the speaker's model of the world.

The three distinctions that limit the speaker's model are:

- Universal Quantifiers
- Model Operators of Necessity and Possibility
- Presuppositions

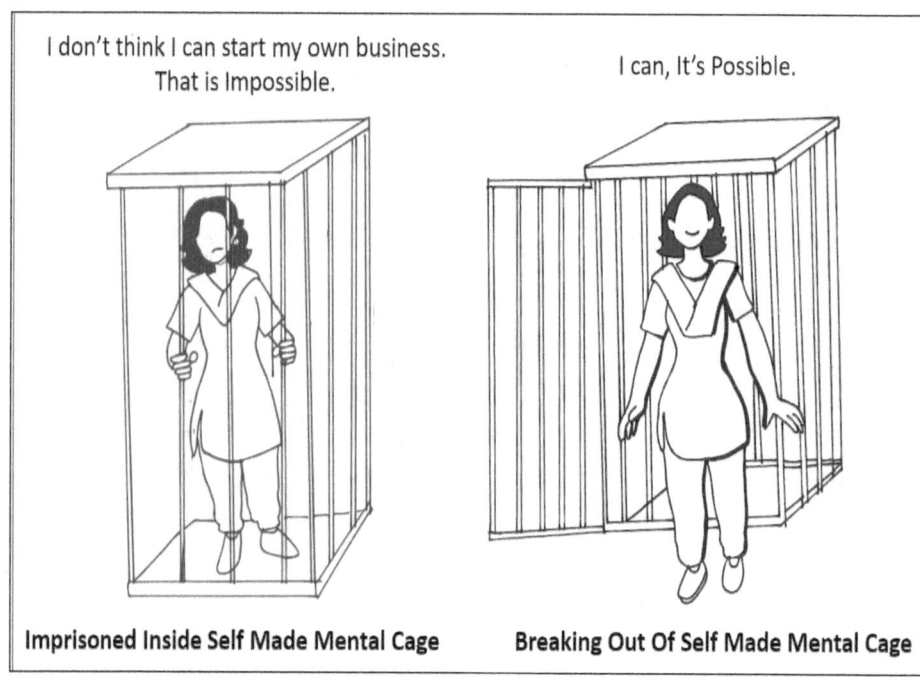

| Imprisoned Inside Self Made Mental Cage | Breaking Out Of Self Made Mental Cage |

## Universal Quantifiers

These are generalizations with cue words—all, every, never, nobody and always. These cue words block out any exceptions. For example, 'nobody listens to me.' Here, the speaker, by using 'nobody,' limits himself or herself. It is like an individual who, while driving home, finds himself stuck on the same road simply because the usual route is blocked for maintenance. Finally, he tries another road, and even that is blocked by the police. He gives up although other roads lead him home. The moment he finds the second road blocked, he tells himself, "There is no way home," even though only two roads were blocked.

A lot of people label their situations with universal quantifiers after just one or two attempts. For example, a salesman who demonstrates a new product to his first prospective customer and fails to make a sale might conclude: "Nobody wants this product." The reality is, it is just one customer who had said 'no.' Or the salesman might conclude: "I can never sell anything," after just one demonstration.

A young boy at a party gets excited and starts dancing with others and enjoys the party till a friend remarks, "How awful a dancer he is," and starts laughing. The young boy carries a belief, after this one incident, that he can 'never' dance and avoids dancing altogether.

## Practice Examples

**Statement:** I can never save money.
**Challenge:** Never?
**Statement:** Nobody listens to me.
**Challenge:** Nobody? What about me now?
**Statement:** Nobody likes me.
**Challenge:** Nobody?
**Statement:** All men are self-centered.
**Challenge:** All? Without exceptions?
**Statement:** Everybody plays politics.
**Challenge:** Everybody?

### On a Lighter Note

*Microsoft Lumia 830 got up in the morning, and he felt a deep knot in his stomach. He sure was depressed. But today he decided to seek psychiatric help. So, with a heavy heart, he got out of bed, put on his light red case and walked out. Finally, he found himself in front of the psychiatrist. "What's bothering you, Lumia?" asked the psychiatrist. "Well, what's not bothering me? Hmm… Everything is bothering me. Nobody likes me. Everybody loves android or iPhones. Nothing works for me. Every update is ignored, and everybody hates me. Oh, god! I am depressed all the time," said Lumia in a depressed tone.*

*The psychiatrist looked at his notes and asked, "All? Nobody? Everybody? Nothing? All the time?"*

*"Oh, come on, doc. All Lumias are trained in NLP. Microsoft ensured that we got thoroughly trained in NLP so that we can handle rejection, criticism and public apathy. I know what you are getting at. You are going to say I am using universal quantifiers. But the fact is that nobody likes me."*

*Psychiatrist replied, "But what about Steve Ballmer?"*

*Lumia said "Oh! I mean... He...might... I think..."*

*Psychiatrist replied, "Oh, come on, Lumia. Steve loves Lumias. Come on, admit it."*

*"Hmmm...well...ok, Steve is an exception. Well, maybe there are other folks, too, who like me. Hmm."*

*The psychiatrist said, "That's it. You are out of your depression. Now you cannot use universal quantifiers. No more can you say nobody likes me. Without the universal quantifier, you cannot go into depression."*

*"So that's it. I can go home now," said Lumia 830.*

*"Yes, of course, you can go home now. But you need to pay the fees before you go," said the psychiatrist.*

## Model Operator of Necessity

The model operator of necessity involves using words such as 'have to, must, it's necessary.' These words reflect the generalizations that the speaker has developed about life.

Ravi felt foggy and dazed. He was not quite sure where he was. "Am I dead or alive?" Suddenly, he heard the alarm ring loudly. It was Monday. Ravi looked at the clock; it was 6.30 a.m. But he felt too sleepy, so he snoozed it and went back to sleep. When he woke up again, it was 8.00 a.m. "Oh, god! I overslept." He felt a sharp pain of guilt pierce through him, sending waves of agony throughout his abdomen and chest.

And then he heard the voice in his head, "You must reach the office on time." He rushed to the bathroom, got ready in a few minutes and thought of a quick breakfast. Again, he heard the voice, "You must reach the office on time." He skipped breakfast, rushed to his car and sped toward the office. "Oh, god! I must reach the office on time. Hope the traffic ain't that bad." How can a road be traffic-free, that too, at around 9.00 a.m.? Ravi felt like he was crawling like a snail as the traffic was so bad. "You must reach the office on time," said the inner voice. His heart rate went up, his breath became shallow, wrinkles created their own landscape on Ravi's forehead. By the time Ravi reached the office, he was half an hour late. Cursing and sweating, he walked into his cabin and slumped exhausted onto his chair.

Ravi didn't realize that he had dozed off on his chair that Monday morning. The colleagues who passed by noticed him but were too busy to wake him up or check on him. What these colleagues didn't see was an angel who had appeared in front of him. The angel carried a magic wand in her right hand. She smiled at him as his body lit up with a radiant light from within. The angle waved her magic wand and words started flying out of Ravi's open mouth. These words were 'have to, can't, impossible, must, it's necessary.'

As these words flew out of Ravi's mouth and vanished into thin air, the angel smiled again and then disappeared.

Ravi got up after a while. He felt very light, and something had changed within him, but he couldn't figure out what.

The next morning when the alarm went off at 6.30 a.m., he woke up to a voice that said, "I choose to wake up on time." He felt alive and could sense the spark of life in his eyes. He felt refreshed after taking a shower and then he heard a voice, "I choose to have a healthy breakfast." He felt light and healthy after the breakfast. He *walked enthusiastically to his car and gunned the engine. "I choose to enjoy my drive to the office," was what the voice said. He listened to a few of his favorite songs as he drove through the traffic. The entire journey was fun and relaxing even as the traffic outside was bad. When Ravi reached the office, he was half an hour early, fresh and eager to start his day at work. "I choose to give my best today. I choose to work with enthusiasm and involvement at work," said the soothing inner voice.*

*As his colleagues passed by, they were shocked to see an energetic and cheerful Ravi fully engaged with his work. But they were too busy and stressed out to walk in to find out what had happened. These colleagues were also too busy to notice the book,* The Life-Transforming Power of NLP, *on Ravi's table.*

## Model Operator of Possibility

Model operator of possibility involves words like 'can, can't, could, couldn't, possible, impossible, will, will not, may, may not.'

### Examples

I can't speak to an audience.

I can't do better than this.

I couldn't have succeeded anyway.

I can get depressed easily.

I can't learn math.

It is impossible for me to cook.

Words like 'cannot' or 'impossible' often indicate that the person saying those words has beliefs about the world which limit their behavior or prevent them from accessing certain choices in their thinking.

2 metamodel questions to challenge these limiting beliefs are:

1. What specifically stops you from _____?
2. What would happen if you did _____?

## Examples

**1. I can't speak to an audience**

Challenge: What would happen if you did?

**2. I can't do better than this.**

What specifically stops you from doing a better job?

**3. I can't succeed.**

What stops you from succeeding?

**4. I can easily get depressed.**

What stops you from staying happy?

**5. I can't learn math.**

What stops you from learning math?

**6. It is impossible for me to cook.**

What would happen if you did cook?

When a person is forced to consider 'what would happen if…' or to identify specific obstacles which they believe prevent them from having a choice, he or she is likely to realize that his or her generalizations don't hold true and that nothing is stopping them from making a choice. This will also open up alternative decisions for the person, which would help them in pursuing their goals.

# Presuppositions

We don't communicate everything explicitly or directly; that would take a lot of words and sentences. Our communication also expresses underlying messages that are not directly stated in the words we use. In other words, part of our communication is not expressed in words but are implied in the way those words are put together. Those portions of our communication that are implied rather than clearly stated in words are known linguistically as presuppositions.

Presuppositions are statements in which some unstated element must be assumed (presupposed) to be true in order for the statement to make sense.

**Example**

1. A tells B: "Tell me what is bothering you."

    Here, it is assumed that B is bothered by something.

2. A tells B: "People who say you are ugly don't know what they are talking about."

    Here, it is assumed that there are people who are saying B is ugly.

3. B tells A: Why are you so possessive?

    Here, it assumed or presupposed that A is possessive.

Joseph Murphy, in his book The *Power of Subconscious Mind*, gives the following example to illustrate how the mind works:

*"Suppose you approach a timid-looking passenger onboard a ship and say to him something like this: 'You look very ill. How pale you are! I feel certain you are going to be seasick. Let me help you to your cabin.' The passenger turns pale. Your suggestion of seasickness associates itself with his own fears and foreboding."*

*Or*

*"If you go to a sailor on the ship and say sympathetically, 'My dear fellow, you're looking very ill. Aren't you feeling sick? You look to me as if you were going to be seasick.' According to his temperament, he either laughs at your 'joke' or expresses a mild irritation."*

'You look very ill. How pale you are! I feel certain you are going to be seasick.' These statements presuppose that the person is ill and pale and that the person is going to be seasick. If the passenger who is listening to these statements doesn't identify the presuppositions, he will take the statements to be true.

Whereas the sailor could well have replied this way, saying, "How dare you assume or presuppose that I am looking very ill? How dare you assume or presuppose that I am going to be seasick?"

Another example: "Let's go for a brisk walk at sunrise tomorrow." Here, the presupposition is that the sun will rise tomorrow.

Any statement contains one or many presuppositions; however, the focus needs to be on identifying negative presuppositions and challenging them as it has a bearing on mental well-being. Recognition of presupposition is vital to maintaining mental and emotional health, whether the language is being used by another or by oneself.

On the positive side, presuppositions are excellent ways to install positive self-beliefs. For example, A to B: "How can someone who is as creative as you do a such a bad job?" Here, one of the presuppositions is that B is creative.

In practice, when we communicate, we use few words or sentences to describe a rich mental representation. For example, let's say you ask a friend, "How was your holiday?" and she replies, "Great. Had a good time."

'Great. Had a good time' is a very shortened representation of a rich experience of a week of holiday in a new destination.

Because of this shortened style of speaking, the listener must fill the gaps to understand the whole communication. And all these happen in the subconscious mind instantly. Because of this shortened language use, every sentence is full of presuppositions.

Learning to hear and recognize presuppositions at first may be difficult because it's what you don't hear that is the presupposition. Presuppositions are not obvious; hence, the brain must do a lot of work to extract them from a sentence. With practice, you can become a pro in figuring out the presuppositions when you are communicating with somebody or with yourself.

## Challenging Presuppositions

**Statement:** Why are you avoiding me?
Challenge: You are assuming or presupposing that I am avoiding you.
Or: What led you to believe that I am avoiding you?
**Statement:** You are as lazy as a buffalo.
Challenge: You presuppose that I am lazy. You also presuppose that buffalos are lazy.
What led you to believe that I am lazy? What led you to believe that buffalos are lazy?
**Statement:** This marriage won't last as my husband is a very self-centered man.
Challenge: What led you to believe that your husband is a very self-centered man?

*Ismael was excited. He had finished his NLP master practitioner program. He decided to practice the key NLP skills every day so that he could master them. He decided to practice one skill at a time for three months, and once he has mastered that, he would pick up another skill to practice for the next three months. The very first skill he picked up to practice was presuppositions.*

*Early morning, he received a text message from his girlfriend Aasma: "Why are you upset with me?"*

**Ismael:** *"You presuppose that I am upset with you."*
**Aasma:** *"What? Do you have a hangover?"*
**Ismael:** *"You presuppose that I got drunk last night."*
**Aasma:** *"What's wrong with you?"*

*Ismael typed, "You presuppose that something is wrong with me" and then he erased that sentence. He decided to communicate in a way that Aasma will understand.*

**Ismael:** *"I am not upset with you."*
**Aasma:** *"Then why didn't you call me yesterday?"*
**Ismael:** *"Yesterday, I was traveling and ran out of battery. Reached home after midnight."*
**Aasma:** *"And what is this 'presupposition'? Why are you using this strange word so many times today?"*
**Ismael:** *"A presupposition is an unstated assumption that is taken for granted when making a statement. We can get misled if we try to answer the question without first clarifying and understanding the assumption. Suppositions can spoil a relationship. Like you assumed that I am upset with you, but in reality, I am not at all upset with you."*

## III. Changing Meanings

"The most dangerous of all falsehoods is a slightly distorted truth," Georg Christoph Lichtenberg. People believe their own distorted belief as truth because they compare the little information they have collected with their own map of the world.

Distortion twists the truth in that the speaker draws conclusions or make assumptions that are sometimes far from reality. By his or her statement, the speaker appears to know the facts about what another person or other people think, believe or do.

This portion of the metamodel questions helps to challenge the speaker's model of the world which are distorted in some way, thus impoverishing the experiences available to the speaker. The four classes of Changing Meanings are:

– Cause and Effect

– Mind Reading

– Lost Performative

– Complex Equivalence

# Cause and Effect

The cause-and-effect-meta-model violation is based on the belief that 'A' causes 'B' when in fact there may be no factual evidence to support that connection between the 2.

As Carl Jung famously remarked, "I am not what happened to me, I am what I choose to become." Do people see choices when they react? Very few can see the choices available to them at the moment of responding to people or events. Many people believe that there are causes out there that 'make' them act or react in a certain way. They believe that they're a victim, blaming others or circumstances. These people live their life at the 'effect' end, just allowing life to happen to them. They believe they have no power to change or alter the outcome.

Some of the characteristics of being at the effect end of the spectrum are: blame, 'can't do' mentality, victim role, complaining, making excuses, negative attitude, etc.

On the other hand, when you decide to live your life at the 'cause' end of the continuum, then you take full responsibility for everything that happens in your life. Being at the cause end means you have choices in your life. It's about being in the driver's seat and starting to steer your life to where you want to go.

Some of the characteristics of being at the cause end are self-empowerment, inner power, 'can do' attitude, grabbing opportunities, confidence and go-getter mindset.

### Solving Electricity Puzzle

*Satya was studying for his 10<sup>th</sup> standard final exams. He lived in a small town called Thanjavur in South India. Looking at all the lessons that he had to study and the time available, he got tensed. There was quite a lot that he had not covered before. He wanted to at least score enough to pass the exam the next day. It was then that the electricity went off. "Oh, god! The electricity goes off at this time of the hour during exams. How stupid of the government. All they know is how to take bribes. Can't this government provide at least uninterrupted electricity? If the officials cannot even ensure the most basic need—electricity at a time like this…" Satya went on and on cursing the government.*

*His mom lit a candle, placed it next to him and said, "Stop it, Satya. How long are you going to curse the government? You don't have that much time. Tomorrow is your exam. Start studying." That shut him up, but he went on cursing the government in his mind, although to others it looked like he was studying.*

*Somehow, Satya passed 10<sup>th</sup> standard with the bare minimum marks and went on to study further. But the power still went off and on time and again in his little town, sometimes for hours together. And every time that happened, Satya would curse the government for hours on end. It didn't matter where he was or with whom. Sometimes, the electricity would go off when he was in a tea shop. Immediately, Satya would start ranting.*

*He would complain about the government's impotence in providing electricity to anyone sitting or standing next to him.*

*Time passed by. After graduating with the bare minimum marks, he got a job as a salesman in a pharma company. Once, when he was in a hospital waiting to meet the doctor to promote his company's products, the electricity went off; the fuse in Satya's mind also went off. "So many governments have changed, but one thing is common; they all know only one thing, that is to take bribes," Satya told a patient sitting next to him and went on a long rant. After five minutes, the electricity came back, but Satya was in no mood to work. He went to a bar, got himself drunk and continued to speak about the government's failure to provide electricity to whoever was in front of him.*

*One day, Satya was with his friends, and the electricity went off. All his friends ran away because they knew Satya would give a long lecture on the government's incompetence. Time flew by, and Satya got married. And thanks to his bad luck, during the first night of his marriage, the electricity went off. Satya had been looking forward to getting to know his wife, but now his mood went off. "The government has only one agenda and that is to take bribes. They cannot even provide basic electricity." He went on and on. After two hours, the power came back. He found that his newlywed wife was not in the room; he was speaking to nobody. She had left to go sleep in another room. He was so busy cursing the government that he hadn't noticed her leaving the room.*

*Time flew by, and Satya grew old. One day, Satya was teaching math to his grandson, and the electricity went off. Satya started cursing the government as usual, and his grandson closed Satya's mouth with his tiny hand. The little 6-year-old boy signaled Satya to be absolutely silent. The little boy brought a white sheet and color pencils and said, "There are 24 color pencils here. Grandpa, I want you to write 24 different things you can do when the electricity goes off. You have five minutes. It is a game, and let's see if you can win."*

*Satya replied, "I accept the challenge."*

*He began writing with a candle next to him.*

1. *Play hide and seek with my grandson*
2. *Go for a drive*
3. *Meditate*
4. *Chit-chat with neighbors*
5. *Go for a walk*
6. *Exercise*
7. *Ignore the power shutdown and sleep*
8. *Cook under candlelight*
9. *Have a candlelight dinner*
10. *Watch a movie. Theaters have generators*
11. *Read a book on kindle*
12. *Pray*
13. *Do yoga*
14. *Listen to music*
15. *Call up your friends on the phone and chat with them*
16. *Play with your pet*
17. *Plan your next day, next week, etc.*
18. *Have a story-telling time*
19. *Indulge in some star gazing*
20. *Enjoy the silence*
21. *Go to the balcony and feel the breeze*
22. *Paint under candlelight*
23. *Write a gratitude letter*
24. *Power off is energy conservation; so, feel happy when there is a power shutdown.*

Satya wanted to write more choices, but he had used all his color pencils. He was not supposed to use a color twice. He had more time to finish the task. Anyhow, Satya decided to tell his grandson that the job was done.

"You have won the game. You are a champion," said the little boy. "Next time the electricity goes off, you know what game to play."

> *The electricity still hadn't come back on. But for Satya, it looked like a bulb had turned on in his head. His own power was shut off all these years, and finally, his grandson had turned it back on.*
>
> – Manoj Keshav

To identify cause and effect, watch for the verbs 'made' and 'cause' and the conjunction 'but.' Challenge this metamodel violation by asking, "How does X cause Y?" This will help the person question his own beliefs and thoughts.

**Examples**

**Statement:** You make me angry when you talk like that.

Challenge: How do you do that? How specifically do you get into this state of anger while listening to me?

**Statement:** I am so disappointed with both my kids.

Challenge: How do you do that? How specifically do you do the process of 'disappointment'? What other responses could you have?

**Statement:** How can I get good grades in school when my parents are fighting every day?

Challenge: How specifically does your parents fighting cause you to get poor grades?

**Statement:** My wife is the cause of all my misery.

Challenge: How do you do 'misery'? How specifically do you do the process of 'misery'? How specifically does your wife cause misery?

**Statement:** Whenever I watch team India play a cricket match on TV, India losses.

Challenge: How do you do that? How specifically does India lose when you watch the match on TV?

## Mindreading

We have all been taught not to judge a book by its cover. But how often do we all make unfounded judgments about another person based on the cover they present to the world? Whether it's yourself or someone else you're mind reading, it is always a good idea to go a little further, to get to know the person better, before you decide that you know what they are communicating.

Mindreading occurs when someone assumes they know what another person is thinking or feeling without direct evidence. It includes the assumptions that are made about another person's thoughts or feelings without the other person specifying it.

It's easy to believe you're good at reading body language and inferring from a person's tone of voice, especially if you never check to find out if you're right. You might continue to believe that you know what's going on in their head, when in reality your assumptions are way off track.

For example, you might assume that the expression you see on a friend's face when you describe your favorite food is disgust. But the fact might be that he or she is having a bad day, indigestion or physical distress at that moment.

If you see a smile on your friend's face when you describe a horribly painful experience you had in a hospital, you might assume he or she is insensitive, rude or sarcastic, but it might be a smile due to recalling a memory of their own experience in the hospital.

Drawing inferences from a small cue such as lack of eye contact, chin raise, raised eyebrow, hands forming a fist, etc., without investigating further can rupture a relationship, create huge misunderstandings and many unforeseen consequences.

Maybe you read an article about how people who don't like themselves and who don't feel safe tend to put on a lot of weight as a protective mechanism. And then you started judging every fat person as someone who doesn't like themselves. It might not be true; maybe it is genetics. There are hundreds of reasons why a person may be obese. Perhaps it is the side effect of some medicine or genetically modified food that the person may have consumed without knowledge. Jumping to conclusions is dangerous.

If someone appears pissed off with you, instead of jumping to a conclusion, it would be more appropriate to discuss your observation with that person. By asking them if they are pissed off or not, you give them a chance to express their side of the story. If they say, "No, I am not pissed off at you. Why do you ask?" then you can tell them, "You haven't smiled at me today. So, I thought maybe you are pissed off at me." This allows the other person to tell you the facts, "Oh! Sorry, it wasn't on purpose. I am upset with my credit card statement. My bill was very high this time. That's why the long face. Nothing to do with you."

### The Betrayal

*John was always suspicious of his wife, Sarah. One morning, she looked happy and excited. "Maybe she is having an affair," he thought. She had just left for work. He thought of following her. "Is she going to the office or on a date?" He looked through the window and could see the road. She hadn't reached downstairs yet. John was confused about whether to follow her or not. He didn't want to be late to work. He looked through the window and got the shock of his life.*

*Sarah was holding another man's hand and crossing the road. "How dare she hold another man's hand and walk around right in front of our home?" John's whole body clenched up. Finally, he saw with his own eyes what he had suspected for long. He rushed to the balcony and tried to identify the man with whom she was having an affair. He was wearing a cap, and from above, John couldn't see his face. "Smart fellow, so he thinks by wearing a cap he won't get caught." He couldn't see further as a bus had blocked his view. He thought of running down and catching them red-handed, but he knew by the time he went down, they both could have taken a taxi and left for their romantic outing.*

The bus moved away, but he could not see Sarah or her boyfriend. "They both must have taken a taxi." He sat down and took a deep breath. "So that's the end of my marriage. She has left me with no other option but to file for divorce." He felt a wave of anger rise through the pit of his stomach. He grabbed his phone and decided to end all of it right now. "Hello. Yes, John?" Sarah answered. "You cheat! Finally, I caught you having an affair. I saw with my own eyes!" screamed John.

"What happened to you? Are you alright?" inquired Sarah worriedly. "I saw with my own eyes. You were holding the hand of your lover and crossing the road. I saw with my own eyes!" screamed John. John was shocked to hear Sarah laughing. "Oh! That! You are stupid. How can I have a lover when I am married to you? Are you out of your mind? Remember the blind old man who works at the corner shop? I just helped him cross the road. He didn't want to miss his 8.00 a.m. bus. Even in my thoughts, I cannot think of another man. What happened to you? Don't you know how much I love you?" replied Sarah with a hint of sorrow and disbelief.

John was taken aback. He stopped breathing. He tried to recollect the man Sarah was holding. Yes, he was holding a blind man's cane. Yeah, he had seen him cross the road earlier. He was Peter, who worked at the corner shop. He himself had, on occasions, helped him cross the road. The whole scene of Sarah holding Peter's hand and helping him cross the road came back to his mind. Yes, it was indeed Peter. He could make out from the memory of his silhouette and gait.

A wave of remorse swept through John. His voice cracked. He wanted to say sorry; his throat constricted and squeezed from within. "Hey, John! I have a meeting right now. I will call you back. We'll talk about this later! Bye for now," Sarah said and cut the line. John sat there in deep remorse and self-pity.

– **Manoj Keshav**

To identify mindreading and what leads a person to mind-read, the listener needs to ask the mind-reader, "How specifically do you know X?" or "How did you arrive at this conclusion?" This helps the person become aware of and even question his or her own assumptions, which he or she believed was the absolute truth.

**Examples**

**Statement:** You are annoying me on purpose.
Challenge: How did you arrive at this conclusion?
**Statement**: I know what's best for him.
Challenge: How do you know what's best for him?
**Statement**: My boss does not like me.
Challenge: How specifically do you know that he does not like you?
**Statement**: You don't like me.
Challenge: How do you know that I don't like you?

Observing body language, breathing patterns and tone of voice are essential to understand another person. At the same time, jumping to conclusions can lead to misunderstanding, hurt and pain. You may carry a grudge for years for something that never happened. "Be careful not to label someone a liar with limited information or based on one observation. Many good relationships have been ruined this way," says Joe Navarro, an ex-FBI agent, body language expert and author of *What Every Body Is Saying*.

## Lost Performative

A lost performative is a personal belief or judgment that is presented as a universal truth. A person who uses the lost performative assumes a personal judgment to be a universal rule. The judge or the evaluator does not own the statement as being his or hers.

The speaker presents his statements as objective knowledge of the situation, while, in fact, the speaker is presenting his subjective knowledge of the situation. These statements are in the form of universal generalizations about the world rather than as belonging to the speaker's model of the world. For example, "Hard work is the only way to success."

The performer (the speaker or the judge) in the sentence is deleted from the sentence, and sometimes the context is deleted as well. Many times, when you hear someone pronounce judgment on someone else, you are likely to encounter a lost performative. The danger of some of these lost performatives is that they bypass our reasoning filters. We may take those ideas as beliefs without considering whether they apply to all people.

To challenge a lost performative, ask: 'According to whom?,' 'For whom is this true?,' 'For whom is this applicable?'

**Examples**

**Statement:** The right place for women is at home.
Challenge: According to whom?
**Statement:** Oldies are cranky to deal with.
Challenge: For whom is this true?
**Statement:** People who don't obey elders will never come up in life.
Challenge: According to whom? Or for whom is this true?
**Statement:** This is the right way to do it.
Challenge: According to whom?

---

### *Never Trust a Man*

*Shanthi didn't like her college-going daughter talking to boys. She had enrolled her daughter, Archana, in a women's college, hoping her daughter would not get a chance to interact with boys. But her daughter still had so many friends who were boys, which was very difficult for Shanthi to digest.*

*"Never trust a man. Never. Never. They all want to sleep with you, use you for their pleasure and then discard you like a used tissue paper," Shanthi told her daughter.*

"Oh! I have been listening to that for years now. I know. Never trust a man. Never. Never. I know, Mom," replied Archana.

"But you still talk to boys; that is wrong."

"Oh! Mom, they are just my friends; nothing more."

"A boy and a girl cannot be friends. Those boys who are talking to you nicely have something else on their mind; they just want to use you for their pleasure. They may take you to someplace lonely and behave inappropriately with you. You might trust them and go out with them because you are so gullible. Never trust a man. Never!"

Archana got up, went to her room and shut the door. She felt irritated with her mom. "Yes, there are bad guys out there, and she wants me to be safe, but Mom's words are getting on my nerves," thought Archana. She decided to cheer herself up because New Year was around the corner. She had decided to take a New Year resolution; she wanted to join a training group and prepare herself to run a full marathon.

At the dawn of a New Year, two weeks later, Archana got up at 4.40 a.m., and she was out of the house in 15 minutes. She was determined to go through the rigorous training program to run a full marathon.

She was in her tracksuit and new running shoes. As she was walking toward the beach, where the group was to meet, a guy on a bike came from behind, touched her inappropriately and sped away. "Yuck!" she said as she felt disgusted and angry. She wanted to hurl abuses at him, but he was already out of sight. "Mom was right. Never trust a man. Never. Never. I should have been alert. I did hear the bike coming from behind. How naïve of me to not have been alert. Even at 5.00 a.m. these assholes can't leave a woman alone."

50 years went by, and Archana celebrated her 72$^{nd}$ birthday in a beautiful hill resort with her husband, Ravi. He had met her when she had joined a marathon training group 50 years ago. Ravi too had joined

> *the marathon training group to run a full marathon that year. And Ravi had expressed his liking for her the very first day. "It was love at first sight," he said later. Archana recalled that day. She was in a foul mood because of the eve-teasing incident. When he had asked her out on a date that same day, she had looked at Ravi, and her mind said, "Never trust a man. Never. Never." Ravi asked, "Why this silence? Is it a yes or no? Archana said, "Of course, let's meet up."*
>
> *That was 50 years ago. Archana felt that it was the best impulsive decision she had ever taken. She had listened to her heart. Ravi was so adoring, caring and affectionate. She felt a deep sense of gratitude as she held her hubby's hand and gazed at the beautiful mountains.*
>
> *"Never trust a man. Never. Never," the thought came to Archana's mind. "For whom? According to whom?" her own mind countered her previous thought just as it had countered it that day when Ravi had asked her out.*
>
> — Manoj Keshav

## Complex Equivalence

Study of the human brain has revealed advanced neural structures, enhanced wiring and forms of connectivity among nerve cells that are not found in any animal. Our ability to think, contemplate, draw inferences and connect the dots is unparalleled. We have the ability to relate events that help us to deal with the world better. For example, we can create a detailed report on the impact of population growth on the planet 50 years from now.

However, in spite of possessing unsurpassed intelligence, we human beings are also known for distortion of reality, believing things that have no logical reasoning and passing on these unscientific, misleading and superstitious beliefs to future generations with tremendous passion.

Complex equivalence is a distortion that involves relating two unrelated experiences or concepts. Here a person takes two unrelated concepts and holds them as equivalents.

To identify complex equivalence, challenge the connection that makes no sense and the assumed meaning of both the events or concepts.

## Example 1

Statement: My husband does not love me…he never introduces his office colleagues to me.

Here, the speaker has concluded that 'not introducing his office colleagues' = 'does not love me.'

Challenge: Does your husband not introducing his office colleagues to you mean he does not love you?

## Example 2

Statement: This carpenter is late…he is not interested in doing our work.

Here, the speaker has concluded that 'being late' = 'not interested in work.'

Challenge: Does coming late mean not being interested in work? Do you know people who are latecomers but who love their work?

## Example 3

Statement: My mom hates me…she is always yelling at me.

Here, the speaker has concluded that 'Mom yelling' = 'Mom hating me.'

Challenge: How does her yelling mean she hates you? Have you ever yelled at anyone you did not hate?

## Example 4

Statement: My boss has not spoken to me the whole day…maybe he is planning to fire me.

Here, the speaker has concluded that 'boss not speaking' = 'getting fired from the job.'

Challenge: How does your boss not speaking to you mean he is planning to fire you?

# Practice Exercise

### I. Learn to Spot Metamodel Violations in Ordinary Talk

Instead of trying to spot all the metamodel violations, it would be easier, in the beginning, to spot any one metamodel violation at a time and using the corresponding challenge-metamodel question. For example, let's take universal quantifiers. During the various conversations you have through the day, keep looking for universal quantifiers. Somebody says, "All politicians are corrupt." That's a metamodel violation. Somebody else says, "All men are perverts." That's a universal quantifier. Another person says, "Nobody likes me." That's another universal quantifier.

Learn to spot 'all,' 'every,' 'never,' 'nobody' and 'always' in everyday conversations. Stick to this practice for a few days. After that, you can take another metamodel. For example, choose nominalization and practice spotting that for a few days. Slowly, you will develop the ability to spot multiple metamodel violations.

### II. Find the Common Violation

Below are 11 sets of sentences. In each group, there is one common violation in all five sentences. Use the codes listed below to mark your answers.

Note: **In each sentence, there is often more than one violation.** Also, note that presuppositions and complex equivalence have been left out.

| SD | Simple Deletion |
|---|---|
| CD | Comparative Deletion |
| LRI | Lack of Referential Index |
| UV | Unspecified Verbs |

| N   | Nominalization |
| --- | --- |
| UQ  | Universal Quantifier |
| MON | Model Operators of Necessity |
| MOP | Model Operators of Possibility |
| CE  | Cause and Effect |
| MR  | Mind Reading |
| LP  | Lost Performative |

**Set 1**

1. It's wrong for women to laugh loudly.

2. Putting your parents in old-age homes is wrong.

3. Criticizing ancient scriptures is bad.

4. Rich girls will not accept a proposal from people like me.

5. Boys don't cry.

**Set 2**

1. I am so upset!

2. I forgot!

3. I am uncomfortable.

4. I got hurt.

5. I am bored.

**Set 3**

1. Rao ignored me.

2. She is driving me crazy!

3. I have lost everything.

4. She rejected me!

5. My boss frustrates me.

## Set 4

1. You wouldn't understand.
2. You do not like me.
3. You know what I am going through.
4. Nobody is going to like my speech.
5. They hate me.

## Set 5

1. I am the best.
2. You are too slow!
3. He is the calmest person I know.
4. My job is the hardest.
5. This restaurant is the best.

## Set 6

1. My boss's perception of me is not right.
2. I am carrying a lot of frustration.
3. I want to make a decision.
4. This needs more attention.
5. I am a failure.

## Set 7

1. They want to destroy my reputation.
2. She didn't speak to me properly.
3. He doesn't care!
4. She didn't come to the airport.
5. They have completed the work.

## Set 8

1. Politicians make me angry.
2. I lose my cool when people brag about themselves.
3. If I watch the cricket match, India will definitely lose.
4. I am alcoholic because my parents never cared for me.
5. If something goes wrong in the morning, then the whole day ends up in a mess.

## Set 9

1. Everybody likes me!
2. Nothing works for me!
3. You are always lazy.
4. He never listens to me.
5. No one listens to me.

## Set 10

1. I have to keep this job.
2. You must pass this exam.
3. I have to complete this project today.
4. I should take care of my parents.
5. I must get promoted this year.

## Set 11

1. I can't tell her everything.
2. I can't live without him.
3. You won't be able to survive without this job.

4. I cannot start a business of my own.

5. It is not possible to change after a certain age.

**Answer:**

| Set 1 | LP (Lost Performative) |
|---|---|
| Set 2 | SD (Simple Deletion) |
| Set 3 | UV (Unspecified Verb) |
| Set 4 | MR (Mind Reading) |
| Set 5 | CD (Comparative Deletion) |
| Set 6 | N (Nominalizations) |
| Set 7 | LRI (Lack of Referential Index) |
| Set 8 | CE (Cause and Effect) |
| Set 9 | UQ (Universal Quantifiers) |
| Set 10 | MON (Model Operator of Necessity) |
| Set 11 | MOP (Model Operator of Possibility) |

# Chapter 10

# The Predicates: Brain's Building Blocks

## The Predicates

Every complete sentence contains two parts: a subject and a predicate. The subject is what or whom the sentence is about, and the predicate says something about the subject. The subject is highlighted and takes the focus, and you will find the predicate often enclosed in {braces}.

**Shiva** {runs.}

**Sneha and her dog** {go for a walk every morning to the beach.}

The predicate (which always includes the verb) says something about the subject.

The word predicate is from Latin, and it means 'to proclaim' or 'make known.'

In both grammar and logic, the predicate serves to make an assertion or denial about the subject of the sentence. For example, Zakir sneezed; Ruby didn't smile.

The subject of the sentence, as its name suggests, is generally what the sentence is about—the topic. The predicate is what is said about the subject.

## NLP Predicates

We experience the world primarily through our five senses—visual, auditory, kinesthetic, olfactory and gustatory. These five senses put together are known as representational systems or modalities in NLP. The words that describe representational systems or modalities are called predicates. An individual's attention, at any moment, will generally be a blend of all five senses—with some having greater dominance on the others based on the current circumstances and which sense the individual habitually gives the greatest attention to.

In NLP, predicates are words and phrases which suggest the activity of seeing, hearing, smelling, tasting and touching. For example, I see what you mean (visual predicate); I am all ears, keep talking (auditory predicate); I feel it in my bones (kinesthetic predicate). In NLP, we listen very attentively and quite literally to what a person says.

You can acquire an increased understanding of how people represent their experiences in themselves. Take a look at these statements from three people whose situations are similar but whose predicates are different.

*Person A (visual):* "*I don't want to go out at this time of the night. It looks so dark outside. I cannot see anything except ghost-like trees. Who knows? They might be actual ghosts.*"

*Person B (auditory):* "*I don't want to go out at this time of the night. The silence outside is scary. I can't hear a human sound anywhere around. All I can hear are the strange sounds of insects and birds. Maybe they are not the sound of insects and other creatures. Perhaps they are ghosts.*"

*Person C (kinesthetic):* "*I don't want to go out at this time of the night. It's cold out there. The ground must be wet and slippery. Also, with so many insects and mosquitoes around, I am sure I would be bitten all over my body. I am already getting goosebumps. Perhaps there is a ghost out there waiting to creep out on me.*"

*To remove fear from A, we may have to work on the visual pictures that he is generating in his mind. To remove fear from B, we may have to work on the sounds and what the sounds mean to B. To remove fear from C, we may have to work at the kinesthetic level.*

Predicates reveal which part of an experience is most relevant to the speaker at a particular moment. If you truly want to understand a person, it is important to pay attention to the predicates he or she is using to communicate. For example, when a person says, "I am not getting the picture," it reveals what's going on internally. The words 'I am not getting the picture' need to be taken literally; you need to explain again, but this time use a lot of visual words and visual information so that this person can 'get the picture.'

## A Conversation

***Husband:*** *Do you see what I mean? You need to visualize how our new home is likely to be.*
***Wife:*** *I think I got a feel for our new home already.*
***Husband:*** *No, no. You really should be able to picture how our home is likely to be before you speak to the architect.*
***Wife:*** *Yeah, I intuitively have a feel of how it should be. That's what you mean, right?*
***Husband:*** *Well, no. Foreseeing all the details and outcomes is important. We need to be crystal clear before we release our check to the contractors.*
***Wife:*** *Right, coming to grips with what we really feel in our bones about our new home is important. Otherwise, we will land ourselves in a sticky situation.*
***Husband:*** *Not exactly. It appears to me that you are not able to see what I want you to see. Just imagine the new home. Can you see it?*
***Wife:*** *Yes, oh! I am so excited. I can feel the warmth of the carpet on the floor. I can touch the concrete wall. And I can feel the positive vibes all over.*
***Husband:*** *I take a dim view of that. If God's is watching, maybe it's the right time for some help. It's evident to me that you are not able to imagine. Wish I can paint the picture that I have in mind.*

**Wife:** *Get a handle on your feeling. Don't get emotional. I sense stress in you. I can handle this. It's time for you to get to work. I can iron out any differences with the architect.*

The above conversation illustrates the importance of 'understanding predicates' in 'understanding each other.' The husband is primarily communicating in visual predicates, and the wife is predominately communicating in kinesthetic predicates.

If we wish to establish an immediate rapport with a person, one of the things you can do is to 'match' them by mirroring their predicates. For example, if the other person is using visual predicates, then it would be a good idea for you to use visual predicates. If the other person is using auditory predicates, then it would be a good idea for you to use auditory predicates. This will help you connect with the person at a deeper level.

## Conversations

**Client A (visual):** *Do you know what I like about a Range Rover? The look of it. I can keep looking at it the whole day.*

**Salesman (matching Client A's visual predicates):** *Truly elegant. Just look at the floating roofline and the continuous waistline. The Range Rover is distinctive and stunning to look at. Also, have a look at the interiors. The finest quilted leathers feature within the cabin. Its muscular, broad-shouldered stance ensures it looks like no other. The Range Rover has a commanding view of the road. It's the very pinnacle of the celebrated British design.*

**Another Client B (auditory):** *Can you turn on the engine? I want to hear it roar.*

**Salesman (matching Client B's auditory predicates):** *The low and rumbly sound of the supercharged V8 engine sounds like a*

> *distant Chinook helicopter. It sounds fantastic and riotous.*
>
> **Client C (kinesthetic):** *I would like to take it out for a test drive. I want to feel this vehicle.*
>
> **Salesman (matching Client C's kinesthetic predicates):** *Sure. You need to feel the Range Rover. Sure-footed and agile, the vehicle drives superbly. Its specially designed interior gives a sense of calm and comfort. (The client gets in the car and grips the steering wheel).*
>
> **Salesman continues:** *The soft, supple leathers, the executive-class seating, cushion adjustments, power recline…all these offer ultimate comfort. How's the drive? How do you feel, sir?*

Sensory-based predicates reveal which sensory system one uses to make sense of his or her experiences. Through the predicates, we can glance into people's internal world. For example:

➢ I see what you mean.

➢ I hear what you are saying.

➢ I have got a handle on it.

All of these sentences pretty much mean the same thing, but they express different sensory systems. Each says, "I understand." Predicates show which part of an experience people are most conscious of at that moment. No one can consciously pay attention to everything around them. For example, try paying attention to how a garden looks and sense the temperature of both your hands simultaneously. You will feel an experience more strongly than the other at the moment.

We cannot process all the sensory stimuli equally at the moment. People can function only if they delete some portions of their ongoing experiences from their consciousness and pay attention only to what is relevant to them. Predicates give us a clue as to what is relevant and what sensory systems people are aware and unaware of.

# Visual Predicates

| Appear | Attractive | Beyond the shadow of a doubt |
|---|---|---|
| Blind | Blurred | Bright |
| Catch a glimpse of | Clarity | Cloudy |
| Concealed | Conspicuous | Demonstrate |
| Displayed | Dream | Enlighten |
| Examine | Exhibit | Expose |
| Bird's view | Fantasize | Flashed on |
| Focus | Foresee | Gape |
| Gaze | Glance | Glow |
| Graphic | Hindsight | Horizon |
| Hazy | Illusion | Illustrate |
| Image | In light of | Inspect |
| Neat | Look | Notice |
| Obscure | Observe | Obvious |
| Outlook | Overview | Peek |
| Peep | Perception | Perspective |
| Picture | Paint | Pinpoint |
| Reveal | Scan | See |
| Shiny | Show | Sight |
| Sketchy | Survey | View |

**Visual Phrases**

- ✓ It appears to me.
- ✓ The message is crystal clear.
- ✓ It actually dawned on me after we spoke.
- ✓ What do you envision for the company five years from now?
- ✓ We need to remain focused at all times.

- ✓ Just imagine how we will feel five years from now.
- ✓ Do you get the picture?
- ✓ How does that look to you?
- ✓ Can you see what I mean?
- ✓ That is an excellent point of view.
- ✓ Just watch what others do.
- ✓ I take a dim view of that.
- ✓ The outlook is bleak.
- ✓ He is in a black mood today.
- ✓ I look forward to seeing you.
- ✓ A colorful expression.
- ✓ Things are looking up.

## Auditory Predicates

| Answer | Announce | Argue |
|---|---|---|
| Articulate | Ask | Audible |
| Babble | Grumble | Resonant |
| Harmony | Resound | Ring a bell |
| Roar | Hear | Hiss |
| Rumble | Sound | Tell |
| Say | Click | Bang |
| Talk | Volume | Snap |
| Call | Discord | Dissonant |
| Drumming | Earful | Echo |
| Explain | Gossip | Growl |
| Hum | Hush | Listen |
| Melodic | Muffled | Murmuring |
| Noisy | Oral | Outspoken |

| Quiet    | Recite     | Shout     |
|----------|------------|-----------|
| Shriek   | Shrill     | Silence   |
| Sing     | Speechless | Squeal    |
| Stammer  | Thunder    | Tone      |
| Tune in  | Utter      | Vocal     |
| Whisper  | Yell       | Deaf ears |

## Auditory Phrases

- ✓ We are on the same wavelength.
- ✓ I tell myself to work out every day.
- ✓ I am all ears; keep talking.
- ✓ Everything we said fell on deaf ears.
- ✓ Can you hear what I am saying?
- ✓ How does that resonate with you? Do you agree with it?
- ✓ Hey, that rings a bell.
- ✓ The silence was deafening.
- ✓ That sounds good to us.
- ✓ We can tell if you are tuned in or tuned out.
- ✓ I am glad to hear it.
- ✓ Things clicked into place.
- ✓ It was music to my ears.
- ✓ I am pleased you said that.

## Kinesthetic Predicates

| Feel        | Touch        | Grasp    |
|-------------|--------------|----------|
| Get hold of | Slip through | Catch on |

| Tap into        | Make contact | Throw out       |
|-----------------|--------------|-----------------|
| Turn around     | Hard         | Unfeeling       |
| Concrete        | Scrape       | Get a handle    |
| Solid           | Active       | Bearable        |
| Beat            | Bend         | Beside oneself  |
| Boil down to    | Bounce       | Break down      |
| Brush           | Burdened     | Callous         |
| Grapple         | Grasp        | Grind           |
| Grip            | Grope        | Hothead         |
| Scramble        | Sensitive    | Sensuous        |
| Shaky           | Shallow      | Shift           |
| Skipped         | Slipped      | Smooth          |
| Soft            | Carry        | Catch           |
| Charge          | Clutch       | Cold            |
| Come to grips with | Concrete  | Crumble         |
| Dig in          | Emotional    | Firm            |
| Flow            | Force        | Fumble          |
| Hug             | Hurt         | Iron out        |
| Kiss            | Lightheaded  | Motion          |
| Nudge           | Panicky      | Play            |
| Plush           | Pull         | Ran up against  |
| Soar            | Stress       | Sweep           |
| Tender          | Tense        | Thick           |
| Tied            | Tremble      | Twist           |
| Unbearable      | Vibes        | Whipped         |

## Kinesthetic Phrases

- ✓ Rubs me the wrong way.
- ✓ Start from scratch.
- ✓ Calm and collected.

- ✓ Get in touch with.
- ✓ Hit me like a ton of bricks.
- ✓ Get in touch with reality.
- ✓ I've got a grasp of what you mean.
- ✓ Warm regards.
- ✓ I was moved.
- ✓ It was a blow to my pride.
- ✓ Let's firm up on this.
- ✓ Hold on.
- ✓ I've got a feel for this place.
- ✓ A sticky situation.
- ✓ A cool customer.
- ✓ I feel it in my bones.
- ✓ One step at a time.

## Olfactory/Gustatory Predicates

| Bitter | Appetizing | Aromatic |
|---|---|---|
| Delicious | Luscious | Fishy |
| Mouth-watering | Flavor | Fragrant |
| Fume | Honeyed | Peppery |
| Perfumed | Pungent | Sour |
| Smoky | Spicy | Sweet |
| Taste | Whiff | Scent |
| Relish | Pungent | Juicy |
| Spicy | Yummy | Savor |

Photography, interior designing, graphic designing, illustration, architecture, industrial designing and fashion designing are some of the jobs in which visual skills and aptitude are the keys to success.

Speech pathologists, translators, broadcast technicians, sound engineers, musicians, singers and acoustical engineers require fine auditory skills and aptitude to succeed in their field.

For those who like to work with their hands, or have a penchant for different textures and the way things feel, it's good to work in an industry that appreciates tactile acumen. Massage therapists, textile experts, food critics (although many assume that taste is the only sense needed to be a good food critic, your ability to judge textures are equally critical), artists, potters and ceramists rely on their kinesthetic skills to succeed.

There are a few jobs that require you have a highly sensitive nose.

**Retail perfume manager:** Someone who differentiates brands and matches the customer's personality with their ideal scent.

**Aromatherapist:** The essence of plants, flowers and herbs have been used for centuries in treatment and therapy. The therapist is required to identify top notes and base notes in a scent and know which one works in favor of the client's well-being.

**Aromachologist:** Rather than using oils and scents to treat someone, an aromachologist is a formulator of scents. This field is gaining more prominence as science discovers more links between scent and the brain. An aromachologist can find the right scent to boost productivity in an office or find the right scent for the locker room to help athletes recover faster.

**Sommelier:** A wine expert who judges wines and also helps pair wines with appropriate food dishes.

A few other jobs that need keen gustatory skills are health & safety inspector, food inspector, food and flavor chemist, professional taste-testers, personal food tasters, chefs, event planners, beekeepers, etc.

Attending to predicates can improve interactions at home, the workplace and schools. Teachers and trainers who use multiple sensory predicates to explain a point are far more effective. They reach out to people with different learning styles. At the workplace, an understanding of different predicates helps improve communication and understanding.

Often, people offer more about what is going on inside them than they are aware of. Listening to the predicates broadens your experience of the person and conversation.

## Practice Exercise

1. **Rapport Building through Matching Predicates:** Observe and listen for predicates while communicating with people; it could be with your family members, colleagues, customers or friends. While responding to them, match your predicates with the predicates used by the other. Observe their non-verbal response as you do so.

2. **Understanding the Root Cause of a Problem through Predicates:** If a German and Chinese professional meet up and communicate with each other in their native language, what would happen? No matter how hard they try, they may not understand each other's words.

Similarly, when a person communicates visually to a person who tries to process it auditorily, there would be misunderstanding or gaps in understanding.

**Example**

*Client:* My boss has these dark, evil-looking eyes. His nose looks like two dark caves placed next to each other. If you look at his teeth, they remind me of sharp, white knives placed in a row. My boss is a baaaaddd man.
*Therapist:* I hear what you say. You don't resonate with your boss.
*Client:* No. You are not able to see what I am saying. Except for a tail, he appears like the devil himself.
*Therapist:* Why don't you tell me what he says that you don't like?

**Client:** *I just don't like this monster. His broad, huge jaw reminds me of a convicted psychopath whose photo appeared on the front page of a newspaper last year.*
**Therapist:** *Now, why don't we focus on what he says to you that bothers you?*
**Client:** *See! You are not able to see my point of view. Would you like to go to my office and see a beast instead of a boss? When I remember his face, my mood immediately dips.*
**Therapist:** *When was the last time you met him and had a discussion with him?*
**Client:** *I never met him fortunately. He is not my direct boss. My boss reports to him, but when I look at him, it makes my world dark. He just looks like my big monstrous stepfather, who used to beat me up mercilessly when I was a child. Same dark evil eyes, broad jaws… Oh! I see a dark cloud.*
**Therapist:** *(shifting to visual) I see your point of view.*
**Client:** *Only you can show me a way out of this. Please help me.*

People sometimes can be very literal in what they say. A child says, "I can see ghosts crawling on the walls. That is why I cannot sleep." Being able to see what the child sees visually leads to understanding his or her world. But simply hearing what the child is saying visually can leave gaps in understanding.

When a person describes a problem, be aware of the predicates. This will lead to identifying the real cause of the problem.

## A Conversation

**Therapist:** *So, after this road accident, you are finding it difficult to sleep.*
**Client:** *Yes. Although, by God's grace, I was spared from any permanent injury. All my wounds have healed. But the flashbacks stop me from sleeping.*
**Therapist:** *So, you see flashbacks, and it stops you from sleeping.*
**Client:** *I see dark cloud gathering around me. I see darkness around me. It's like a huge black hole. I don't know if it is real. But that's what I saw*

*before I became unconscious during the accident. I keep seeing this darkness flash before me as soon as I close my eyes to sleep. I fear I will never wake up. This dark hole wants me dead. So, I open my eyes, and I am scared to close them again.*

**Therapist (notices all the visual predicates):** *Close your eyes and see the darkness around you. Can you see the huge black hole?*

**Client (in a shaky voice):** *Yes.*

**Therapist:** *You told me you've been through the Gotthard base tunnel in the Swiss Alps. Now imagine yourself there. Consider the dark gray cloud to be the tunnel when you enter it. Slowly, you will see a little light through the huge black hole. If you don't, visualize it. Your mind is capable of drawing any image it wants. There, do you see it? Good. That's the end of the tunnel. Let the light become bigger and bigger. And see yourself slowly moving out of the dark, gray space—the tunnel. Soon, you see yourself coming out of the tunnel. There is light all around you. You can see the stunning Swiss mountains. There is Mother Nature all around you. The Alps is beautiful and inspiring. Now bring yourself back to the present. You are in the room here with me. Gently open your eyes. How do you feel?*

**Client:** *Okay, I guess. At least, the darkness turned to light. Couldn't enjoy the Alps though. I was scared the darkness might flash back again.*

**Therapist:** *Let it flash again. That's another tunnel you are passing through. Just see the sunlight at the end of the tunnel and don't forget to enjoy the Swiss Alps after you come out of the tunnel. Enjoy the sunlight and Mother Nature.*

**Client:** *That's it. Will this imaginary exercise solve my problem?*

**Therapist:** *There is no real dark cloud. There is no real black hole engulfing you. It is your imagination. Of course, it occurs because you have gone through a traumatic experience. And your subconscious wants you to be safe. But the dark cloud is still your imagination. And if the image in your head can give you anxiety, then all we need to do is change the image.*

*What if the dark cloud becomes pink cloud? What happens then? What if the dark cloud becomes a green cloud? How would you feel? What if, through a magic wand, you turn the big dark cloud into a small Hershey's dark chocolate? Play around with the image you see and you will see that you control it, not the other way around.*

**Predicates as a Tool of Influence:** While communicating (written or oral), effectiveness increases when we use sensory-based language. By referring to any one or all five sensory predicates, we can make communication come alive.

For example: *The soft amber glow of the sunrise filled the sky with mighty colors of red and splashed the clouds with endless rays of pink. As the sun fully revealed itself, it seemed to swell, pouring warmth onto his smiling face.*

Take away all the visual predicate words from the above example, and the sentence would be bland without any appeal.

Whether it is communicating your vision to your team, making a sales pitch, convincing your boss or proposing to someone, the NLP-predicate words can add impact. It can leave a deep impact on the mind of your listener.

# Chapter 11

# Submodalities: Key to Transformation

We have five primary senses: visual, auditory, kinesthetic, olfactory and gustatory. In NLP, these are referred to as representational systems or modalities.

> *"One of Bandler and Grinder's stroke of genius in NLP was in formatting 'thought' in terms of the representational systems or modalities."*
>
> – **Michael Hall.**

How do we make sense of the world around us? We collect information through our five senses and 're-present' these things on the screen of our mind. This information tells us how to respond and how to feel.

A closer look will reveal that it is not the modalities but the submodalities, the finer distinctions, that tell us how to respond and how to feel. For each of these modalities, there are subtler distinctions. Submodalities are how we structure our experiences. In other words, submodalities are the internal characteristics and details in each modality that together comprise the structure of an individual's experience.

We don't store reality as it is. The images of a happy experience may be far bigger and brighter than the reality. A person you are afraid of may be taller and bigger in your memories. Some memories are fuzzy, black/white or small in size while some memories are bright, rich and bigger than reality. These distinctions play a vital role in how you feel about these memories.

When we create memories we don't just take reality as it is, we zoom in, zoom out, add special effects, sometimes exaggerate

Submodalities refer to the subjective structural subdivisions within a given representational system. For example, for visual modalities, the key submodalities are size, brightness and distance. For auditory modalities, the key submodalities are volume, pitch and distance. When you are aware of the submodalities, you suddenly have more choices about how your inner experience is structured. It is in these submodalities that you will find 'the difference that makes a difference.'

The key submodality distinctions for visual, auditory and kinesthetic modalities are:

| Visual | Auditory | Kinesthetic |
|---|---|---|
| 1. Brightness | 1. Tempo | 1. Temperature |
| 2. Color/Black & White | 2. Volume | 2. Pressure |
| 3. Size | 3. Pitch | 3. Location |
| 4. Shape/Panoramic | 4. Rhythm | 4. Texture |

| | | |
|---|---|---|
| 5. Framed/Unframed | 5. Associated/Dissociated | 5. Movement |
| 6. Location | 6. Duration | 6. Intensity |
| 7. Associated/Dissociated | 7. Location | 7. Extent |
| 8. Single/Multiple | 8. Distance | 8. Shape |
| 9. Distance | 9. Mono/Stereo | 9. Frequency |
| 10. Simultaneous/Sequential | 10. Clarity | 10. Number |
| 11. Still/Moving | 11. Punctuation | 11. Balance |
| 12. Speed | 12. Resonance | 12. Symmetry |
| 13. Focus | 13. Echo | 13. Weight |
| 14. 3-D/Flat | | 14. Distribution |
| 15. Contrast | | |
| 16. Duration | | |
| 17. Perspective | | |

Changing submodalities is an effective way of changing how we feel about an experience. Submodalities are the key components in many of the NLP change technics. Submodalities, by themselves or as part of other technics, are integral to help people work on compulsion issues, stop addictions like smoking, work on their belief systems, cure phobia as well as set powerful goals and visions.

Among the various submodalities, each individual has a few 'critical' submodalities that, when changed, lead to a huge transformation in that person. Identifying those few critical submodalities in an individual is an important step to quicker and faster change.

## Questions To Elicit Submodality Distinctions

Exercise 1: Pick an image from a pleasant incident in your life and note down the answers to all the questions listed below.

Exercise 2: Once Exercise 1 is completed, pick an image from an unpleasant incident and note down the answers to the same questions below.

Exercise 3: Compare and contrast the similarities and differences in the answers. What's your learning? How are the submodalities of pleasant memories different from the submodalities of unpleasant memories?

## Visual

1. Is the image bright or dim?
2. Is the image black and white or in color?
3. Is the image life-size, smaller than life or larger than life?
4. Does the image have a shape or is it panoramic?
5. Is the image framed or unframed?
6. If not panoramic, where is the image located in your visual field (e.g., above/below or right/left or center)?
7. Are you seeing the image as associated (i.e., as if you were actually there) or dissociated (i.e., Do you see yourself in the image)?
8. Do you see a single image or multiple images?
9. How near or far is the image from you?
10. Are there are multiple images? Are they simultaneous (i.e., do you see them all at the same time) or sequential (e.g., like a slideshow)?
11. Is the image itself still or moving?
12. If there is movement, how fast or slow is it?
13. Is the image clear or fuzzy?
14. Is the image 3-dimensional or flat?
15. Is there a notable contrast between the background and foreground?
16. How long does the image stay in your visual field?

17. From what perspective do you see the image (e.g., above, below, from one angle or another)?
18. Are there any other visual aspects of this experience that you believe are important to note?

## Auditory

1. Is the tempo fast, slow or moderate?
2. Is the volume quiet, loud or in between?
3. Is the pitch high, low or normal?
4. Is there a rhythm to the sound? If so, can you describe it?
5. Is the sound coming from within you or from outside of you? If it is outside, do you hear yourself out there?
6. How long does the sound last?

## Kinesthetic

1. If there is a temperature associated with this experience, what is it?
2. Are you aware of any pressure associated with this experience?
3. Where do you sense energy in the image?
4. Do you sense a texture associated with the image (e.g., smooth or rough)?
5. Do you sense any movement associated with this experience?
6. Do you sense any intensity associated with this experience?

> ### Larger Than Life
>
> *Suman screamed loudly; it was 4.00 a.m. Her scream woke up not just her husband but also her neighbors. Since they were used to her screaming in the middle of the night, all of them, including her husband, went back to sleep.*

Suman was panting hard. She managed to step out of the bathroom. Her body was still tensed. She looked at her husband lying on the bed.

"You are the most insensitive person ever," yelled Suman. "Is it a cockroach?" he asked without opening his eyes. "Yes, but a huge one. It was a giant; its head was so big, like the devil. It has so many ugly looking legs, with poisonous thorns all over. It was so scary and so big. It was right in front of my face and was ready to jump on my face and kill me. It is a monster. Get up now. Go to the bathroom and kill that monster, please," pleaded Suman.

He got up and went to the bathroom muttering, "The cockroach in your head is not the cockroach in the bathroom." He found a tiny cockroach, managed to trap it in a shower cap and put it into a glass jar and closed the lid. He returned with the jar behind his back. He saw that his wife was still panting.

He said, "You are good at drawing. Take a piece of a paper and draw the cockroach you saw."

Suman replied, "Are you out of mind?"

"Please, Suman. I will take care of that cockroach for you. Do what I say. I will explain the reason later. Trust me. Also, draw the soap that is in our bathroom next to the spot you found the cockroach," said her husband.

Suman got up hesitantly, took a pencil and paper and quickly drew the cockroach and the soap bar. She was very good at sketching. Once she finished, she handed over the paper to her husband. Suman's husband was shocked to see the picture of a cockroach on the paper. The drawing of the cockroach was a highly exaggerated picture of a real cockroach. It was bigger than the soap. The legs looked like mini dinosaur legs. It was a lot uglier and menacing than the real one.

After half an hour of persuasion and by repeatedly assuring her that the cockroach in the jar can in no way harm her, Suman finally agreed to *look at the cockroach in the jar. Suman's husband asked her to compare the drawing and the real cockroach. Suman's body tensed up at the sight of the real cockroach. Suman's husband asked her to keep half her attention on the glass jar, and this helped Suman relax a bit. She started comparing the drawing with the real cockroach and soon found that in her drawing, the cockroach was far bigger than the actual cockroach. In fact, the real cockroach looked so small compared to the drawing. "Oh, my god! I am distorting the reality in my head. How is it happening?" Soon, she realized that her mind was making it appear far bigger, much uglier and deadlier than the real cockroach. Why was her mind adding all these special effects?*

*"Can you reduce the size of the image of the cockroach that you have in your head? Can you adjust everything about that image to make it look like the real cockroach in the jar?" Suman closed her eyes. She reduced the image's size and made it look like the real cockroach. Her husband asked her to do that 10 times. Then he asked her to visualize any two objects like a mobile and a pen.*

*"Now think of the cockroach, and freeze that picture in your head. Is it like the real cockroach or is it far bigger than the real one?" he asked.*

*Suman responds, "It looks real. Not exaggerated."*

*"How is your breathing? Your muscles…are they tensed?" he asked.*

*"I still don't like the look of a cockroach, but I am not that scared. My body also is a little more relaxed."*

*"Next time you see a cockroach, you will still not like it, but I am sure you will not fear it as much or scream."*

*"Why you didn't teach me this before?" asked Suman.*

*Her husband replied, "Well, only yesterday I learned about the power of submodalities. Wish I had learned about it before."*

**– Manoj Keshav**

A man plays Jesus in a movie. This actor's face gets imprinted on the audience's mind as Jesus Christ. Before people saw Christ's movie, some other image represented Jesus Christ in their head. Later, many people, while praying or thinking about Jesus, might recall the actor's face as Christ. Our memories aren't static but pliable or malleable and easily manipulated.

Many advertisements and movies show highly exaggerated images of things, and later, the image stays in our mind. Ads and movies distort and exaggerate, but the most important insight is that we ourselves distort reality and add special effects while storing memories. Everybody does this; some people do a little distortion of reality and some distort a lot.

We have all the resources we need to facilitate change. Familiarizing ourselves with submodalities helps us understand the structure of our experience. Submodalities help us change the very structure of our experience and give us the power and confidence to change different aspects of ourselves.

Imagine a red rose which is colorful, bright and clear. Now Imagine a rose in black and white without any colors; a picture that is faded, not clear. When you imagine the red bright rose, you feel elated and joyous. It is so pleasant to see the red rose, but the black and white faded rose is dull, unpleasant and boring to look at.

The same thing happens in the way we store our memory; two people looking at the same rose may store the image of the rose in their head differently. One may store it as rich, colorful and detailed. Another person may store the same rose picture as dull, hazy and lifeless. This is exactly how the two might experience other life situations as well, which determines how they experience life itself—colorful and vibrant or boring and dull.

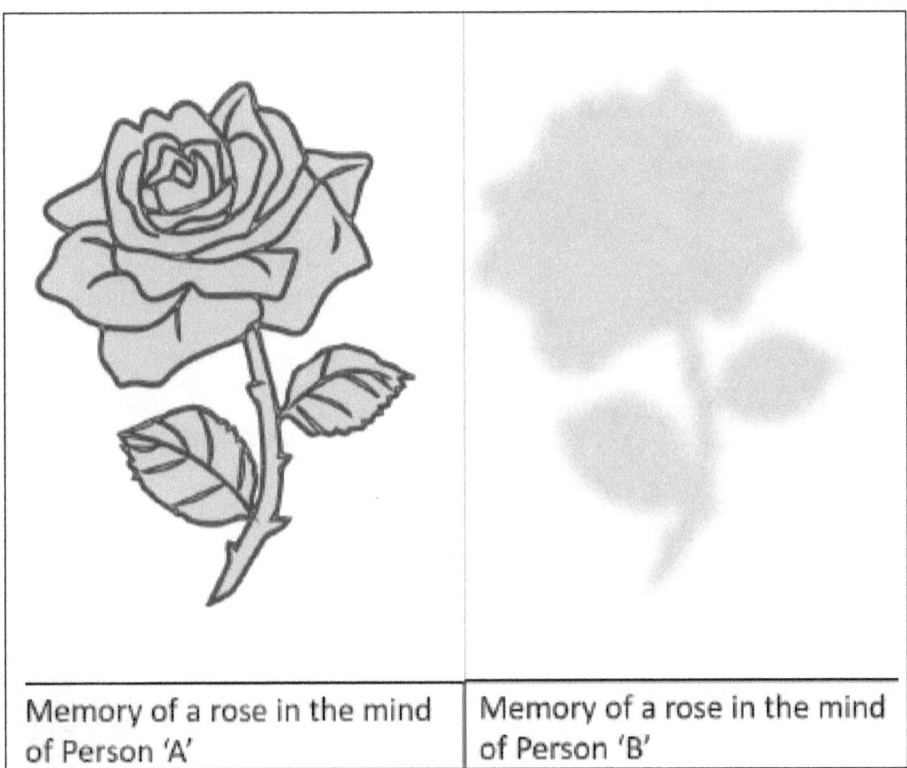

| Memory of a rose in the mind of Person 'A' | Memory of a rose in the mind of Person 'B' |

The rose picture that is colorful is something you are drawn to whereas the rose picture that is black and white and faded is something you want to move away from and look elsewhere. Now imagine two people have the same goal in life. One person pictures his or her goal in vibrant, colorful and detailed images. While the other person has the same goal, he or she picturizes it as dull, black/white and hazy. The first person, whose goal is colorful, will find the goal inspiring and he or she would be drawn to it. Whereas the other person, whose goal is in black/white, would find his or her goal uninspiring and find ways to distract himself or herself away from the goal.

This is what we mean in NLP when we say that the content alone is not the experience. Two people may experience the same reality, but because of the changes in submodalities, their experience of the reality will be very different.

The picture of Ice Cream displays two ice cream sundaes. The bigger one triggers your senses, and you might feel an appetite for it. You would be tempted to have it if you are an ice cream lover. But the small picture on the right is not something you are likely to be drawn to. It is not as appealing as the other although it is the picture of the same ice cream. Hence, although both pictures are the same, one is enticing and the other is not. The only difference is the size of the image; that's all. The size of the picture that we take of reality makes a lot of difference in how we experience the reality.

Let's do an exploration exercise. Think of a mildly unpleasant experience. For example, think of a time when you were a little irritated, frustrated, angry, sad or stressed. Now hold that image in your mind and change the brightness of the image from one extreme end to the other slowly. Notice your internal response. How do you feel when the picture becomes brighter and brighter? Then notice when the image becomes increasingly dim and dark. Do you feel the same throughout this exercise or do you feel changes in your feelings? At what point was your unpleasant feeling at the peak? Make a mental note. And at what point was your unpleasant feeling minimum? Make a mental note. Now bring the image back to its original state of brightness.

Now let's take the same image of the unpleasant experience. This time, instead of the brightness, let's experiment with the size. Now hold that image and change the size of the image from one extreme end to other slowly. That is, initially make the image bigger and bigger and notice your feeling. Are you getting more irritated, frustrated, angry, sad or stressed? Is the unpleasant feeling increasing or decreasing every time you increase the size of the image? When you feel you have made it as big as you can, do the reverse. Make the picture smaller and smaller till the picture becomes a small dot. Keep observing what happens to your feeling. At what point is your unpleasant feeling maximum? Make a mental note. And at what point is your unpleasant feeling minimum? Make a mental note. Now bring the image back to its original state of size.

Now let's take the same image of the unpleasant experience. This time, let's try playing with the distance. Hold the image of the unpleasant experience in your mind and check out where exactly the image is for you. For some people, it will be in front of their eyes. For some folks, it is above their head. For some people, the image is toward their right, about a foot from the face. For some people, the image is toward the left, about a foot from the face. If need be, close your eyes and just sense the location of the image. Once you have located the image, move it a little away from you and keep moving it away from you. At one stage, the image might be far away in space and look like just a dot. Then you can do the reverse. Bring the image closer and closer right in front of your eyes. As you are exploring with the distance, notice what happens to your feeling inside.

At what point is your unpleasant feeling at the maximum level? At what point is your unpleasant feeling at the minimum level? Now bring back the image to its original distance.

Now adjust the brightness, size and distance in such a way that there is no unpleasant feeling inside you. Take a break. Think of something neutral like how many windows are there in your house. Again, see the adjusted image of that unpleasant image but because you have adjusted the brightness, size and distance, there is no unpleasant feeling inside you. Take a break state. Think of something neutral like your mobile number backward. Keep doing this exercise three to five times more. Then forget the whole thing for a day or two. After two days, think about the unpleasant experience. You will be surprised to find that the experience does not create any unpleasant feeling because this time you will see the image in which you have adjusted the brightness, size and distance.

The ability to zoom out and see the big picture and to zoom in and get a close look at select details is leadership ability. Both perspectives—worm's eye and bird's eye—have virtues. Leaders need multiple perspectives to get a complete picture. Distortion of reality helps us to innovate. A cartoonist exaggerates certain features to make a point. Our ability to play around with the images and movies in our head is our strength. At the same time, using this strength to make life miserable is an option that many people have taken without their knowledge.

Zooming in on all the things you are scared of, exaggerating all the things that can go wrong, making larger than real images of all the villains in your life, zooming out all the good things that happen in your life, dismissing all the things that go right in your life and replaying disturbing experiences again and again and adding more and more special effects each time to make it look even more horrible are sure-fire recipes for misery in life.

## Exploration Exercise

The way to dive deeper into submodalities is to get curious about the submodalities. "Scientists exhibit a heightened level of curiosity," according to a 2007 report on scientific creativity for the European Research Council. "They go further and deeper into basic questions, showing a passion for knowledge for its own sake." According to astronomer Carl Sagan, "Everybody starts out as a scientist. Every child has the scientist's sense of wonder and awe."

This exercise requires a heightened level of curiosity. Let's explore the world of submodalities with a sense of awe and wonder. Every time you have felt confident, what are the submodalities? Wouldn't you like to know? What about an unresourceful state like being stuck, being scared, etc. What could be the submodalities of being stuck? Wouldn't you want to know?

While exploring, we shouldn't assume that whenever we take an image or movie of a happy experience and make it bigger and brighter, the happy feeling will increase. And whenever we take an unhappy experience and make it smaller, dim and dull, the unhappy feeling will decrease. This may be the case in some situations but not in all cases. For example, if we take an image of a romantic candlelight dinner and make it brighter, what happens? Does it enhance the romantic feeling? For most people, it will reduce the romantic feeling. Hence, we shouldn't fall for a generic theory that for happy experiences, increasing brightness always leads to a better mood and decreasing brightness takes away the happy feeling.

There are no general rules as such; every person is different, and the way we respond to various submodality changes is different. Also, we need to take the context into consideration. Let's explore:

1. Think of a pleasant experience. Choose any one submodality (for example, temperature).

2. Change only one submodality at a time, from one extreme to the other, and notice the changes you feel. For example, if you choose the temperature, try reducing the temperature to a very low degree and then increasing the temperature to a very high degree.

3. Note down the following as you modify the selected submodality:

    ➢ At what point is the pleasant experience at its peak? That is, when are you the happiest during the change in temperature?

- When you are changing the temperature from one extreme to another, what was happening to the other submodalities? Were they changing on their own or were they all static?

- What did you discover and notice?

4. Do the first three steps with an unpleasant experience. What did you discover and notice?

## Did You Notice A Threshold?

The threshold is a level or a point at which something starts to change. For example, you can chill water until it reaches a freezing point. At that threshold, it changes to ice. You might have discovered the same with submodalities as well. For example, let's take the submodality 'size.' Let's think of ice cream. Now make it bigger, and chances are that you will like it more. Keep making it bigger and bigger. At a certain stage, it will cross your threshold, and you will no longer like it.

What is important to realize is that changing submodalities changes the experience, and changing submodalities is within our capacity. We can change submodalities at will. Hence, we can change our experiences at will. A traumatic incident will stop being traumatic once you have changed the submodalities enough. This opens up a whole new world for us.

## Mapping Across Submodalities

1. Think of a situation in which you feel stuck, and you want to feel more resourceful. For example, you are a student, and you find it difficult to motivate yourself to study. Or you find it difficult to be assertive with your spouse or find it hard to pull yourself out of bed and exercise.

2. Now think of a time when you were in a resourceful state that would be particularly useful in the problem or the stuck state that you thought of while you were at Step 1 of this exercise.

A few examples of being in a stuck state and its corresponding resourceful state:

- A student not able to study: As a student, think of a time when you were at your best, very focused and studied really well. Or you participated in a play/drama, and while going through the dialog, you were so focused and motivated that you memorized all your dialogs in no time.

- Finding it difficult to be assertive with your spouse: Think of a time when you were assertive with your spouse. It might be an exception, but you did assert yourself. Or think of a time when you were assertive with somebody else, when you expressed yourself fully.

- Finding it difficult to pull yourself out of bed and exercise: Think of a time you did get out of bed and were off to do what you wanted to do that day. Maybe it was a picnic day organized by your friends, and you got up in a jiffy and were out on your way for the trip.

3. Identify the similarities and differences in visual, auditory and kinesthetic submodalities of both the stuck state and resourceful state. You can do this by recalling the stuck state and noting down all the submodalities. Then recall a similar event during which you were resourceful and note down all the submodalities. Compare and contrast and note down the differences.

4. Map Across: Now put yourself back in the stuck state. Keeping the same content, change the submodalities one at a time to match the submodalities of the resourceful state. Once you have completely shifted all the submodalities, the result will be that all the submodalities of the stuck state match those of the resourceful state.

5. Test: Now when you think of the stuck state, how do you feel? Are you feeling resourceful? If you are not feeling resourceful, check if any of the submodalities of the stuck state and resourceful state are still different? If so, complete the mapping by shifting all the submodalities to match the resourceful state.

Or it is also possible that you may have picked a wrong resourceful incident. That is, it is not resourceful enough or is inappropriate in the context. That's the reason why even after mapping across the submodalities, you still don't feel resourceful. In such a case, you need to pick up a more appropriate resourceful incident.

Once you've finished mapping across everything and you feel resourceful, you are ready for the next step.

6. Future Pace: Think of a time in the near future when you will face the situation where you used to feel stuck. Are you feeling resourceful? If yes, the mapping across has been successfully completed.

Think of all the situations where the 'mapping across' NLP method can be useful for you.

## Create a Compelling Future with Submodalities

1. Choose a goal that is important to you. The goal can be one you intend to accomplish over any time frame.

2. Close your eyes. Imagine that you have already achieved your goal. What do you see? What are you hearing? How are you feeling? For example, you want to clear a particular exam. So, see yourself holding the scoresheet in your hand. You have cleared the exam. People are congratulating you and such.

3. Now play around with the submodalities like making the pictures larger, closer or brighter. Add more details to the picture. Work on the sounds in the image. Increase and decrease the volume. Play around and explore. The goal is to shift your submodalities in such a way the pictures, sounds and feelings become more compelling, and you feel better.

*For example, your goal is to run a marathon. See those pictures in a way that is inspiring. Zoom in on your toned muscles, the confidence on your face, your energy, the way your body moves like a natural athlete. You are experiencing a runner's high. You are in the 'zone.' Enhance those feelings, make those pictures brighter. How does it feel to complete a marathon? Receiving the medal. Zoom into those pictures. Feel the pleasant weight of the medal hanging around your neck. Increase the body warmth. Make the pictures and movies of you running a marathon come alive. Make it very inspiring and compelling. Keep adjusting the visual, auditory and kinesthetic submodalities till the experience of having achieved your goal is compelling and certain for you.*

4. Finally, try to think about what you would think once you have achieved your goal. What will be your inner dialogs? For example, you may tell yourself, "I did it." Work on the submodalities of those internal dialogs until they become compelling.

5. The brain cannot distinguish between something that's vividly imagined and something that's real. Visualize the whole experience of achieving your goal by putting it all together, fine-tuning the submodalities that you explored in the previous steps. Visualize the whole experience vividly.

For example, Michael Phelps, the Olympic swimmer, is extraordinary. He won 22 medals in total, of which 18 were gold medals, which is one of the greatest achievements in Olympic history. According to Bob Bowman, Michael Phelps' coach, "For months before a race, Michael gets into a relaxed state. He mentally rehearses for two hours a day. He sees himself winning. He smells the air, tastes the water, hears the sounds and sees the clock. Phelps takes visualization a step further. He sees himself from the outside, as a spectator in the stands. He sees himself overcoming obstacles, too. For example, what would he do if he fell further behind in a race than he intended? Phelps mentally practices all potential scenarios."

Coach Bowman believes that all of us—regardless of our field—have a firm belief in who we are today and who we'd like to be tomorrow. When we set goals for our business, sport or any area of achievement, there's a gap between where we are and where we want to be. According to Bowman, "If you can form a strong mental picture and visualize yourself doing it, your brain will immediately find ways to get you there."

# Chapter 12
# NLP: Belief Change Exercise

*"It ain't what you don't know that gets you into trouble. It's what you know for sure that just ain't so."*

— **Mark Twain**

It is common wisdom that if someone really believes that he or she can accomplish something, he or she will move confidently toward achieving the goal. But if he or she believes something is impossible, no amount of nudging, coaching or encouragement is going to convince him or her to take a step forward. All of us have beliefs that serve as resources and as beliefs that limit us.

According to Dr. Bruce Lipton, "If cells are in a healthy environment, they are healthy. If they're in an unhealthy environment, they get sick." Dr. Lipton goes on to explain that the chemistry of blood determines the nature of the environment of the cells within you. The blood's chemistry is largely impacted by the chemicals emitted from your brain. The brain chemistry adjusts the composition of the blood based upon your perceptions of life. This means your perception of any given thing, at any given moment, can influence the brain chemistry, which, in turn, affects the environment where your cells reside and controls their fate. In other words, your thoughts and perceptions have a direct and overwhelmingly significant effect on the cells of the body.

According to Dr. Lipton, "The function of the mind is to create coherence between our beliefs and the reality we experience." What that means is that your mind will adjust the body's biology and behavior to fit your beliefs. If you have been told you will die in six months and your mind believes it, you are more likely to die in six months. That's called the nocebo effect—the result of a negative thought causing a negative result. This is the opposite of the placebo effect, where a positive effect mediates healing.

Since most of the beliefs operate outside our awareness, we don't see their impact on our daily life. Therefore, we don't see ourselves incapacitating our own lives and take responsibility for the lives we lead.

## Power of the Mind

According to Frank Putman, a psychiatrist at the National Institute of Mental Health and a leading researcher in the field, "The multiple personality offers a special window into psychosomatics. With a multiple personality, you can do research that holds the body constant while you vary the personality so you can sort out how psychological states affect the body. Multiples exhibit some remarkable medical phenomena." Bennett Braun, another doctor who directs the unit that treats multiple personalities, added, "Some multiples carry several different eyeglasses because their vision changes with each personality." Another woman with multiple personality who was admitted to a hospital for diabetes, baffled her physicians by showing no symptoms of the disorder when one of her personalities who was not diabetic was dominant.

If beliefs are such a powerful force in our lives, how do we set the right beliefs so that we are not slaves to unhealthy beliefs?

NLP provides, perhaps, the most powerful and transforming set of tools to elicit our deep-seated limiting beliefs and transform them.

## Beliefs: Can Empower Us or Imprison Us

When a baby elephant is caught from the forest and brought to the city to perform in a circus, the baby elephant tries his best to break the chain that has him chained to a pole. After repeated attempts to break the iron chain, the baby elephant finally realizes that the chain is just not possible to break.

After many years, the baby elephant grows to an adult, and his human master just throws the chain around the legs. He does not even bother to tie that chain to a pole. He knows that the elephant would not even try to move away from the chain because now the elephant believes that he won't be able to break free.

"Belief has been the most powerful component of human nature that has somewhat been neglected," says Peter Halligan, a psychologist at Cardiff University. "But it has been capitalized on by marketing agents, politics and religion for the best part of two millennia."

## Beliefs vs. Reality

What you believe can be completely detached from actual, objective reality. How do we come to believe things that are absurd, self-destructive, wrong and have no basis in reality? Perfectly normal and reasonable people believe all kinds of bizarre things. The feeling of certainty has nothing to do with ground reality. Beliefs have nothing to do with rationality or reasoning but more to do with emotionality.

## Beliefs vs. Delusions

Belief is something that you feel is true. Belief provides stability. A delusion is a false belief, but for the person who has those delusions, the content of it is true.

In Cotard delusion, people believe they are dead. Fregoli delusion is the belief that the sufferer is constantly being followed by people in disguise. Capgras delusion, named after its discoverer, the French psychiatrist Jean Marie Joseph Capgras, is a belief that someone emotionally close has been replaced by an identical impostor.

### Rain and the God of Death

*Sunil started sweating profusely. He felt his heart had fallen off into his trousers. He was gripped with fear. He knew Yama, the Hindu God of Death, was nearby. Maybe his time to die had come, or perhaps it was someone close to him that was nearing death. But he sensed that tonight death was certain. He peeped out through the window; it was raining heavily. He could hear thunderstorms far away. The rains had been relentless for three whole days; the roads were starting to flood. For three days, Sunil stayed indoors, too scared to go out. He had called in sick and not gone to work. All that Sunil could do these three days was to pray continuously. He didn't want to die so young. He was only 28-year-old. But he felt the God of Death, Yama, walking toward him. Sunil's heart rate went up. He closed his eyes. He heard the thunders and heavy rain pouring down. He felt the darkness and then nothing.*

*Sunil woke up the next day. Daylight filled the room; it was noon. He peered out through the window. The rain had stopped. He walked to his balcony and looked up; the sky was clear. He breathed out in relief. He felt his whole body relax. He kept breathing out in relief. He was not dead; he was alive. He walked to the main door, opened it and picked up the newspaper. The headlines spoke nothing of the rain. He skimmed through other pages, and then he found what he was looking for: Seven people had died as one of the old buildings' roof came down due to heavy rain. So, Yama, the God of Death, did come. He had taken seven souls with him. He knew it; he had sensed Yama yesterday. Thank god, he was alive.*

*His friends had laughed at his belief that 'rain happens so that Yama can take away souls.' But they were all so wrong. Every time it rained heavily, people died. Yama did come, and he did bring death. How can these people be so stupid and so relaxed when it rains? Don't they know they can die when it rains? Some crazy people get happy while it rains. Oh! God! Can't they see the facts? He looked again at the newspaper. He knew he was right.*

*His mind drifted to the time when he was 6-years-old, and he was jubilant that day because a school holiday was declared due to heavy rain. He had already put on his uniform and was waiting for the school bus when he heard the news from the neighbors. He was so jubilant. Yay! No school! He wanted to run outside and play. But it was raining so heavily. Little Sunil peered outside the window. His face was cheerful for there was* no school, an unexpected holiday. He was still in school uniform and hadn't bothered to change yet. He stretched his hands through the window grills and felt the heavy rain. It was then he heard his mom's scream. He quickly pulled his hands inside and ran looking for his mom. Why was Mom screaming? He couldn't find her in the drawing room. He could hear his mom's cries coming from outside.

Little Sunil ran outside into the rain and couldn't believe what he saw. His dad was lying on the road with his face down, and his mom was trying to lift him up. His dad was wearing a raincoat. Neighbors rushed to help him, and together they pulled up his dad and put him in the car. Little Sunil was drenched entirely and frozen out of fear. Sunil's mom lifted him and got into the car. A neighbor got into the driver's seat. They rushed toward the hospital. All that Sunil felt was the sound of the heavy downpour of rain and thunder and lightning all the way to the hospital. The hospital had declared his father dead on arrival and later told his mom that he had suffered a massive heart attack while kick-starting his motorcycle. But all that was said to little Sunil at that time was that God had come to take his dad away. When he asked why he couldn't see God coming, his mom told him that he couldn't see Yama due to the rain. Little Sunil sat there numb, eyes filled with tears, and knew Yama came that day when it was raining so that no one could see him. That's how the God of Death operates. He comes when it rains.

Next year, when his grandma passed away during a rainy day, Sunil knew for sure how the God of Death operated. He comes when it rains. Since then, whenever it rained, Sunil experienced a morbid fear in every cell of his being. The dark fear had been growing within him every year and with every rain. Something within told him that the God of Death was looking out for him. And the only reason he was alive was because he did not venture out when it rained. His friends had laughed at him and said his belief had nothing to with reality. But he knew.

> *He stopped telling people to stay indoors during rains. He stopped telling people that the God of Death was walking outside, looking for souls. No one would believe him, but every time it rained, the next day the newspaper reported a few deaths. But nobody could see the common thread.*
>
> *Up in the sky, way above, the God of Death—Yama—laughed. "Stupid fellow has more than 40 years to live, and he is going to spend those golden 40 years looking out for me."*
>
> *"Unquestioned beliefs are the greatest cause of human misery," said the Goddess of Knowledge, Saraswathi.*
>
> – Manoj Keshav

## The Nature of Beliefs

A scientist thinks in terms of probabilities. Normal people want to believe in absolutes because probabilities can be confusing. The nature of belief is certainty.

British psychologist William Sargent suggested that beliefs largely stem from an accident in our environment rather than being personally worked out and adopted. The accepted dogmas and prevailing beliefs in the environment that we are born into are injected into us right from our childhood. Belief and knowledge might look the same, but they are very different. Belief has a feeling of certainty, and because a belief feels strong, we assume it must be true. For example, indigenous people believing that a plane is another big bird.

We can create false beliefs through generalizations from a single incident in life or just a few incidents. A little boy who is called ugly by a friend, teacher or aunt might develop a belief that he is ugly, and he may carry this belief throughout his life with a sense of certainty just because a person in his childhood called him ugly. Thereafter, any comment that goes with him being ugly is received and any comment that showers appreciation toward him being handsome is discarded and he ponders over the ulterior motive of the person who is showering appreciation of his looks.

When you begin to look at the nature of beliefs itself, rather than just the content of your beliefs, you start to become more objective not only about yourself but also about the environment in which you find yourself.

## The Role of Emotions in Belief Formation

Beliefs have to do more with your emotional state than your intelligence. Intentionally and successfully introducing or implanting a belief in another person requires an impact at the emotional level, where their feelings are stirred rather than a calm, reasoned argument. Once a belief is introduced in the mind of a person, that person will come up with reasons and logic in favor of his or her beliefs, which is called 'rationalization.' Emotion is the glue with which beliefs stick.

Unless you do away with the emotions that hold a belief, there is no way you can change a self-destructive belief. Believing something with all your heart does not necessarily mean that it is true. There are beliefs that are based on facts, which have empirical foundations. And there are beliefs that have no factual basis. It is difficult to change beliefs because it is the absolute truth for the person, which is emotionally felt with a sense of certainty. Hence, beliefs are hard to shift.

## Emotional Intensity Is Infectious: Can Spread like Wildfire

Researchers found that young men and women find one another more physically attractive if they meet high up on a swinging rope bridge. The emotional intensity and raised heartbeat that they experience are wrongly attributed to physical attraction rather than to the precariousness of their situation.

Cult leaders whip up emotions because that's how false beliefs can be implanted in another person; politicians do the same. Remarkably few people look at things with objectivity. Many rely on their emotions to get a sense of right or wrong. And when they get a sense that something is absolutely right, then the belief in that 'something' is hard to shake off, even though it has no grounding in facts.

We know that depression runs in families. It was long believed that it must, therefore, be genetic. However, despite occasional media hype, no actual depression gene has ever been found. Dr. Michael Yapko, a world authority on depression, shows that it is just as, if not *more*, likely that depressive thinking and attitudes are passed on from one generation to the next through emotional contagion. In other words, it runs in the family.

Similarly, beliefs are passed on from generation to generation through emotional contagion; it runs in the family. A grandfather who believes 'poverty is a way of life, and there is no way out' will pass on these beliefs through emotional contagion. And this belief will continue to get passed on to the next generation unless someone in the family wakes up and challenges this self-destructive belief system. But very rarely do people awaken to false beliefs. It's the other way that's more common. People will go to great lengths to protect their beliefs from being assaulted.

Dr. Robert Cialdini, in his book on influence, describes the feeling that we are behaving consistently with our previous and publicly stated position can, for some people, become more important than discovering the real truth about something and risk being accused of back-pedaling by others. Many people also value consistency over accuracy. Admitting that you are wrong can be too much for some people. People, families and communities are more likely to stick to their beliefs even if they don't make sense.

## Awakening to Self-Destructive Beliefs

When a person is dreaming, he totally believes that the dream is real. The dreamer has no idea that he is dreaming; he completely believes that the dream is actual objective reality. And when this person wakes up, he or she realizes that the dream was just fantasy and has no connection with reality. Similarly, it is necessary to awaken to the false beliefs that we carry in our head as absolute truth with certainty.

A belief is something through which we perceive the world around us. It is our recognition that some idea or thing is true and valid. Just because we see something a certain way, it does not necessarily mean that it actually is the reality. For thousands of years, it was a widespread belief that the earth was flat and that if you were to go to the edge of it, you would fall off.

> *"When Columbus lived, people thought that the earth was flat. They believed the Atlantic Ocean to be filled with monsters large enough to devour their ships, and with fearful waterfalls over which their frail vessels would plunge to destruction. Columbus had to fight these foolish beliefs in order to get men to sail with him."*
>
> **– Emma Miler Bolenius,**
> *American Schoolbook Author, 1919*

Every culture holds certain beliefs; some of it is grounded in reality, and some of it is illusions, just like our dreams. **We must not equate the intensity of our feeling of certainty as indicative of accuracy or truth.**

Beliefs can be infectious. If many people believe in something, you too are more likely to end up believing the same. Societies are founded on certain belief systems; they function and sustain on these belief systems. They may perish as well, holding on to these belief systems. Conflicts between groups, including war, may be defined as a battle between belief systems. Symbols emerge strongly in such conflicts. They may be revered objects like stones, writings, buildings, flags or badges. Whatever they may be, they symbolize the central core of belief system of a particular community.

## The Belief System

The belief system is nothing but a body of concepts. Every human being makes sense of their world through their belief system. People construct all kinds of individual beliefs in order to explain how the world works. These belief systems help us make decisions and move forward through life. Beliefs are often reinforced by society, religion, culture, experience and training. A belief system needs no basis, in reality, to exist as long as it feels right and provides an explanation of a phenomenon in life.

The lifespan of a belief system is, in some cases, longer than the lifespan of believers. Belief systems generally may have an evaluative component. Certain beliefs have the 'good' component, and certain beliefs have the 'bad' component. For example, 'praying is good; stealing is bad.'

Our brains have an affinity for attachment, not just to people and places but to ideas. Once we hold a belief in our mind, we tend to discard any evidence against it and lap up any evidence that supports it.

The bias that causes us to pay more attention and assign greater credibility to ideas that support our current beliefs is called confirmation bias. We gobble up evidence that supports our argument and beliefs and ignore evidence that argues against it. We spend a considerable amount of energy to disapprove ideas that contradict our beliefs systems. The accuracy of belief is not our goal. Validating our pre-existing belief is our goal.

Humans are not the only species to have beliefs. Animals have beliefs too, although they may not be aware of them. Animals will run from predators because they know—that is, believe—that they will be eaten if they don't run. Even protozoa can be said to believe things. That is, they will move toward energy sources rather than away because they know or believe that engulfing such sources will continue their existence.

The most important thing is to weed out unhealthy beliefs and nurture healthy beliefs. This starts with being honest with ourselves in recognizing how biased we truly are.

We humans are scared of the unknown. We like order. We like to feel safe and comfortable. We don't like it when something comes along that threatens to change the way we see the world, even if it is for the better because we just want to keep things the same.

## How Do Beliefs Originate?

*"A state of no mind is meditation. When you can look without your mind interfering, distorting, interpreting, then you see the truth. The moment the mind is dropped, a great silence arises because the mind carries your whole past. All the memories of the past go on hankering for your attention, they go on crowding upon you, and they don't leave any space within you."*

**– Osho**

Beliefs may not be facts at all. They are perceptions formed through our own experiences and the views of others. We need not carry around redundant or destructive beliefs that belong to others. We can create our own empowering set of beliefs instead.

By the time we are adults, most of us have developed very entrenched, deep-rooted and fundamental beliefs about ourselves. Psychologists refer to these as our core beliefs. Once established, they can prove difficult to change.

The body reflects our beliefs. According to Lynne Forrest, what we believe determines not only our health but the physical stance and posture we assume, and that physicality becomes the way we communicate to others about who we are and what we believe. Our body reflects our beliefs, and because this is so, we can use our body as a doorway to identify our negative, limiting core beliefs and clear them. How? By identifying the part of the body where the beliefs can be felt as physical symptoms and using those places of discomfort to identify the belief that we are carrying there. Through observation and inner-body awareness, we begin to bring ourselves back into healthy alignment within.

Most of our beliefs originate in childhood. Often, they come from a thought lineage that has been passed down to us from previous generations; this consists of both positive and negative beliefs.

A traumatic childhood, especially one that involved us being rejected and unloved by our parents, can leave deep scars in the psyche of a person.

**Few Examples of Limiting Beliefs**

- o Others will abandon me: This belief may develop if one/both parents abandoned us.
- o I am not worthy of others' care and love: This belief may develop if our parents focused only on their needs and ignored ours.

- I must be self-sacrificing: This belief may develop if our parent/s parentified us. Parentification is the process of role reversal, whereby a child is obliged to act as a parent to their own parent. A parentified daughter may conclude that:
  - If I am compliant, quiet without needs, then the mother will finally see me and take care of me.
  - If I give what mother wants, she will stop abusing me.
  - Girls grow up believing that love, approval and validation are very scarce, and one must work to the bone in order to be worthy of it. Then, as adults, they attract situations that replicate this pattern over and over. The daughter does not receive affirmation for herself as a person, rather she receives affirmation only if it relieves mother of her pain.
- I must subjugate myself to others: This belief may develop if our own views and needs were dismissed as unimportant by our parent/s.
- I am intrinsically unlovable: This belief may have developed if we were unloved or perceived ourselves to be unloved by our parents.
- I am vulnerable and in constant danger: Such a belief can develop if we spent a lot of our childhood feeling anxious, under stress, apprehensive or in fear.
- I must always keep to the highest of standards: Such a belief may develop if our parents only loved or accepted us *conditionally*.

## Beliefs at the Identity Level vs. Beliefs at the Capability Level

There are certain beliefs that you hold at the identity level. For example, "I am not creative." And there are certain words that we hold at the capability level. For example, "I cannot lose weight easily."

There are many beliefs that people hold at the identity level. You can discover that by filling this sentence with all your self-beliefs: "I am too…"

One way to make a person awaken to a false, limiting belief at the identity level is to sow doubt. How do you create doubt for the person who believes in statements such as the following?

A: I am a very, very lazy person.

You can sow doubt by going for the context.

Response: Are you always lazy? Can you think of a time when you were not lazy?

So, the client may modify it by saying, "I am a very, very lazy person when it comes to household work."

By doing so, the client has shifted from the identity level belief (I am) to the capability level belief (household work).

## Beliefs and Their Role in Shaping Our Life

Do you want a pilot to believe that he can fly or do you want him to develop that capability? I am a great programmer, carpenter, author, etc., can be installed as a belief. Is that ecologically correct? Shouldn't a person focus on developing competence or capability rather than just changing his or her belief system?

Beliefs are derived from experience and the interpretation of those experiences. Generalization, deletion and distortion play a role in belief formation. Just like how maps need to be updated from time to time so that they match the changing territory, beliefs must also be updated from time to time to match the current environment and new insights you gather through life. For example, most people believed that the earth was the center of the universe and that the sun went around the earth. But later, when scientific evidence pointed to the fact that it is the earth that rotates around the sun, everybody had to update their belief about the sun and earth.

Beliefs are built like any other thing we learn from our experiences. We learn through direct experience, modeling other's experience and indirect experience. For some people, just a single experience is good enough to form a strong belief. Others have more rigorous requirements for building a belief, needing multiple examples or repeated experiences over time in order to believe it to be true.

It is common for children to build beliefs based on what they are told by parents, siblings or teachers. Beliefs can also be formed by reading about something. Most people also have beliefs that conflict with one another. When a person has conflicting beliefs toward a person or situation, he or she may experience mixed feelings, mixed reactions or indecision. A general discomfort is felt as a result of this incongruence or dissonance.

Beliefs are perceptual filters, the lens through which we view our world. It's the primary factor that shapes one's personality and life.

## Difference between Beliefs and Values

Beliefs are generalizations we hold to be true. They arise from our past experiences and the cultural and environmental situations we have faced. For example, the belief 'I am good at nothing' is an interpretation of one or more past experiences. When we use our belief to make decisions, we assume that the past successes of decisions made this way will also apply in the future. For example, Kodak believing in film roll based on past successes. Of course, there are empowering beliefs that help an individual excel in life.

When a person thinks of a belief, he can feel in his body a sense of certainty. This feeling or this body state gives him the feeling of absolute truth in his belief. Beliefs can influence our behavior, thoughts and emotions in a powerful way.

The main difference between values and beliefs is that values are ideals or standards of behavior, while beliefs are convictions that we generally accept to be true. Values are principles or standards that are considered valuable or important.

Belief is a conviction that we generally accept to be true, especially without actual evidence or proof. Beliefs can develop from what we see, hear, read and experience. But they could also stem from how we interpret these sensory inputs and experiences. On the other hand, they can also sprout from what is taught.

Values are not based on our past, and they are not contextual; they arise from our needs. Values describe what we need and what we desire or seek to achieve. And human needs are universal. Every human being has a need for safety, meaning, connection and companionship. For example, 'excellence in everything I do is my life motto' is a value that reflects a human need for self-efficacy. 'Family first' is a value statement that reflects the need for safety, connection and intimacy.

Value is the measure of importance or worth a person attaches to something. A few more examples: I value freedom of speech; I value my family; I value my time alone; I value native culture.

## Surface Beliefs vs. Core Beliefs

Surface beliefs: These are beliefs about doing and capability. For example, I cannot dance.

Core beliefs: These are beliefs at the identity level. For example, I am worthless, or I am lovable.

A belief is an idea that guides your actions, filters your experience, gives or denies you permission to act and lets you know how things work and what things mean.

# Belief Classification

According to NLP, beliefs fall into three main categories: causation, meaning and boundaries.

## Causation Beliefs

As per businessdictionary.com, 'Causation is the connection between two events or states such that one produces or brings about the other; where one is the cause and the other its effect. Also called causality.'

There are beliefs that a person holds that are certain that an event causes another event to happen. Causation words are those words that help us to uncover 'Causation Beliefs' in a person.

- You make me angry (make)
- I am a failure because my parents never encouraged me (Because)
- Indian culture forces a person to be obedient to his or her parents (Forces)
- Rain always creates traffic jams in my town (Creates)
- I am sure to get diabetes at some point in my life because it is in my genes (Because)
- Flight delays drive me nuts (Drive)
- Smoking causes cancer (Causes)
- If you go out in the rain, you will get cold (If)
- Hard work leads to success (Leads)
- Your attitude determines your altitude (determines)

Limiting causal beliefs act as a chain that holds a person down from exploring his or her full potential. These limiting causal beliefs need to be changed to release one's full potential. Writing down one's internal dialogs and identifying limiting causal beliefs can be one of the ways to move forward in weeding out unwanted beliefs from our mind.

## Meaning Beliefs

Human beings have a great desire to understand the phenomena around us. We seek meaning, explanation, clarification and description to make sense of the world around us. It is not just Isaac Newton who wanted to understand a specific phenomenon, we all have that desire in us to make sense of the world around us, and we do so by relying on all the existing knowledge and experience we have had so far. When we equate an event or phenomenon with another, we might conclude that 'This = That' or in other words, 'This' is equivalent to 'That.' This process leads to the creation of 'Meaning-based Beliefs.'

- Fasting is discipline (is)

    (This is that or X = Y)

- Arguments is a sign of a healthy marriage (is)

- Late coming means lack of interest (means)

    (This means that or X means Y)

- Silence is consent (is)

    (This is that or X = Y)

- Junk food is slow poison (is)

    Junk food = Slow poison

- I am a slow learner (I am a)

    I = Slow learner

- I am a procrastinator (I am a)

    I = Procrastinator

## Boundary Beliefs

A boundary is a line which marks the limits of an area. The word 'boundary' is commonly used a lot in relation to geographical area markings like a nation's boundary or a city's boundary. Not all barriers are physical. There are also mental boundaries that exist in our mind beyond which we may not want to step out. They may be about how much we can do some things, what is possible or not possible to do, what is safe to do and what is not safe to do, etc.

### Example

A person might believe that he can become a millionaire. He may believe that he can make a couple of million dollars in his lifetime. At the same time, he may believe that few millions are possible but beyond that is impossible. If he is asked whether there is a possibility of him becoming a billionaire, this particular individual will emphatically reply, "No chance. Not in this lifetime," because this individual has put certain boundaries around his financial goals. There are things that are possible for him, and there are things he considers impossible. In reality, there are no limits. Limits exist for this individual because he has boundary-based limiting beliefs.

### Another Example

A person might believe that he is average-looking and might believe that a very beautiful lady will not want to have a relationship with him. Hence, he puts a boundary in his mind and does not approach a gorgeous girl even though he may like her very much.

Most of the boundary-based beliefs are about skills, capabilities, how high goals are set, the type of people with whom you want to have a relationship, etc.

### Few More Examples

- Setting a goal to become a CEO is not at all practical for me. I don't think I can ever achieve that.

- Maximum I can run a 5 km marathon. Beyond that, I will collapse.
- Singing in front of more than 50 people is something I just can't do.

Words like can, can't, will, won't, may, might, could, would are to be given notice to identify limiting beliefs.

# Exercise 1

## Uncovering Limiting Beliefs

Our limiting beliefs are problematic, not because they are hard to change, but because they are hard to find. The reason it's hard to identify a self-limiting belief is because the ones that have the most impact on us are usually outside our awareness. Our limiting beliefs are often unconscious and unquestioned; a part of the fabric of our perceptions, which makes them hard to find.

In order to identify limiting beliefs, you need to choose an area of your life where you are going through some difficulty. It could be your health, family, relationship, business or money. Pick a specific problem or difficulty you are going through now.

**Step 1:** Choose a problem or difficulty you are going through now.

Please write down the difficulty or problem on a piece of paper.

**Few Examples**

My marriage is a mess.

This financial problem never leaves me.

I am lazy, and I just don't have it in me to put my plans into action.

I might lose my job in the days to come. I am feeling very insecure about my job.

**Step 2:** Write down the reasons why you have this problem. Use the word 'because' to describe the reason for this particular problem.

**Few Examples**

- My marriage is in a mess because…

- This financial problem never leaves me because…

- I am lazy, and I just don't have it in me to put my plans into action because…

- I might lose my job in the days to come because… I am feeling very insecure about my job because…

Write down as many reasons as possible for that one problem till you find yourself unable to come up with any more reasons. For one problem, write down 15 to 20 reasons. Focus on writing a whole lot of reasons quickly. This will allow you to keep your conscious analytical mind aside and allow ideas to float up from your subconscious mind.

**Step 3:** Pick out the beliefs that you have written.

Now, we need to pick out the beliefs that you have written from the whole list of reasons. Some of the reasons may be facts, and some may be junk thoughts. But among them are strong beliefs. What is a belief? A belief is a generalization that feels true in the body; there is an emotional charge to it.

Take your list and read each sentence that you have written. Tick those sentences that you feel true in the body, those that have an emotional charge to it. Don't tick based on how true it is logically. Tick based on how you feel within.

**Example**

For Shailesh, a middle-aged corporate executive, these are the notes:

Problem statement: My marriage is in a mess…

- Because my job demands I travel often.
- Because my wife is not understanding.
- Because I am so busy.
- Because both of us are not earning enough.
- Because life has become a routine.
- Because we couldn't go on a vacation.
- Because I am self-centered.
- Because I just don't know how to make my wife happy.
- Because women are difficult to understand.
- Because women are emotional, and they are miserable by nature.
- Because I am drinking every night.
- Because I am not attractive.
- Because I am not talented.
- Because I have a big tummy now.
- Because we are not made for each other.

In the above examples, some of the statements are limiting beliefs that have no grounding in facts and need to be worked on.

After you have written your problem statements and a lot of possible causes, go through your list and separately write down all your limiting beliefs. Now you can use NLP to transform these limiting beliefs into empowering convictions.

## What Happens If Limiting Beliefs Are Not Worked On?

The scary thing about limiting beliefs is that they turn out to be a self-fulfilling prophecy. It is not because they are really true but because our actions or inactions follow the belief, making it true. For example, if you believe you cannot stick on with one thing, your action or inaction will follow this belief, thereby making the belief turn out true for you.

If you believe you are not good at engaging strangers in a conversation, you will avoid parties and situations where you will be required to talk to strangers. Even if you go to a party, you might stick to people you know. At the end of the day, with your action or inaction, you will demonstrate that the belief is true for you.

But you can come to recognize that the belief isn't actually true. The ability to distinguish between one's belief and the truth is a step forward. This realization is not enough by itself. The conscious awareness doesn't actually eliminate them from where they reside—the subconscious mind. Beliefs don't come with expiry dates; they don't self-destruct. Active intervention is required to transform limiting beliefs. Change your belief, and you will upgrade your life forever.

What you believe has a huge impact on how you think, feel and respond in any given situation. Most of what we do or not do in life are based on the beliefs that we carry in our subconscious mind. Beliefs are not facts. They are generalizations that help us or limit us. Instead of getting stuck in life due to limiting beliefs, you can choose empowering beliefs that will get you where you want to go.

We don't declare a belief as right or wrong; we only classify them as useful or not. The beliefs that are useful to us in life are empowering beliefs, and the beliefs that are not useful or get you stuck in life are limiting beliefs. We don't see the world the way it is. We see the world in a distorted way that reflects our beliefs. All that we see in the world are proofs that our beliefs are correct. Most of our thinking can be termed as a process of rationalization to prove that our beliefs are correct.

People can accomplish extraordinary things if they have an empowering belief system. More people are derailed by their own beliefs than by any external circumstance or limitation. In order to take the first step toward a goal, you need to believe that you can do it before you go about achieving it.

When a person clears a limiting belief, there is a visceral shift in her/his feelings and thinking. Mental blocks disappear and motivation soars. Self-doubt, confusion and hesitation vanish; optimism, self-belief and enthusiasm expand. Imagine being able to reach down into your subconscious mind and simply deleting the early limiting beliefs, programs and indoctrination you got when you were young. Our limiting beliefs block the free flow of love, truth and wisdom in our lives. When you learn to change and transform your own limiting and negative beliefs, you will become unstoppable.

Your belief creates your reality. If this statement is true, you should be able to shift your reality by changing your beliefs. When you transform a limiting belief seated deep in your subconscious mind, your experience of reality changes, too. You see the world differently, feel differently and experience a shift, both in body and mind.

## Discovering a New You

*"One of the greatest discoveries a man makes, one of his greatest surprises, is to find he can do what he was afraid he couldn't do."*

—**Henry Ford.**

Beliefs are as necessary to us as air and water; we cannot live without them. We need beliefs to make sense of what is happening in life. One could never be without beliefs, nor would you want to be. What you do want is to have beliefs that work for you just like a leader on an important mission would like to recruit people who are positive, talented and capable of producing results.

Maybe your past experience led to a belief that 'you are worthless, that people will trample on you because you deserve it.' You are not at the mercy of this belief. You are free to break away from this belief.

Maybe your past experience led to a belief that 'you just don't have it in you to be a leader. You can do a job assigned to you, but you can never lead people.' You might have even created a belief that it is very stressful to be a leader and is not worth it. But you are not at the mercy of this belief. You are free to break away from this belief.

Maybe your past experience led to a belief that 'health issues are a part of life—that you cannot be completely healthy. There is something inherently wrong with your body.' This could be your conviction and belief, but you are not at the mercy of this belief. You are free to break away from this belief.

Maybe your past experience led to a belief that 'you can never stick to a goal—that you have a wavering mind. Consistency is not in you. Setting a goal and changing your mind prematurely before the goal is achieved is who you are, and that's how life is going to be.' That could be your conviction and your belief, but you are not at the mercy of this belief. You are free to break away from this belief.

When you change your belief, you change everything. Your life is forever being molded and created from your beliefs. You hold within your beliefs your own destiny. Change your beliefs and change your future.

### Death of a Belief

*"I know I am an average performer. I never got the first rank, a gold medal or first prize for anything in my entire life. I have always been an average performer. I know that for sure." These were the first lines Harish put on paper. He kept writing whatever came to his mind. He just wanted to pour out his feelings. During his school days, one of his classmates, Ram, was always the first-rank holder; he always got the highest marks. Harish had wondered how he did that. At the same time, he knew he couldn't fare well. If he could just pass, it would be great. He knew he had always been an average guy. Another guy in the class, Sathish, was the first in sports. On sports days, he got one medal after another. Swimming first, 100 m race*

*first, shot put first… Harish had wondered how he did that. At the same time, he knew he was an average performer in sports. If he got selected just to play in a team, it was a big achievement. Being recognized or receiving appreciation from somebody that he played well, na…that never happened. If he remained in the team without being thrown out for non-performance, well that was an achievement by itself.*

*"My life sucks. Well, not that much. Just about average." But he felt an emptiness within. In his fantasy, he would think of being an achiever. But in reality, he could not sing. He was an average dancer. He could not paint. He could not crack jokes. He had always shied away from public speaking and presentations.*

*He went on to get a desk job; he was an accountant. Now he had reached 40 and had stagnated for years in the corporate world as an accountant, never getting promoted to be a manager as he lacked leadership skills. "Well, life sucks…well, not that much." He was not a failure. He was just an average performer. Whenever he felt an emptiness within, he would just write about his life, his thoughts and his feelings. He would pour it out on paper. Sometimes he wouldn't get sleep and would go on writing till dawn.*

*Harish had gone to a self-improvement workshop where he learned to put his thoughts on paper. The trainer of the workshop had said that when we put thoughts on paper, we get clarity in life. Harish did get clarity. Now he was certain he was an average performer and will remain an average performer. Even in that self-improvement workshop, he was an average participant.*

*As usual, his wife and his teenage daughter were in deep sleep, and he was awake. The emptiness had taken over his mind. He got up and as usual, started to write. He had written everything about his life. So, he decided to write about his future. He thought of his last days, his funeral. How will a funeral be for an average person? How many people will turn up for the funeral of an average person? As he continued to write about his end, he felt even more depressed about his life. He soon realized that his depression was also average. He excelled at nothing in life. Even in misery, he remained average and would die average. He wrote for hours about his death as an average person. By midnight, he was done with his death, but he was still awake. "Now what? I have written everything about myself from birth to death." He thought of writing about after death. He would turn to dust. Average dust, part of the earth, but average. Then he continued to write his thoughts, "Well, how can dust or any part of the earth be average? Everybody turns to dust after death, whether it is a king or a slave. Everybody turns to dust and dust is not average. It's not just dust, but the sky, a leaf, the clouds, a drop of water, a rock or anything is not average. Nothing is average. At least after death, I won't be average anymore. Well, if no rock, no leaf, no cloud is average, then how can a human being be average?" He paused and thought over this for a long time. "Death has brought death to my 'I am average' story," he further wrote.*

*After that, he couldn't write anymore. He felt a shiver running through his spine. His whole body shook. He felt an intense sense of relief. He felt an enormous burden evaporate into thin air. He just sat there for an hour. Then he went to bed because he felt very sleepy. As he was slipping into sleep, he knew he will be another person the next day because his 'I am average' story had died forever.*

– Manoj Keshav

# Exercise 2

## The NLP Submodality Belief Change Process

This process takes a limiting belief, implants doubt in it and makes you see that there is no truth in it. It then takes an empowering belief that you want to have and transforms it into a belief that your body feels is absolutely true.

**The Process**

1. Think of an empowering belief that is a resource to you, which gives you a sense of optimism, capability and a sense of self-worth.

2. Write down the visual, auditory and kinesthetic submodalities of the above-stated empowering belief.

Break state.

3. No longer true: Think of a belief that is no longer true for you. A belief that you believed in completely but you now know to be not true. For example, you might have believed in your childhood that Santa Claus flies down from the North Pole to give you a gift, but now you know that it is not true.

4. List the visual, auditory and kinesthetic (VAK) submodalities of the belief that you know is not true. Write them down.

Break state.

5. Compare and contrast analysis: Do a compare and contrast analysis of the submodalities of the belief that is true for you and the belief that is no longer true for you.

Break state.

6. Think of a limiting belief that disempowers you.

7. Write down the submodalities (VAK) of the above-stated limiting belief.

8. New belief: Think of the many empowering beliefs that you would like to have instead of this limiting belief. Choose a new belief that is apt to replace the limiting belief that you want to transform.

Break state.

9. Turning the limiting belief into a belief that is no longer true: Keep the content of the limiting belief constant, but change the submodalities of

the limiting belief to that of the submodalities of the belief that is no longer true for you.

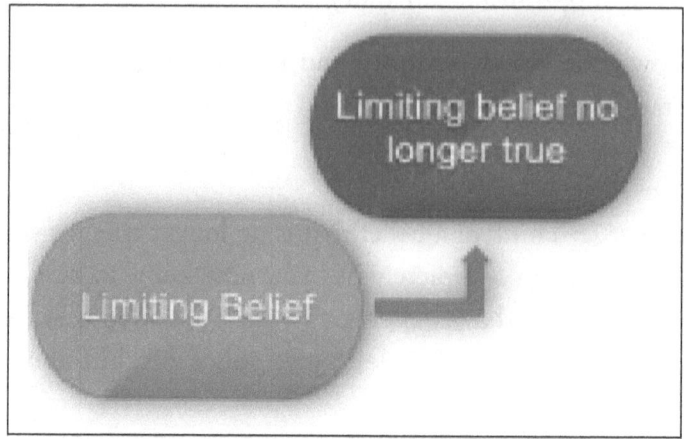

10. Content change step: Send the limiting belief that is now no longer true for you into the distance, far away into space. Then see the picture coming back from the distance, containing the content of the new empowering belief.

11. Turning the content of the new belief into an absolutely true state: Now you have this picture containing the content of the new empowering belief. Go ahead and change the submodalities into the submodalities of your empowering belief (submodalities you wrote down in Step 1 and Step 2).

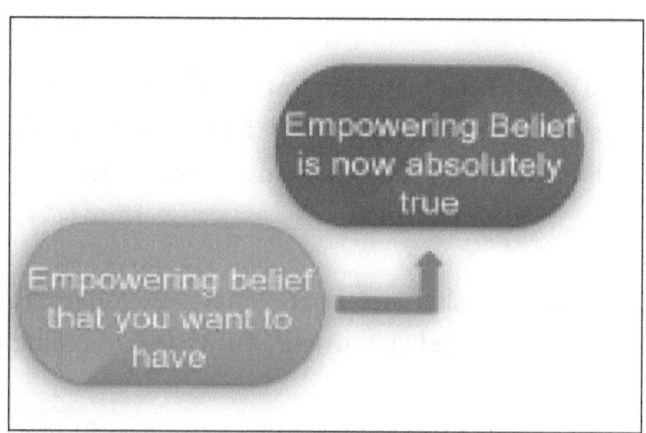

Break state.

12. Think about this new empowering belief. How does it feel in the body? If you don't feel a sense of certainty about the new belief, repeat Step 11 a few times.

13. Future pace: Think of a time in the future when having this new belief will add value to your life.

# Exercise 3

## Creating a Belief Board

When you set a new goal, an important step in order to achieve your goal is to check if you have the right set of beliefs to get you there. If you don't believe you will succeed, then some parts of you will resist your goal, and your progress will encounter one roadblock after another. Creating a belief board is a powerful way to ensure you have the right set of beliefs to get you to your goal.

You can create a visual belief board and put all your beliefs that you want to install in your subconscious mind. How is a belief board different from a vision board? A vision board is a collage of pictures and words that represent your goals. A belief board is a collage of pictures and words that represent your empowering beliefs about yourself and the world. A belief board includes the beliefs that you want to install in your subconscious mind. A belief board visually reminds us of what we believe to be important. It's a way to be clear about the beliefs that we hold, allowing us to remain focused and not get derailed.

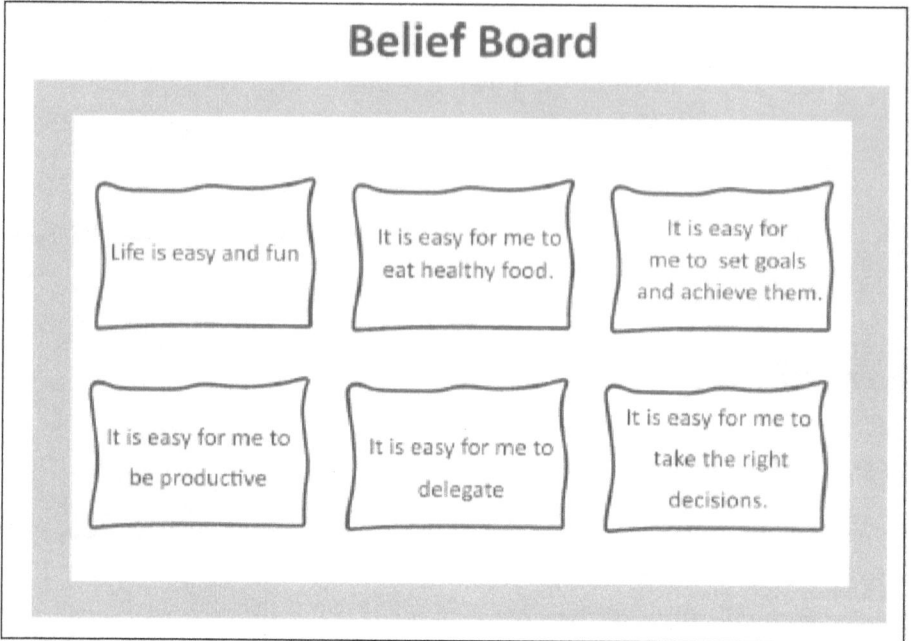

## Guidelines to Create a New Belief with Which to Replace the Limiting Belief

1. State the new belief in the positive.

2. Ensure the belief is ecologically right for you. For example: 'I am super productive 20 hours a day' does not take into consideration the body's need for rest, sleep, fun, etc. Hence, a belief like this is not healthy. Ecologically right beliefs are the ones that respect the balance of all our needs and don't tilt into the 'excessive' zone.

3. Choose the words that inspire you. Sometimes, a lot of rewriting, tweaking and reflecting are required to get the words right.

4. Give it enough flexibility to deal with exceptions. For example, 'I am a lively and highly enthusiastic person' may not fit in a funeral, and that's ok. Allowing flexibility based on context is very essential.

5. Do what works for you. Be open to making changes and rewording your belief board till you feel it is just right.

# Exercise 4

## The Walking Belief Change Exercise

The walking belief change process is like the NLP submodality change process. For example, it involves identifying limiting beliefs, turning them into a belief that is no longer fully true for you and finally replacing them with empowering beliefs. What is unique about the walking belief change exercise is that it incorporates the use of spatial anchors by allowing you to experience various levels of belief and disbelief.

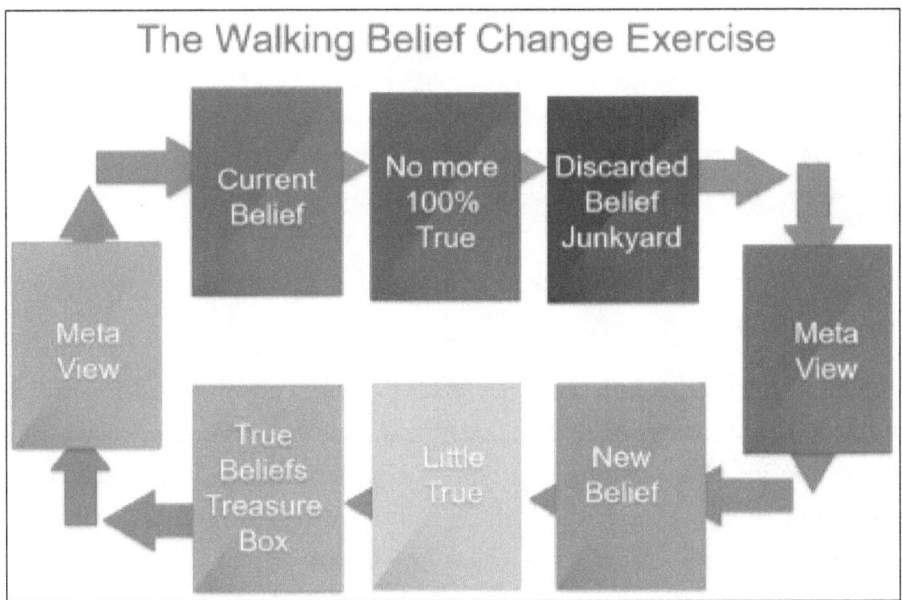

**Step 1:** Use eight pieces of paper and label each piece as follows: Meta View 1, Current Belief, No More 100% True, Discarded Belief Junkyard, Meta View 2, New Belief, Little True and True Beliefs Treasure Box.

**Step 2:** Using these eight labeled pieces of paper, create eight specific locations as described in the diagram above.

**Step 3**: Identify the limiting belief about yourself that limits you in some way. Examples: I cannot cook. I cannot get up early in the morning. Losing weight is not possible for me. I cannot control my anger. I always procrastinate.

Now, it would be worth an effort to dig a little deeper and come out with the belief that is at the core of yourself. To do that, answer this question with, "I am…"

Now, what does having this belief say about you?

Answer: I am…

The answer that you came up with has far more influence on you. Hence, it would be better to work on those beliefs.

**Step 4**: Identify what you would rather believe in as your empowering belief. An empowering belief needs to be constructed as a positive statement. For example, instead of saying, "I am not a worthless person," you can make it positive: "I am precious." Also, ensure that the new empowering belief feels ecological for you and ensure no part of you objects to this new belief.

**Step 5**: Step onto the paper or space that's labeled 'Current Limiting Belief' and state your limiting belief. Notice how it feels in your body. Notice your breath. Notice your feelings, any body movement or involuntary reaction. Notice where in the body this belief resides. In the throat or stomach? Or is it at the back of your neck? Notice which part or parts are holding this belief. Also notice the visual, auditory and kinesthetic submodalities of this experience.

Break state: Leave all the feelings and energy in that space, step into 'Meta View 1' space and take a few deep breaths. Think of something unrelated, like how many times it rained last year or how many windows are there in your house.

**Step 6**: Step onto the spot that's labeled 'No More 100% True.' Flip the belief to its opposite end and think of at least three occasions or situations when the opposite or contradictory belief was true for you. For example, if you believe you suck at math, think of at least three occasions when you did well in math. Maybe you did well in math in 4th grade. Perhaps you taught your daughter math very well.

Also, you can think of things you were really bad at, which you later mastered. Maybe you were very bad at playing table tennis, and later you improved dramatically. So, if you suck at math, perhaps there is room to improve if you work on it.

Keep exploring till you feel that the limiting belief is actually not true. And once you experience this doubt, notice your body, notice your breath, notice how you feel and be aware of the visual, auditory and kinesthetic submodalities.

Break state: Leave all the feeling and energy in that space and step into 'Meta View 1' and take a deep breath. Think of something unrelated, like how many trees are around your house.

**Step 7**: Now step onto the spot that's labeled 'Discarded Belief Junkyard.' Think of a few beliefs that you once believed that are no longer true for you. You have discarded those beliefs into the junkyard because you know the belief is not true. For example, you experienced chest pain one night and you rushed to the hospital. You knew for sure it was a heart attack. You 100% believed you had a heart attack. Your whole life was flashing in front of you. You knew you might die before you reached the hospital. But later, the doctor who examined you said you were fine. She also confirmed that your heart was perfectly fine. Your whole body relaxed, and your mind discarded the belief that you had a heart attack into the 'Discarded Belief Junkyard.'

When you were a little kid, your mom told you that if you waste your food, Mastan—a huge elephant —will come and trample you to dust. You believed that 100%; you were so scared of the monstrous elephant Mastan that you wiped your food plate absolutely clean. Later, when you grew up, you realized Mastan is a figment of imagination and that elephants have better work to do than to check on you. Off went your belief, right into the Discarded Belief Junkyard.

Now think of a couple of beliefs that you have put in the 'Discarded Belief Junkyard.' Once you have done that, see your current limiting belief in that 'Discarded Belief Junkyard.' Notice your body. Notice your breath. Notice your feeling and notice the submodalities.

Break state: Leave the feeling and energy in that space, step onto 'Meta View 2' and think of something unrelated and neutral, like the color of your first laptop or the color of your first pen.

**Step 8:** Now step onto the paper or space that's labeled 'New Empowering Belief' and state the new empowering belief. Notice your body, breath, feeling and submodalities.

Break state: Leave the feeling and energy in that space and step onto 'Meta View 2' and think of something unrelated and neutral, like how many buttons are there on your outfit.

**Step 9**: Now step onto the paper or space that's labeled 'Little True' and state the new empowering belief. Now think of at least three evidence to support this new empowering belief. So, instead of the limiting belief—I suck at math—you decide to replace it with 'I am an excellent learner' or 'I am intelligent, and I can master math if I put in enough effort.'

Now look for at least three evidence to support the belief 'I am an excellent learner.' For example, you learned much about the Japanese culture in a very short time when you were in Japan. Or you learned to cook a new dish quite well. And soon, you get a *feeling* associated with 'I am an excellent learner.'

Then look for at least three evidence to support the belief 'I am intelligent.' For example, you solved an organizational problem by coming out with an excellent solution. Or you received an appreciation letter from your boss in which he mentioned how intelligent you are. And soon, you get a feeling that 'I am intelligent' is somewhat true.

The same process is to be followed for the third belief statement. Once you have found evidence for all your empowering beliefs and you get a feeling that the new empowering beliefs are somewhat true, notice your body, your breath, your feelings and submodalities.

Break state: Step onto 'Meta View 2' and think of something unrelated and neutral, like guessing the weight of your watch in grams.

**Step 10**: Step onto the paper or space labeled 'True Belief Treasure Box.' It is the space where all your empowering beliefs are held in reserve, to be utilized by the subconscious mind whenever it is needed. Once you are standing in this lovely space, think of a few beliefs that are already in the 'Treasure Box.' Beliefs that you know are true for sure. For example, the earth rotates around the sun. Or anything else. Like your eyes are brown, you know that's true for sure. There is no confusion there. Once you have thought of a few beliefs that are present in the 'Treasure Box,' state the new empowering belief and see that in the 'Treasure Box.' Notice your body, your feeling, your breath and submodalities.

Break state: Step onto 'Meta View 1' and think of something unrelated and neutral.

Repeat this entire process two more times but faster each time. In the second and third time, there is no need to step into the 'Meta View' space. From the limiting belief, you can directly step into 'Beliefs That Are No Longer 100% True' spot. Once you have reached the 'Treasure Box,' step into 'Meta View 1' space. Repeat the whole process one more time.

**Step 11**: Last step: future pacing.

Now see yourself going forward into the future with your newfound empowering belief system. What will it allow you to be, do and have? Notice the feel-good sensation in the body. Notice your breath, emotions and submodalities.

# Exercise 5

# Re-Imprinting Belief Change Exercise

## Originated by Robert Dilts

An imprint is a significant experience from the past through which an individual formed a belief or cluster of beliefs. An experience by itself is neither positive nor negative. The way we process the experience is what makes an experience positive or negative. For example, when an individual receives criticism for her work, she can process it as a failure or as incompetence and conclude that she cannot do anything right because she was not born intelligent. Or she could take that criticism and use it as a feedback to improve her performance and conclude that she is a good learner and that there are always people to guide you to get things done in better ways. Hence, no experience is positive or negative; it is our thinking that makes it so.

Re-imprinting is to relook at those significant experiences and re-process those experiences in a way that transforms limiting beliefs into empowering beliefs. The twin benefits of this process are freedom from the emotional pain associated with the experience as well as freedom from the limiting beliefs that were formed because of the experience.

### Time Travel, Now Open to Public

*Micheal was baffled to learn that Newlink Robotics Research firm had developed a time machine that lets one go back into their past. This technology not only allows a person to go back into the past but they can also change their past. Micheal threw his mobile onto his bed. "Every type of false message is spread through the internet. In fact, one should never get carried away by the messages that appear on social media." What baffled Micheal the most was that Newlink Robotics Research was not far from his house. And time travel was open to the public for a fee of 250 USD. "Must be some financial scam. Somebody is looking for a quick buck."*

*Although he believed that this was a joke, a part of him still wanted to visit the firm. Plus, he was pretty depressed since his relationship ended a few months ago. And nothing else seemed to work well for him. Sometimes he felt even God had abandoned him. He felt lonely and often scared, not knowing why exactly. Every time he felt lonely and scared, he felt his muscles turn numb. He was hardly breathing. He felt like he could choke as if somebody had gagged him.*

*He checked out the address again. Yes, he was at that very address. He went in, and there was this security guard who asked him to fill up half a dozen forms and then he led him to a lift. It looked like he had gone over 20 floors down. Or was this lift very slow? There were no buttons and no display boards. There was no way of knowing how many floors he was going down. But he was sure he was going very deep down.*

*Finally, the lift stopped and the door opened. Micheal stepped out of the elevator. He felt he had stepped inside a space station or something like that. One of the scientists walked up to him and said, "Micheal, this way please." Micheal was shocked to hear his name. "How did this guy come to know my name? Oh! The forms I filled up before getting into the lift."*

*Micheal was hooked up to all kinds of sensors and crazy-looking computers. Micheal felt like he was an astronaut ready to travel through the Milky Way.*

*The scientist asked Micheal, "Are you ready to travel into your past?" "Yes," replied Micheal. His whole body got tensed up, and beads of sweat appeared on his forehead as he closed his eyes in anticipation of going into his past. The scientist turned on many gadgets, and Michael felt his whole body shaking. Then he heard the scientist saying loudly, "Here you go, Micheal. Good luck and bon voyage." Micheal felt as if he was spinning in empty space, and everything around him was whirling round and round.*

*He found himself in a school. Soon he realized that it was his school, the school where he had studied. All the kids were of age seven or eight. He soon* *realized that he was in his 3$^{st}$ grade class. He was not the only adult in the class, there was this female teacher who was taking the class. He walked up to her and introduced himself to her. It looked like she didn't notice. So, he introduced himself again. She turned toward him and looked through him as if he didn't exist. Micheal soon realized that he was invisible to everybody and nobody could hear him. Still, to be sure, he yelled and screamed in front of everybody, but nobody even noticed him. But Michael could hear everything and could see everything. Soon, he saw…little Michael in the fourth row; head down in shame and guilt. Memories came back to him. He had failed every test. He just could not score good marks. Micheal remembered that day in his life as one of the saddest days. He knew what was going to happen. He knew a very terrible thing was going to happen that evening.*

*Micheal stayed in the classroom till all the classes got over. He quietly followed little Michael. Little Michael had no interest in going home. He didn't want to get scolded by his mom and dad. Micheal could see the little boy dragging his feet and slowly walking toward his home with fear and dread in his little heart.*

*His home was just a 15-minute walk from school, but little Micheal took more than an hour to reach home. Micheal walked behind little Micheal, just observing the little version of himself and knowing that the worst was yet to happen.*

*Little Micheal knocked on the door, and immediately, the door was opened by his mom. She looked very anxious. "Where were you? I was so worried. I was just about to go out looking for you. Why did you take so much time to come home?" asked his mom, her voice a little shaky due to distress.*

*Little Micheal just stood there in silence. Micheal knew that little Micheal was controlling his tears and a storm of emotions was swelling up inside although his face showed nothing much. "Come inside, are you hungry?" asked Mom while taking the school bag from him. She served him snacks and then went over his school notebooks. Every notebook had lots of red marks, and then she saw the marks and notes written by the class teacher. Little Micheal and Micheal saw tears welling up in Mom's eyes. "Why are you not able to do well in school? That too 3rd grade is not that difficult. I taught you all this yesterday. Still, you could not remember and write. Look at your handwriting. It is so horrible. Nobody can make out what you wrote. And your class teacher wants to meet your father. Oh, my god! Why is this happening?"*

*That night, his dad and mom were discussing little Micheal's school performance; it soon turned into a full-blown argument. Little Micheal closed his ears with his little hands, but he could still hear both of them screaming at each other in the next room.*

*Micheal wanted to comfort little Micheal. But he could neither touch him nor speak to him. Little Micheal had gone to sleep, but Micheal couldn't. He knew the worst part of his life was to happen the next day.*

*Next day, Micheal saw little Micheal wake up to the sound of his mom sobbing. He walked out.*

*Mom said, "Your dad has left us forever. He has packed his things and gone away. He is not going to come back. He left us, Mike." Little Micheal could not control his tears anymore. He ran into his mother's arms, and all that came to his mind was, "I am no good. I am bad. Dad left because of me. I am not good enough for anyone." Little Micheal felt everything had gone dark around him. He felt his muscles turn numb. He was hardly breathing. He felt like he could choke, like someone had held him by his throat.*

*Micheal, who was watching little Micheal, also felt darkness around him. He felt his muscles turn numb. He was hardly breathing. He too felt like he could choke. He walked out of this house and started taking deep breaths. It was still quite dark around him, and his vision was blurred. It took him more than half an hour to feel normal. Micheal knew how this incident shaped his entire life. He always considered himself worthless. He believed nobody liked him, and nobody wanted to stay with him. When his girlfriend broke up with him, it brought the same anxiety, fear, isolation and darkness that he felt when his dad had left him and his mother.*

*Micheal walked out of the house. He no longer wanted to see little Micheal. "This is the reality. How can I change my past? How can I change the belief that I acquired because of this incident? My dad did leave us because I made them fight due to my poor performance. How can I change reality?"*

*Suddenly, Micheal felt strange noises and a weird sensation before he went blank. He regained consciousness and realized he was back in the present.*

*The scientist asked, "Are you all right?"*

*Micheal replied, "I am alright. It did look like I actually went back to my childhood. It was a very real experience for me. I now know that a single incident in my childhood has shaped my personality in a big way. But how do I change that incident? That incident has already occurred and is the reality. Even if do imagine changing that, it would just be an illusion."*

*The scientist said, "We are not going to change the reality. The reality never causes pain. What causes pain is the interpretation of the reality. We could see the incident you went through with our advanced technology. No experience is good or bad. Our thinking makes it good or bad. Your dad left you and your mom; this is the reality. To interpret it as your dad left because of you and to conclude that you are worthless is not reality. Dads don't leave because their sons or daughters score low marks in school. There must be more to it than just your marks. And no human being is worthless. Every human being has unlimited potential. So, what we are going to change is the interpretation of the whole event by a little child with a limited understanding of the world. The moment you remove the pain associated with this incident, your beliefs that you are worthless and that you are no good will collapse on its own. You will be a new you. Are you ready to go back, but this time to change the whole experience?"*

*Micheal felt the world spin around him again. And in a few seconds, he was back in school.*

*He knew nobody could see him or hear him although he could see and hear everybody. Everything was the same except one thing: he was holding a small device with a very prominent green button. Micheal thought, "How come I have this strange device? Where did it come from? Maybe the scientist has included this device this time. What does this device do? How come the scientist never told me about this? Anyhow, let me focus on the task at hand. My job is to re-interpret the whole experience so that the pain associated with this experience is released."*

*Soon, he saw little Micheal in the fourth row; head down in shame and guilt. He had failed all his exams. Micheal thought, "How do I change the situation? Little Micheal cannot hear me." He looked at little Micheal and saw him going through fear, shame, guilt and darkness. "How do I change this darkness that has engulfed little Micheal? How?" thought Micheal. Suddenly, he remembered the strange device with a button in his hand. "Maybe this time I am supposed to change the whole situation by using this device." He made up his mind and pressed the green button. As soon as he pressed the green button, he was filled with fear, shame and guilt. "What's happening?" thought Micheal. "Oh, I get it. I am feeling what little Micheal is feeling right now. We are connected. What do I do now?" thought Micheal.*

*"If I change these dark feelings within myself, maybe the feeling within little Micheal will change as well. Let me try." Micheal got in touch with the fear, shame and guilt within him and started churning these feelings within. He looked at little Micheal sitting in the fourth row. Micheal realized that little Micheal was also experiencing the same thing; he could make out from the body language of little Micheal.*

*Slowly, Micheal churned the fear, guilt and shame into determination, into a resolve to do better next time. Micheal felt the fear and darkness within him transforming into courage and faith. He felt grit and strength. He felt optimistic.*

*Micheal saw little Micheal walking up to the class teacher and saying, "Ma'am, I promise I will do better next time." Seeing the resoluteness in little Micheal's eyes, the class teacher gave him a hug and said, "Sure you can. God bless. Bring your notebook." Little Micheal gave his notebook to his class teacher. She struck off what she had written in red. Instead, she wrote, "Do it better next time. You are very talented. You can."*

*The class teacher looked affectionately at Micheal and said, "No need to bring your father to school. Ok? Study hard and do it better next time."*

*That evening, Micheal saw little Micheal walking happily home. Little Micheal showed his class books to his mom and said, "Mom, I am going to study well and get good marks next time." His mom looked at the note his class teacher had written and then lovingly looked at little Micheal. "Sure, sweetie. You can," she said and gave him a hug. Little Micheal, after having snacks, decided to study first and then play. On his own, without being prompted by his mom, he started to study. Seeing this, his mom gave him more hugs and kisses. Little Micheal was beaming with happiness.*

*That night, little Micheal heard his mom and dad fighting. They were yelling and shouting at each other. Little Micheal was curious to know what had happened. He went near the door of his room and tried to listen to what was happening. Mom was mentioning another woman, Riya, again and again. Little Micheal couldn't make out much. But Micheal, who was standing beside little Micheal, understood it all. Suddenly, Micheal felt a heavy burden, which he was carrying all this while, fall off from his shoulders. He felt light, liberated and free.*

*Next day, Micheal got up early morning. He felt refreshed from a good night's sleep. He had never slept so peacefully before. He was full of energy*

> *and was eager to take on this day. He felt deep gratitude to Newlink Robotics Research group. They did help him clear a very important incident from his past. "Life is beautiful," thought Micheal as he sprang out of his bed.*
>
> *– Manoj Keshav*

## The Effects of Limiting Self-Beliefs

1. Lower ambitions and aspirations: If you believe deep in your heart that you are not capable and don't deserve success, lower ambitions and aspirations are the consequences. Even to visualize yourself actualizing your full potential will create dissonance in you because it is not aligned with your beliefs. Mediocrity can become a way of life unless those limiting beliefs are challenged.

2. Self-sabotage: While attending a training program or reading a motivational book, in the presence of a motivational coach or friend, you break out of the boundaries you have set for yourself and aim high in life. You set high goals, and you start sweating it out to execute one task after another. You start inching closer toward your goals with commitment and hard work. But the limiting belief that you are actually not capable and you don't deserve success will slowly pull you down. You start making mistakes, missing deadlines, conflicts arise, and finally, you end up sabotaging yourself. And finally, when you experience failure, you also experience a sense of resonance (inner alignment) with your deeply held limiting self-beliefs. You feel vindicated because you always knew you are a failure, and no matter what you do, failure is what is destined for you. That's how powerful a limiting belief can be. Hence, it is imperative that one transforms these limiting beliefs into empowering beliefs.

3. Procrastination and avoidance mindset: If you hold limiting beliefs like 'I am a failure' and the prospect that failure is what is ahead of you, then the best way to avoid this painful outcome is through procrastination.

It will keep failure out. For example, a person who wants to start a business on his own may keep procrastinating, and that way, he can keep failure away. The more you procrastinate, the more the failure seems to be far away. Letting go of these limiting beliefs is essential to overcome procrastination and the avoidance mindset.

Note: To achieve your goals, it is necessary that you first believe that you can achieve them, that it is possible and attainable. You must believe that you deserve it and you have all the resources within you to achieve it.

## Belief Change Exercise: Re-Imprinting Method

**(This is how a typical session would proceed with a client.)**

### Step I

1. Think of a limiting belief you presently have. Pick a belief that stops you from living a fuller life and being your best.

2. Now, think of a recent event when you experienced this limiting belief. Once you have identified the event, you are ready to move on to the next step.

3. Now, I want you to experience the event as if it is happening now. Think of the images, sounds and feelings associated with this experience. Write these down in a notebook (examples of feelings: unease, fear, sadness, disappointment, anger, etc.)

### Step II

1. Stay with this feeling. Think of another incident that happened five years ago when you had the same feeling, while the circumstances could have been completely different. Once you have recognized one such experience, look for another incident where you experienced the same feeling 10 years ago. Stay with the feeling. Now find an incident where you experienced the same feeling 15 years ago. Stay with the emotion.

# NLP: Belief Change Exercise | 275

Now find an incident where you experienced the same feeling in your childhood. Now gently explore if there was a time in your initial days or early childhood where there was a critical incident during which you felt the same feeling.

For example: If you experience a strange fear and sense your stomach churning while thinking about the event, then look for an incident about five years ago when you had the same feeling of strange fear. The circumstances could have been completely different. Then look for an incident that happened 10 years ago, then 15 years ago and then all the way to your childhood. Keep looking for an incident in your childhood where you experienced this strange fear with a feeling of churning in your stomach. The earliest incident is the one that you need to work on.

Note: It is crucial to keep your feeling as the guide while searching for the original childhood incident. The content of the incident is not important. It is the feeling that is important.

2. Now, I want you to become that younger self and re-experience that chosen incident.

3. Stay with that feeling/feelings and write down the beliefs you have about yourself, starting each sentence with 'I am…' For example, 'I am helpless.'

## Step III

1. Now, dissociate yourself from that chosen original incident and see the whole experience as if it's a movie. See your younger self in the movie going through that incident from beginning to end. As you are watching this incident, I want you to write down any other beliefs you have about yourself after that original incident and because of that incident. Check to see if you have formed any other beliefs later on because of this incident. You can look for self-beliefs and beliefs about others and the world you formed a few years after the incident occurred.

2. When all the beliefs are written down, you are ready to move on to the next step.

3. Now, get up and walk around, shake your body, take a few deep breaths and sit on another chair.

## Step IV

1. Now, recall that childhood incident again and watch the incident as a movie. How many significant people are there in the event besides your younger self?

    For example, let's assume the client says that besides his younger self, his father and mother are there and that his father is of primary importance. Then the process would go like this:

    a. I would like you to start with your father. As you see that incident as a movie in front of you, focus your attention on your father and find the positive intention of your father's behavior. (Write down the positive intention.)

    b. Now, take your attention to your mother and see what she is doing in that experience. And then find the positive intention of your mother's behavior during the incident.

    c. Now, see your younger self in the movie in front of you. See his or her exact behavior. Find the positive intention of your younger self's exact behavior and write it down.

(It is important that all the significant people's positive intentions are written down, not just recollected.)

## Step V

In this step, you will identify and anchor the resources (inner resources like creativity, confidence, etc.) needed by all the significant characters in the original incident individually, including your younger self out there. You can give them any resources, in whatever measure, that would help each character deal in a highly resourceful way.

In this example:

a. Let's start with your father. What resources do you want to give him? With these resources, your father, in this incident, will be able to change the whole situation. So, give him adequate resources. Now, visualize your father having all these resources.

b. What resources do you want to give your mother? With these resources given by you, your mother, in this incident, will be able to change the whole situation. So, give her adequate resources. Now, visualize your mother possessing all these resources.

c. What resources do you want to give your younger self? With these resources given by you, your younger self will be able to change the whole situation. So, give your younger self adequate resources. Now, visualize your younger self possessing all these resources.

## Step VI

Please close your eyes and visualize each character in the original incident changing the whole situation with these newly given resources.

In this example:

a. See your resourceful father changing the whole situation. Your mother and your younger self do not have any resources. Watch your father with the resources change the whole situation.

b. Now, see your resourceful mother changing the whole situation. Your father and your younger self do not have any resources. Watch your mother with the resources change the whole situation.

c. Now, see your younger self changing the whole situation. Your father and mother do not have any resources. Watch your younger self with the resources change the whole situation.

Now, I would like you to relax and write down the new beliefs you would like to choose about yourself as a result of this new experience. State your new beliefs starting with 'I am...'

## Step VI

In this step, you will step in the shoes of each character in the original incident and see the situation from that character's point of view. And you will change the whole situation by becoming each character, one at a time.

In this example:

a. Close your eyes and step into your father's shoes in that original incident. Become your father and see the situation from his point of view. You are your father with all the resources you need. The other 2, your mother and your younger self, do not have resources. With your resources, go ahead and change the whole situation.

b. Now, step into your mother's shoes. Become your mother and see the situation from her point of view. You are your mother now with all the resources you need. The other 2, your father and your younger self, do not have any resources. With your resources, go ahead and change the whole situation.

c. Now, step into your younger self's shoes and see the situation from his or her point of view. You are your younger self with all the resources. The other 2, your father and mother, do not have any resources. With your resources, go ahead and change the whole situation.

Repeat this whole process three or five times, faster each time.

Now, I would like you to relax. Write down what new beliefs you choose to make about yourself because of this last experience. State your beliefs with 'I am...'

## Step VII

Now, retaining the added resources given to your younger self and the new beliefs that arose, move forward through time to the present and then imagine the future. Notice how these new resources and new beliefs will impact your life, career, future decisions, relationships, etc.

# About the Author

Manoj Keshav is a leading international NLP Master Trainer, psychologist and therapist with more than 20 years of training experience in conducting life-transforming, experiential workshops.

His approach to training is the 'Inside-Out' approach. He believes that to bring about deeper change, we need to dive deeper into one's mind; it involves uncovering one's inner drives, paradigms and deeply held belief system.

## Unique Training Methodology

*A little boy brags to his sister that he taught his dog to whistle. When the sister hears nothing, she quizzes him on his statement, only to be told 'I said I taught him; I didn't say he learned.'*

**– As illustrated by Piskurich**

Manoj is a firm believer that training enables transformation. Covering the syllabus is easy; transformation is no easy task. It's an art form—one that requires craft, creativity and mastery of specific skills. His unique blend of multi-faceted pedagogy involving experiential exercises, discovery learning drills, well-thought-out role plays and process integration has the ability to facilitate great results.

Contact Details
Email: mk@manojkeshav.com
Author website: www.manojkeshav.com

www.ingramcontent.com/pod-product-compliance
Lightning Source LLC
Chambersburg PA
CBHW020732180526
45163CB00001B/211